Readings in
FOUNDATIONS OF GIFTED EDUCATION

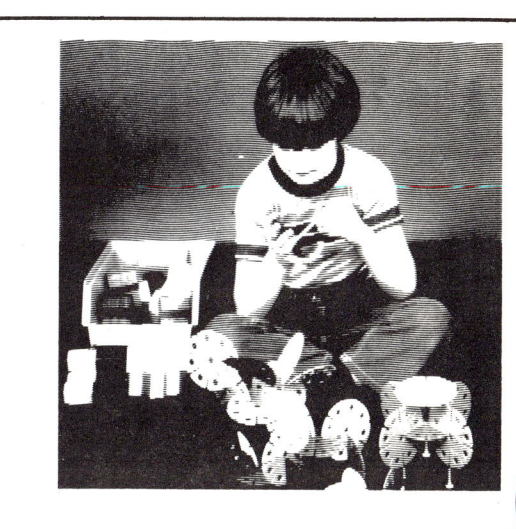

David M. Jackson
Former Executive Director,
National/State Leadership Training Institute
on the Gifted and Talented
Reston, Virginia

Special Learning Corporation
42 Boston Post Rd. Guilford, Connecticut 06437

Special Learning Corporation

Publisher's Message:

The Special Education Series is the first comprehensive series designed for special education courses of study. It is also the first series to offer such a wide variety of high quality books. In addition, the series will be expanded and up-dated each year. No other publications in the area of special education can equal this. We stress high quality content, a superb advisory and consulting group, and special features that help in understanding the course of study. In addition we believe we must also publish in very small enrollment areas in order to establish the credibility and strength of our series. We realize the enrollments in courses of study such as Autism, Visually Handicapped Education, or Diagnosis and Placement are not large. Nevertheless, we believe there is a need for course books in these areas and books that are kept up-to-date on an annual basis! Special Learning Corporation's goal is to publish the highest quality materials for the college and university courses of study. With your comments and support we will continue to do so.

John P. Quirk

0-89568-189-7

©1980 by Special Learning Corporation, Guilford, Connecticut 06437

All rights reserved. No part of this book may be reproduced, stored, or communicated by any means--without written permission from Special Learning Corporation.

First Edition

1 2 3 4 5

SPECIAL EDUCATION SERIES

* ● Abnormal Psychology: The Problems of Disordered Emotional and Behavioral Development
* ● Administration of Special Education
* ● Autism
* ● Behavior Modification
* Biological Bases of Learning Disabilities
* Brain Impairments
* ● Career and Vocational Education for the Handicapped
* ● Child Abuse
* ● Child Psychology
* ● Classroom Teacher and the Special Child
* ● Counseling Parents of Exceptional Children
* Creative Arts
* ● Curriculum Development for the Gifted
* Curriculum and Materials
* ● Deaf Education
* Developmental Disabilities
* ● Developmental Psychology: The Problems of Disordered Mental Development
* ● Diagnosis and Placement
* ● Down's Syndrome
* ● Dyslexia
* ● Early Childhood Education
* ● Educable Mentally Handicapped
* ● Emotional and Behavioral Disorders
* Exceptional Parents
* ● Foundations of Gifted Education
* ● Gifted Education
* ● Human Growth and Development of the Exceptional Individual

● Hyperactivity
* ● Individualized Education Programs
● Instructional Media and Special Education
● Language and Writing Disorders
● Law and the Exceptional Child: Due Process
* ● Learning Disabilities
● Learning Theory
* ● Mainstreaming
* ● Mental Retardation
● Motor Disorders
Multiple Handicapped Education
Occupational Therapy
● Perception and Memory Disorders
* ● Physically Handicapped Education
* ● Pre-School Education for the Handicapped
* ● Psychology of Exceptional Children
● Reading Disorders
Reading Skill Development
Research and Development
* ● Severely and Profoundly Handicapped
Social Learning
* ● Special Education
● Special Olympics
* ● Speech and Hearing
Testing and Diagnosis
● Three Models of Learning Disabilities
● Trainable Mentally Handicapped
● Visually Handicapped Education
● Vocational Training for the Mentally Retarded

● Published Titles *Major Course Areas

TOPIC MATRIX

Readings in Foundations of Gifted Education provides the college student in special education, the classroom teacher, and persons invovled in organizing a gifted education program with a comprehensive overview of the subject. The book is designed to follow a basic course of study, and cover various theories of gifted education.

COURSE OUTLING:

Foundations of Gifted Education

I. Introduction to the Education of the Gifted
   A. History
   B. Issues

II. Screening and Identification Procedures

III. Evaluation of Programs

IV. How to Find Support for a Program

Readings in Foundations of Gifted Education

I. Theoretical Bases of Intervention

II. Identification of the Gifted

III. Problems in Evaluating Special Programs

IV. Building Professional and Public Support for the Gifted

Related Special Learning Corporation Titles

I. Readings in Gifted and Talented Education

II. Readings in Curriculum Development of the Gifted

III. Readings in Special Education

IV. Readings in Administration of Special Education

Photo: Office of Human Resources, Department of Health, Education and Welfare

CONTENTS

1. Theoretical Bases of Intervention

Overview   3

1. **Pre-Sputnik to Post-Watergate Concern About the Gifted,** Abraham J. Tannenbaum, *The Gifted and the Talented: Their Education and Development, The Seventy-eighth Yearbook of the National Society for the Study of Education,* Edited by A. Harry Passow, The University of Chicago Press, 1979.
A historical overview of the status of gifted education through the last three decades.   4

2. **Issues in Education for the Gifted,** James J. Gallagher, *The Gifted and the Talented: Their Education and Development, The Seventh-eighth Yearbook of the National Society for the Study of Education,* Edited by A. Harry Passow, The University of Chicago Press, 1979.
Issues yet to be adequately resolved include: implications of the broadened definition, provision of curriculum materials, and ambivalent feelings about giftedness in American society.   20

3. **The Gifted Student: A Researcher's View,** Elizabeth Monroe Drews, *Developing Elementary and Secondary School Programs,* Council for Exceptional Children, 1975.
The author presents her view of young people who may be "...more fully human..." than many others.   32

4. **Educational Non-Acceleration and International Tragedy,** Julian Stanley, *G/C/T,* No. 3, May/June 1978.
Evidence is summarized making the case of acceleration of youths who reason extremely well in mathematics and are eager to move ahead educationally.   40

5. **Are We Educating Only Half the Brain?** John Curtis Gowan, *The Gifted Child Quarterly,* Vol. XXIII, No. 1, Spring 1979.
Using knowledge of the brain's functioning, the author describes processes by which creativity is produced.   53

Focus   61

2. Identification of the Gifted

Overview   63

6. **What Makes Giftedness? Re-examining a Definition,** Joseph S. Renzulli, *Phi Delta Kappan,* Vol. 60, No. 3, November 1978.
A research-based definition is offered.   64

Focus   70

7. **Young Handicapped Children Can Be Gifted and Talented,** Merle B. Karnes, *Journal for the Education of the Gifted,* Vol. 2, No. 3, Spring 1979.
A project that has developed procedures for identifying and programming for handicapped children is described.   72

8. **Factors Compounding the Handicapped of Some Gifted Children,** Charles Meisgeier, Constance Meisgeier, Dorothy Werblo, *Gifted Child Quarterly,* Vol. XXII, No. 3, Fall 1978.
Schools must strive to be sure that a gifted child's educational program is meeting the child's total needs, regardless of handicaps.   83

9. **The Culturally Disadvantaged Gifted Youth,** Addresses by Shirley Chisolm and Moshe Smilansky, G/C/T, No. 5, November/December 1978.
In two addresses given Ms. Chisolm and Mr. Smilansky discuss the present and future situation for the gifted culturally disadvantaged youth.   89

3. Problems in Evaluating Special Programs

Overview   97

10. **Issues and Procedures in Evaluating Programs,** Joseph S. Renzulli and Linda H. Smith, *The Gifted and Talented: Their Educa-*   98

tion and Development, The Seventy-eighth Yearbook of the National Society for the Study of Education, Edited by A. Harry Passow, The University of Chicago Press, 1979.

The authors provide an overview of the field of evaluation, special problems of programs for gifted students and evaluative study model.

Focus   112

11. **Evaluation of the Alexandria, Virginia Program for Talented Elementary Students, 1974-77,** Frank Morra, Jr., and Richard Hills, Frank Morra and Associates, Inc., 1978.   114

    Methodology and findings of a program evaluation are presented.

Focus   119

12. **The Ferrell Gifted Program Evaluation Instrument for Teachers and Evaluation of Instructional Programs for Gifted and Talented Children,** in *Sample Instruments for the Evaluation of Programs for the Gifted and Talented,* TAG Evaluation Committee, March 1979.   120

    Copies of an instrument for teachers and a set of instruments for assessing a program are provided.

4. Building Professional and Public Support for the Gifted

Overview   139

13. **The Emerging National and State Concern,** David M. Jackson, *The Gifted and Talented: Their Education and Development,*   140 *The Seventy-Eighth Yearbook of the National Society for the Study of Education,* Edited by A. Harry Passow, The University of Chicago Press, 1979.

    Describing what has happened as a beginning, the author outlines some of the activities of the federal government--the ERIC Clearing House on Handicapped and Gifted and the National/State Leadership Training Institute, and the growing scope and diversity of state activities.

14. **It's a New Day for Gifted Children,** Dorothy Sisk, *G/C/T,* No. 8, May/June 1979.   153

    "True equality demands that we maintain equal awareness, respect and freedom for each individual to develop his or her uniqueness."

15. **Parent Talk,** Willard Abraham, *Gifts, Talents and the Very Young,* National/State Leadership Training Institute for the Gifted and Talented, 1977.   157

    The author advises parents of young children and gives behavioral examples.

16. **Constructive Ways to Work with the Establishment: How "Organized Persuasion" Works for the Gifted in Public Education,** Carol Nathan, *Parentspeak,* National/State Leadership Training Institute for the Gifted and Talented, 1976.   161

    A community leader discusses issues related to social and institutional change.

17. **How Media Can Assist in Raising Public Consciousness About Education of the Gifted,** Raymond P. Ewing, *New Directions for Gifted Education,* National/State Leadership Training Institute for the Gifted and Talented, 1976.   171

    Insights from the field of public relations provide some clues for those interested in better understanding of the needs of the gifted.

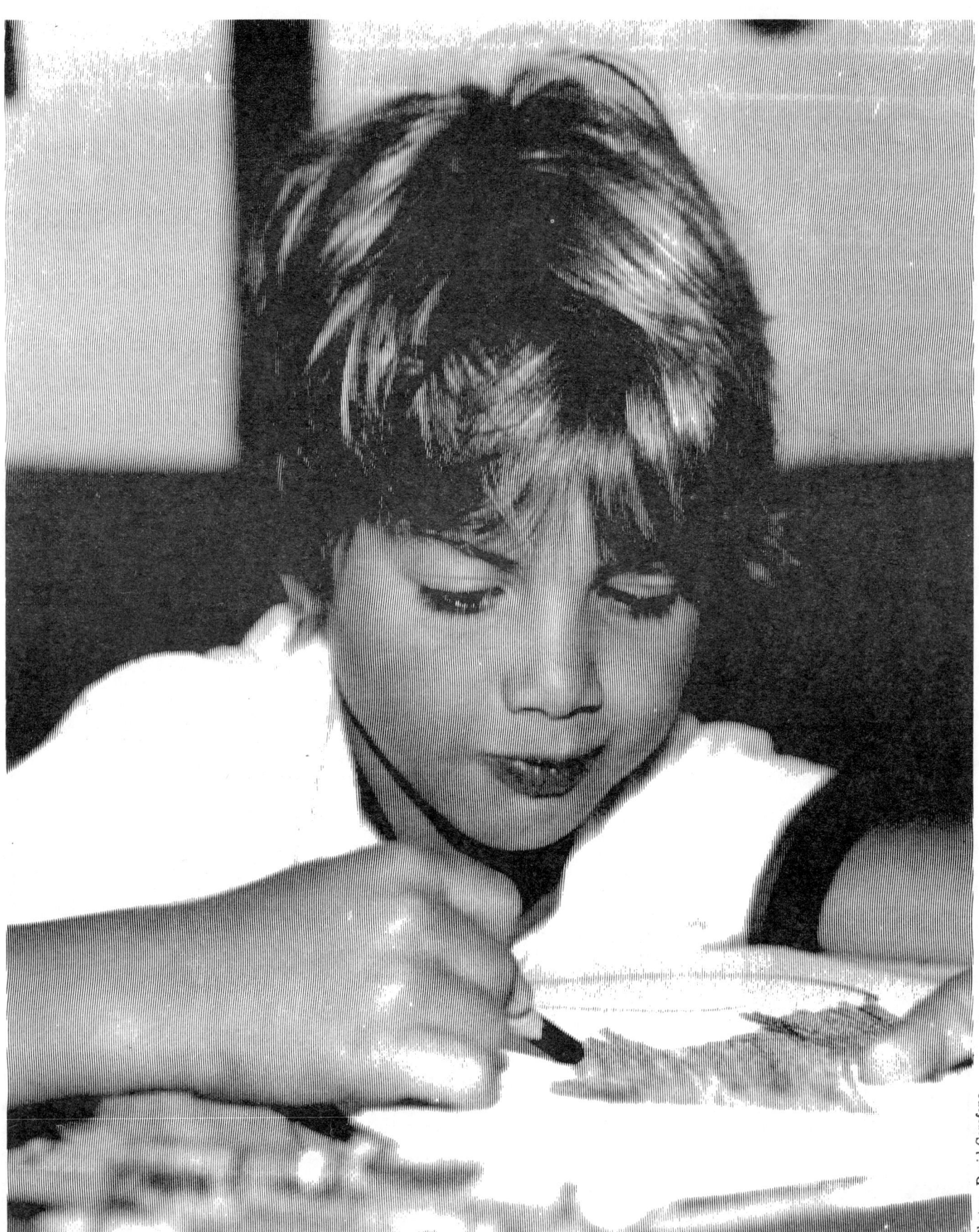

Photo: David Carofano

PREFACE

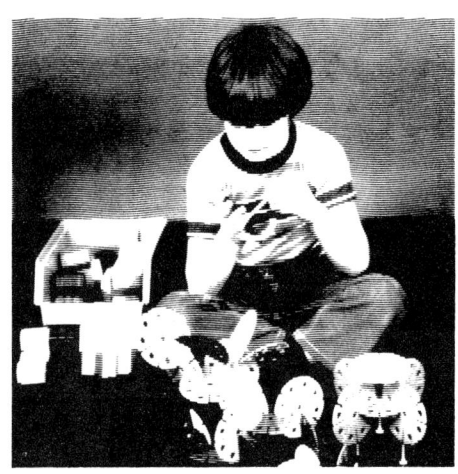

More than two decades ago, the late English historian of civilizations, Arnold J. Toynbee, raised the question, "Is America neglecting its creative minority?" In Toynbee's view, the progress and even the ultimate survival of a civilization depends upon a small group of people who are different, people whose inventions and problem-solving abilities are central to the welfare of a society. If we were to assume that America's creative minority includes those children of unusually strong intellectual abilities, high creative potential, and a high degree of task commitment, we might ask, "What is the probability that in today's schools and communities, such a child will be recognized and offered educational opportunities commensurate with his or her abilities and interests?"

Available data do not fully answer this question. Yet some clues are seen in the national survey discussed in Section IV, and we might strongly suspect that a majority of our gifted children are not being discovered and educated in ways that challenge their abilities. Thus the rising amounts of interest in gifted children noted by Tannenbaum in the Introduction are most welcome, as is the diversity of views of giftedness and its nurture in the current literature represented in this volume.

Photo: David Carofano

THEORETICAL BASES OF INTERVENTION

Section I begins with a historical overview of the developments in public/educational attitudes towards the gifted student for the past three decades. This general introduction takes the reader into the broad area of issues facing the administrator, teacher and parent of the gifted child today. From the evidence at hand, we now know more than enough to acknowledge the need for gifted programs. But we also need to know more about such areas as familial influences, both environmental and genetic.

James J. Gallagher's "Issues in Education for the Gifted" explains that we are in the process of establishing a broader definition of gifted and talented, including valuable talents other than academic. The identification of gifted cannot be limited to a few tests, but needs to become an integrated network of skills evaluation, tests, and interviews. The author feels that educational programming must focus on content, special skills, and a modified learning environment. The underachiever and the culturally different need special assistance in reaching their full potential. "A Researcher's View of the Gifted" further expands on these ideas. Elizabeth Monroe Drews suggests three ways of exploring and discovering talents; by inquiring into interests, by judging performance, and by administering tests. She feels that we must strive to create an "ideal" learning environment.

The section ends with a Focus that contains quotes from Philip M. Powell's review of *The IQ Controversy* (edited by Ned J. Block and Gerald Dworkin). The reviewer tries to summarize the country's need for such a controversy, and concludes with a suggestion that we try to teach the gifted to develop as "total human beings," that we someday, may all realize our full potential.

PRE-SPUTNIK TO POST-WATERGATE CONCERN ABOUT THE GIFTED

Abraham J. Tannenbaum

The half-decade following Sputnik in 1957 and the last half-decade of the 1970s may be viewed as twin peak periods of interest in gifted and talented children. Separating the peaks was a deep valley of neglect in which the public fixed its attention more eagerly on the low functioning, poorly motivated, and socially handicapped children in our schools. It was not simply a case of bemoaning the plight of able and then disadvantaged learners, with each population taking turns as the pitied underdog or the victim of unfair play. Rather than *transferring* the same sentiments from one undereducated group to another, the nation found itself *transforming* its mood from intense anxiety to equally profound indignation: anxiety lest our protective shield of brainpower became weaker, rendering us vulnerable to challenge from without, followed by indignation over social injustice in the land, which could tear us apart from within. Now we are experiencing a revival of earlier sensitivities to the needs of the gifted. Judging from these vacillations in national temperament, it seems as if we have not yet succeeded in paying equal attention simultaneously to our most and least successful achievers at school.

The cyclical nature of interest in the gifted is probably unique in American education. No other special group of children has been alternately embraced and repelled with so much vigor by educators and laymen alike. Gardner saw signs of public dilemma rather than fickleness when he commented that "the critical lines of tension in our society are between *emphasis on individual performance and restraints on individual performance.*"[1] Such conflict would arise logically from a failure to reconcile our commitments to excellence and to equality in public education. Fostering excellence means recognizing the right of gifted children to realize their potential, but it also suggests something uncomfortably close to encouraging elitism if the ablest are privy to educational experiences that are denied all other children. On the other hand, promoting egalitarianism will guarantee increased attention to children from lower-status environments who are failing at school. As we concentrate more exclusively on raising the performance levels of these minorities, however, there is danger of discriminating against the minority of gifted students by denying their right to be challenged adequately on grounds that they are advantaged. Perhaps because we cannot live exclusively with excellence or egalitarianism for any length of time and tend to counterpose rather than reconcile them, we seem fated to drift from one to the other indefinitely.

The 1950s: Pre-Sputnik and Post-Sputnik

From the current perspective, the 1950s are viewed as sedate, conservative years, at least in contrast to the convulsive 1960s. But this kind of hindsight is fairly myopic. While it is true that America was spared too much internal dissension, except for McCarthyism and some grumbling about our involvement in Korea, still it was the age of cold warfare at its worst and its threat to the psyche

---

1. John Gardner, *Excellence: Can We Be Equal and Excellent Too?* (New York: Harper and Row, 1961), p. 33 (italics in original).

From *The Gifted and the Talented: Their Education and Development*, ©1979 by the National Society for the Study of Education, reprinted with permission.

1. Pre-Sputnik

seemed lethal. Two superpowers, determined to undo each other's political systems, possessed the ultimate weapon of destruction, and each feared that the other would use that weapon as a deterrent if it imagined itself about to be attacked.

Unlocking secrets of the atom to produce the bomb represented a scientific as well as a military breakthrough, increasing the dependency of armed power on the innovativeness of the scientist. Americans had grown confident that our country's leadership in science and technology was unchallengeable. We expected ourselves to be always the first in creating new gadgetry to make life and death easier, whether through sophisticated home appliances, computer systems, communications equipment, or explosives with the power of megatons of TNT. Image the shock, then, when this illusion was shattered by the successful launching of Sputnik by none other than our arch enemy in the midst of a cold war that at any moment could turn hotter than any conflict in history. Sputnik was not simply a demoralizing technological feat; it had potential military applications as well. Suddenly, the prestige and survival of a nation were jeopardized because the enemy's greatest minds of the day had outperformed ours, and the Russians capitalized on this coup by broadcasting to every nation on earth its success, at long last, in reducing America to a second-class power.

Although the shock of Sputnik in 1957 triggered unprecedented action on behalf of the gifted, educators had already expressed their lament over public indifference to these children much earlier in that decade. In 1950, for example, the Educational Policies Commission decried the school's neglect of mentally superior children and the resulting shrinking of manpower in the sciences, arts, and professions.[2] A year later, the Ohio Commission on Children and Youth revealed that only 2 percent of the schools in that state had special classes for the gifted and a mere 9 percent reported any kind of enrichment in the regular classroom.[3]

Criticism of the elementary and high schools eventually came also from the academic community. In 1953, Bestor, an academician, published a sensational indictment of public education for practicing what he considered its special brand of fraudulence on America's children.[4] Because of what he regarded as a misplacement of power in the hands of know-nothing "educationists," Bestor was convinced that schools provided meager intellectual nourishment or inspiration, especially for the gifted who often marked time in their studies until graduation released them from boredom and euphoria.

To some extent, the eagerness among educators to increase the nation's talent supply was inspired by politicians and economists who had worried about our diminishing reservoir of high-level manpower in science and technology even before Sputnik dramatized the problem. For example, Wolfle, Director of the Commission on

---

2. Educational Policies Commission, *Education of the Gifted* (Washington, D.C.: National Education Association, 1950).

3. Ohio Commission on Children and Youth, *The Status of the Gifted in Ohio* (Columbus: Ohio Department of Education, 1951).

4. Arthur E. Bestor, *Educational Wastelands* (Urbana, Ill.: University of Illinois Press, 1953).

1. INTERVENTION

Human Resources and Advanced Training, asserted that the United States failed to prepare enough men and women in the natural sciences, the health fields, teaching, and engineering.[5] Only six of ten in the top 5 percent and only half of the top 25 percent of high school graduates went on to earn college diplomas. At the more advanced levels, a mere 3 percent of those capable of earning the Ph.D. actually did so. What made matters worse were expectations that the shortages would become even more acute in the late 1950s unless the schools succeeded in encouraging gifted students to continue on to advanced studies.

Manpower statistics confirmed the existence of shortages in key professions. Again, the cause of this alarming situation was attributed to the commitment of the schools to deal with mediocrity rather than superiority. Allegedly, teachers were geared to work with average or even below average students, with the result that the ablest were often disregarded. Many dropped out of school before graduation or refused to go on to college after four years of high school.

Aside from the exhortative statements and surveys dramatizing the failure to educate gifted children, there is also evidence of scholarly activity in the early part of the decade. Few people could forecast the impact of Guilford's paper on creativity on the subsequent research pertaining to the nature and measurement of productive thinking.[6] That paper encouraged psychometrists to abandon the assumption that tests of general intelligence, such as those developed in the early part of the century by Lewis Terman, could be used to locate the pool of children out of which virtually all of the gifted would probably emerge. Rather, Guilford's model brought attention to multiple aptitudes, including divergent production or "creativity," as it is sometimes called. His ideas about creativity and its measurement were later adapted by Getzels and Jackson in their comparison of "high creative-low IQ" and "high IQ-low creative" students at the University of Chicago High School.[7] This study had a stunning influence on educational researchers because it announced a breakthrough in the use of so-called "creativity" measures to identify a talent resource that would be overlooked by tests of general intelligence. The question of whether instruments for assessing creativity can locate otherwise undiscoverable talent has never been fully settled,[8] but protagonists for the use of such tests have inspired the kind of general enthusiasm that today would greet an announcement of new sources of energy.

Much of the work in the early 1950s was codified in *Education for the Gifted*, the fifty-seventh yearbook of the National Society

---

5. Dael Wolfle, *America's Resources of Specialized Talent* (New York: Harper and Row, 1954).

6. Joy P. Guilford, "Creativity," *American Psychologist* 5 (1950): 444-54.

7. Jacob W. Getzels and Philip W. Jackson, "The Meaning of 'Giftedness': An Examination of an Expanding Concept," *Phi Delta Kappan* 40 (1958): 75-77.

8. Susan B. Crockenberg, "Creativity Tests: A Boon or Boondoggle for Education?" *Review of Educational Research* 42 (1972): 27-45.

1. Pre-Sputnik

for the Study of Education. Published in 1958, it was the first yearbook of the Society on the topic since 1924.

Despite the work of specialists on the gifted and the portents and premonitions concerning Russia's strides in building its talent reservoir, there was no serious action in America's schools until Sputnik was launched in 1957. At that time, the rhetoric started to become more strident and the research more abundant, and together they either produced or accompanied radical changes in public education. We were convinced that the Russians slipped ahead of us in space technology because we had insufficient manpower to advance the sciences. Predictably, the schools were singled out as scapegoats.

While the nation kept careful watch on scientific developments in the Soviet Union, it also monitored the rate at which Soviet education was producing new scientists and the kind of training they received in the process. Invariably, invidious comparisons were made between the enemy's system and ours. One report claimed that before graduating from a Russian high school, a student had to complete five years of physics, biology, and a foreign language, four years of chemistry, one year of astronomy, and as many as ten years of mathematics.[9] Our own graduates were woefully undereducated by comparison. Worse than that, the young people in American colleges earning science degrees and committing their talents to defense-related professions did not compare in number with their counterparts in the Soviet Union.

It was essential to build up our supply of high-level human resources quickly or else risk seeing a national emergency deteriorate into a national catastrophe. In time, school officials began to acknowledge that something was wrong with public education and that there was much overhauling to be done. It was probably the mounting exposés of malpractice in the schools, capped by Sputnik and its ominous implications, that moved them out of their complacency and made them more reform-minded. Indeed, the reaction to Sputnik might not have been so swift and strong if the critics' cries for change in our schools had not had a cumulative effect.

When the educational community finally took action on behalf of the gifted, it did so with alacrity. Public and private funds became available to assist in the pursuit of excellence, primarily in the fields of science and technology. Academic coursework was telescoped and stiffened to test the brainpower of the gifted. Courses that had been offered only at the college level began to find their way into special enrichment programs in high school and subsequently in elementary school. Even the self-contained classroom, which had been a tradition in elementary education, briefly gave way to limited departmental instruction in a few localities. Attempts were made to introduce foreign languages in the elementary schools, but that too did not last long after an auspicious begin-

---

9. *Soviet Commitment to Education*, Report of the First Official U.S. Education Mission to the USSR, Bulletin 1959, No. 16, Office of Education, U.S. Department of Health, Education, and Welfare (Washington, D.C.: U.S. Government Printing Office, 1959).

1. INTERVENTION

ning. Also making short-lived appearances were courses with such attractive titles as the Mathematics of Science, Opera Production, Seminar in the Humanities, Integration of the Arts, World Affairs, Structural Linguistics, and Critical Thinking. There were even special efforts made to locate and nurture giftedness among the socially disadvantaged, most notably through the P.S. 43 Project in New York City, which later became the widely heralded but eventually ill-fated Higher Horizons Program. Interest spread also to school systems in rural areas and to colleges and universities where the gifted were provided with enrichment experiences never before extended to them.

There is no way of knowing precisely what percentage of our schools offered something special to the gifted in the years immediately after Sputnik. Many of the crash programs were never taken seriously enough by their sponsoring institutions to last long. But there were prominent exceptions that started out as enrichment experiences for the gifted only and later changed the curriculum for all children. Much of what is taught today in the mathematics and sciences, for example, is a legacy of post-Sputnik designs in gifted education. Similar influences can be felt in current secondary school programs that are comprehensive enough to accommodate human diversity without shortchanging the gifted. Conant expressed the sentiment of the late 1950s in a report entitled *The American High School Today*.[10] He offered a broad, twenty-one step plan for changing secondary education with special emphasis on core courses that were challenging in content and required of all students regardless of their career plans. His proposals took special note of the academically gifted (the upper 15 percent) and the highly gifted (the upper 3 percent). The tougher standards he suggested for them were far more acceptable to school officials than were those recommended by Bestor and his fellow critics.

In addition to the plethora of special enrichment activities initiated in the schools during the late 1950s and early 1960s, there was an upsurge in research activity dealing with the characteristics and education of gifted children. Investigations in vogue at the time focused primarily on such topics as the relative effectiveness of different administrative designs (for example, ability grouping, enrichment in regular classes, and acceleration); the social status of the gifted at school and its effect on their motivation to learn; the causes and treatment of scholastic underachievement among children with high potential; achievement motivation and other nonintellective factors in high-level learning; and the psychosocial correlates of divergent thinking processes. Professional journals were deluged with research reports and with exhortations to do something special for the gifted. So rapid was the buildup of literature in the field that one writer claimed there were more articles published in the three-year period from 1956 to 1959 than in the previous thirty years.[11]

---

10. James B. Conant, *The American High School Today* (New York: McGraw Hill, 1959).

11. Joseph L. French, ed., *Educating the Gifted* (New York: Henry Holt, 1959).

High scholastic standards and standing, academic advancement, studiousness, and career-mindedness were conspicuous themes in our schools. It became virtually unthinkable for a gifted child to bypass the tougher courses in favor of the less demanding ones. It certainly was no time for youth to do their own thing or to enjoy the privilege of doing nothing. Instead, they were brought up in a period of total talent mobilization, requiring the most able-minded to fulfill their potentials and submit their developed abilities for service to the nation.

The 1960s: A Decade of Turmoil

The 1960s opened with John F. Kennedy's election to the presidency amid promises and dreams of a modern utopia. There was excitement in the air as the nation prepared itself to sweep away the stodginess of the 1950s and create a new age of excellence. Kennedy's earliest presidential messages made it clear that brains and loyalty to the flag were among our most precious assets. He announced boldly his intention to put a man on the moon by 1970, a clear sign that we were accepting Russia's challenge for supremacy in space exploration and that the most brilliant scientists would be called upon to make such a feat feasible. This meant encouraging the largest possible number of able students to enroll in science programs that offered them the best possible special education. For who else but the gifted could yield from their ranks a cadre of scientists qualified to honor the President's commitment?

There were other hints of meritocracy in the air. Kennedy gathered around him some of the most precocious men (although few women) of his generation to advise him on governmental matters. Known then as the "Whiz Kids," some had earned their reputations as scholars at leading universities and others as promising idea men in industry. All of them projected an image of braininess with a zest for unraveling the chief executive's knottiest problems. They were gifted children grown up and enjoying the glamor of fame and power rather than living in relative obscurity as so many other gifted people must do, even in their most productive years. At last, able children had their own celebrity role models to emulate, much as budding athletes and entertainers have theirs.

It would, of course, be naive to suggest that we had reached a point in history when the brilliant student was taking his place alongside the sports star as a hero on campus. Far from it. Research by Coleman[12] and Tannenbaum[13] demonstrated that acclaim among peers was far more easily achieved on the athletic field than on the honor roll. Still, the Kennedy years were making good on promises of social and economic rewards for those willing to cultivate their superior scholastic abilities despite the lack of enthusiastic cheering from schoolmates.

The bids were high for brains in the early 1960s, but there was a string attached. President Kennedy himself expressed it best in

---

12. James S. Coleman, *The Adolescent Society* (Glencoe, Ill.: The Free Press, 1962).

13. Abraham J. Tannenbaum, *Adolescent Attitudes toward Academic Brilliance* (New York: Teachers College Press, 1962).

1. INTERVENTION

his immortal admonition to his countrymen: "Ask not what your country can do for you—ask what you can do for your country." It was a call for unselfish accomplishment, to dedicate the work of our citizens to the greater glory of the nation. Those with higher abilities had more to contribute and were therefore under pressure not to bury their talents or even to indulge in creative productivity that was impractical. The feeling during that cold war period was that the scientist could better serve the nation than the poet.

Judging from the career plans of gifted children in the late 1950s and early 1960s, they evidently believed that the nation was worth serving. By far the largest number of students with high tested intelligence majored in the sciences, and many of them aspired to enter fields of technology that could somehow help the defense effort. The lure of employment opportunities in these industries and professions was reinforced by the glamorization of science as man's most exciting modern frontier.

Yet, the flurry of activity on behalf of the gifted has left some unfinished business to haunt us. Even the threat of Sputnik and the indulgence of excellence during the Kennedy era were not enough to guarantee that the needs of the gifted would be cared for perpetually at school. Instead, enrichment was considered a curricular ornament to be detached and discarded when the cost of upkeep became prohibitive. Moreover, the fervor with which guidance counselors ushered gifted youths into science programs backfired to some degree as large numbers of these students switched their academic majors by the time they reached their sophomore year in college,[14] and many who did stay on to pursue the careers mapped out for them became victims of the shaky fortunes of the aerospace industry. On the other hand, little more than lip service was paid to the needs of a special breed of students not gifted academically but possessing exceptional talent in the arts, mechanics, and social leadership. Also, whatever work was done in defining and measuring divergent productivity remained in the research laboratory. Few people attempted to develop ways of cultivating this kind of intellective functioning and translating it into curriculum sequences. Finally, the national talent hunt failed to penetrate the socially disadvantaged minorities whose records of school achievement were well below national norms and whose children with high potential were much harder to locate because their environments provided too little of the requisite encouragement and opportunity to fulfill whatever promise they might have shown under other circumstances. A notable exception to this general neglect of talent among the underprivileged was the aforementioned P.S. 43 project in New York City, which was then modified to become the Higher Horizons Program.[15] But these efforts were shortlived, coming to an end when a subsequent evaluation revealed no special accomplishments of the program, perhaps due to an underestimate of costs, personnel, curriculum plan-

---

14. Donivan J. Watley, *Stability of Career Choices of Talented Youth* (Evanston, Ill.: National Merit Scholarship Corp., 1968).

15. Jacob Landers, *Higher Horizons Progress Report* (New York: Board of Education of the City of New York, 1963).

ning, and just plain hard work needed to duplicate on a much larger scale the earlier successes at P.S. 43.[16]

Focus on Underprivileged Minorities

The 1954 Supreme Court decision to desegregate public schools set off an inexorable movement toward updating the Constitution and the Bill of Rights. Once again, education became the linchpin of a national priority, this time for social justice, as it had formerly been for the Great Talent Hunt. Separatism and equality were declared an impossible combination and therefore unconstitutional. Educators and social and behavioral scientists placed the cause of disadvantaged children at the top of their priority list, even ahead of the gifted. We were now more concerned with bolstering freedom and equality within our borders than with playing the lead on the world stage despite the unabated pressures of cold warfare that brought confrontations between East and West in Europe, Southeast Asia, and the Middle East.

In addition to diverting interest away from the gifted, the advocacy movement for the socially disadvantaged actually contested at least two features of special programs for the ablest: (a) the use of intelligence tests and other conventional measures of aptitude as a means of determining who deserves to be called gifted; and (b) grouping children in special classes for the gifted on the basis of their performance on these kinds of assessments. The intelligence test, a major instrument for determining academic potential ever since Terman initiated his monumental studies of genius in the early part of the century, came under heavy attack for being biased against some racial minorities and the socioeconomically depressed. It was charged that the problem-solving tasks, which are mostly verbal, favor children with experience in higher-status environments. Consequently, these children obtain higher scores, thus creating the delusion that they are basically more intelligent and perhaps even born with superior intellect. As a result of these charges, some urban centers with large racial minorities, notably New York and Los Angeles, discontinued the use of such tests.

The push toward greater egalitarianism aggravated a mild distrust of intelligence testing that had always existed in this country. Many suspected that it is vaguely antidemocratic to declare, on the basis of a test score, that a child is fated to become an achiever or a failure, economically comfortable or uncomfortable, and a high- or a low-status person, even if such forecasts allowed broad limits of error. Such an idea did not square with our traditional faith in this country that one is given the freedom and opportunity to make of himself what he will. The residual aversion to testing intelligence on grounds that it predestines inequality among *individuals* was compounded by charges that the measures discriminate against racial and socioeconomic *groups* as well. It was enough to threaten the use of mainstay instruments for identifying gifted children.

---

16. J. Wayne Wrightstone et al., *Evaluation of the Higher Horizons Program for Underprivileged Children* (New York: Board of Education of the City of New York, 1964).

1. INTERVENTION

Since racial minorities, such as Hispanics, Blacks, Chicanos, and Native Americans, traditionally performed less well at school than did white majorities, it was logical to regard ability grouping for the gifted as de facto racial segregation. Critics argued that schools were practicing blatant favoritism by creating separate classes for children who rated superior on conventional measures of intellect and also by offering those chosen few a kind of enrichment in their curriculum that was denied everyone else. The objections were not against special ability grouping per se for the gifted, or even the unique educational experience reserved for them because of their ability. What created the furor was the practice of denying enough children from disadvantaged subpopulations their rightful access to these classes. There was an overwhelming sentiment favoring the idea that high potential is equitably distributed among all races, privileged and underprivileged, but that life's circumstances in some groups are oppressive enough to cast a shadow over their innate competencies.

Thus we see that American education was not able to reconcile its interest in the gifted with its concern about the disadvantaged, nor could it design a satisfactory methodology for locating and cultivating giftedness among these minority groups. The dilemma was easy to resolve inasmuch as it reduced itself to a choice between battling for social justice or pursuing excellence, and there was no doubt as to which of the two would better fit the mood of the 1960s.

VIET NAM AND DISSENTING YOUTH

During the brief Kennedy era, the United States faced the communist world in several near-conflicts. In each instance, we emerged with our self-image intact as the champions of the free world against forces of darkness. The subsequent adventure in Viet Nam turned out to be disastrously different, despite the fact that President Johnson justified our entanglement on the same grounds that his predecessor defended his risks of war in Berlin and Cuba. Eventually, the nation grew tired of the war, suspicious of politicians' promises of a quick victory, and increasingly convinced that our country was meddling in affairs of other nations rather than serving as a judge and enforcer of what was morally right in the world.

Among the many casualties of the Viet Nam conflict was our perception of giftedness in political leadership. The Whiz Kids of the Kennedy years, many of whom had stayed on in the Johnson era to help formulate strategy for the war effort, rapidly lost their image as people who could become heroes in public life by virtue of their brainpower alone. In fact, their sad history seemed to prove that being supersmart in the scholastic sense of the term was no guarantee of superunderstanding of man's most serious problems and how to solve them. Gifted youth on campuses throughout the country learned to despise them for their role in the Viet Nam debacle rather than revere them as graduated honors students distinguishing themselves as national leaders.[17]

---

17. David Halberstam, *The Best and the Brightest* (Westminster, Md.: Random House, 1972).

1. Pre-Sputnik

A far more serious by-product of Viet Nam was a growing unrest among students in the colleges. Kenneth Keniston, who studied these young people in great detail, made it quite clear that a complex mix of personal attributes, familial influences, peer associations, and school environments set them apart from their more conforming age-mates.[18] It is noteworthy, however, that a disproportionate number of disaffected youth on campus distinguished themselves in their studies at school and were frequently enrolled in some of the more enriched and prestigious programs. Their immediate targets were the colleges they were attending, which represented to them an establishment with archaic standards for success and unreasonable controls over their lives. Yet these same gadflies in centers of learning were themselves described in one study as possessing high degrees of intellectualism.[19]

The unrest on campus underwent some dramatic changes over a relatively short period of time. As one observer remarked, "The key difference between the Berkeley riots of 1964 and the Columbia crisis of May, 1969 is that in the pre-Columbian case the major impetus for unrest stemmed from the perceived abuse or misuse of authority ('Do not bend, fold, or mutilate'), whereas the later protest denied the legitimacy of authority."[20] The revolt was not only against institutions (educational or otherwise) and their leaders; it was also against a tradition of rationalism that sanctified ivory-tower scholarship. When Columbia rioters willfully destroyed a professor's research files, the act may have carried a message that goes beyond ordinary vandalism. It seemed to imply that all the work invested in accumulating those files was a waste of the professor's talent, which ought to have been dedicated to building a better society rather than dabbling in trivia and esoterica. And to make matters worse, the educational establishment expected its brightest students to follow in the footsteps of professors like him.

Many questions were raised among gifted college students as to whether they ought to funnel their psychic energies into a life of the mind. Many were attracted to the sensitivity training movements, which told them that "talking is usually good for intellectual understanding of personal experience, but it is often not effective for helping a person *to experience*—to feel."[21] Accordingly, man should not be seen simply, as though he were a machine, but rather as a complex biological, psychological, and social organism who can fulfill himself through all of these dimensions of his being. Every part of the body has to be exercised to its fullest potential, which means building up the strength and stamina of its muscles, its sensory awareness and aesthetic appreciation, its motor control, and the gamut of its emotional and social feelings. Inhibiting other aspects of self for the sake of the intellect amounts to robbing life

18. Kenneth Keniston, *Youth and Dissent: The Role of a New Opposition* (New York: Harcourt, Brace, Jovanovich, 1971).

19. Richard Flacks, "The Liberated Generation: An Exploration of the Roots of Student Protest," *Journal of Social Issues* 23, no. 3 (1967): 52-75.

20. Warren G. Bennis, "A Funny Thing Happened on the Way to the Future," *American Psychologist* 25 (1970): 595-608.

21. William C. Schutz, *Joy: Expanding Human Awareness* (New York: Grove Press, 1967), p. 11 (italics in original).

1. INTERVENTION

of its multidimensionality, so the task of the individual is to make something of all his capacities, even if in so doing he cannot make the most of any of them.

Significantly, a new utopia emerged in the form of Consciousness III, depicted by Reich in his best seller, *The Greening of America*. One of the postulates of this new world was described by Reich as follows:

> Consciousness III rejects the whole concept of excellence and comparative merit. . . . It refuses to evaluate people by general standards, it refuses to classify people, or analyze them. Each person has his own individuality, not to be compared to that of anyone else. Someone may be a brilliant thinker, but he is not "better" at thinking than anyone else, he simply possesses his own excellence. A person who thinks very poorly is still excellent in his own way. Therefore people are in no hurry to find out another person's background, schools, achievements, as a means of knowing him; they regard all of that as secondary, preferring to know him unadorned. Because there are no governing standards, no one is rejected. Everyone is entitled to pride in himself, and no one should act in a way that is servile, or feel inferior, or allow himself to be treated as if he were inferior.[22]

Thus we see how life for campus dissidents became strangely paradoxical. Many of them espoused the habits of intellectualism generally associated with gifted students. At the same time they rejected excellence and its trappings as violations of democracy and too stultifying to the attainment of total joy and liberation. Even those consenting to live the life of the mind learned an unforgettable lesson from the events in Viet Nam. No longer could they be adjured to cultivate their talents for the sake of their country's prestige and need for survival. The immoral war in Southeast Asia tarnished the nation's image enough to discourage such commitments among many who could potentially be counted among our high-level human resources. Besides, some may have felt it faintly dehumanizing to be treated like natural resources; it simply did not fit well with the new spirit of selfhood and individuality.

THE DEVALUATION OF SCIENCE

For many years, consuming or producing scientific knowledge was regarded as a human virtue, particularly if it helped conquer nature in order to make man's life more comfortable. There was hardly much doubt that gifted children would derive great personal satisfaction and a certain measure of power and freedom if they became highly informed about the secrets of the universe or contributed significantly to unraveling some of these mysteries. In the 1960s, however, serious doubts were raised about the value of scholarship as it had been traditionally transacted in the schools. Significant segments of campus youth began to sour on knowledge factories, and Herbert Marcuse, one of their most influential spokesmen, warned about the mechanizing, denaturalizing, and subjugating impact of knowledge.[23]

---

22. Charles A. Reich, *The Greening of America* (New York: Random House, 1970), pp. 226-27.

23. Herbert Marcuse, *One-Dimensional Man* (Boston: Beacon Press, 1964).

1. Pre-Sputnik

Gifted youth in the age of Sputnik were bombarded with the message that a lifetime devotion to achievement in science was not only in the interests of the state, but of mankind in general. Such pursuits have their own built-in ethic, that any efforts at pushing back the frontiers of theory and research deserve the highest commendation because they attest to man's divine-like power of mastering his environment and creating his own brand of miracles in it. Suddenly the nation was told that man's science is as fallible as he is himself. Among the most vocal critics were the environment-minded scientists who warned that, in our enthusiasm for conquering nature, we may be destroying ourselves in the process unless we impose restraints on such activity.[24] Perhaps the best-known writer to forecast doom if science were to continue on its conventional course was the biologist Commoner, whose book, *Science and Survival*, enjoyed wide circulation and influence. Commoner took the ecological point of view that the elements of nature are integrated but our knowledge of these elements is so limited that we do not see their connectedness. Expressing deep concern about the preoccupation of science with the elegance of its methods rather than the danger of its products, he directed much of his fire at the polluting effects of such symbols of technological giantism as nuclear testing and industrial waste. He acknowledged the need for brainpower to enrich scientific thinking, but he also warned that "no scientific principle can tell us how to make the choice, which may sometimes be forced upon us by the insecticide problem, between the shade of the elm tree and the song of the robin."[25] With such caveats, it became more difficult to convince gifted children that a life dedicated to science is the kind of high calling it once was unless closer links were made between the intellect and the conscience.

Besides being tarnished because they failed to take account of their human consequences, careers in science lost more of their glitter when the job market in various related fields began to tighten. The manpower crisis dramatized by Sputnik gradually calmed down when we began to overtake the Russians in the technology race and achieved a victory of sorts by transporting the first man to the moon in 1969. Manpower shortages in the various fields of science were no longer critical, partly because the flood of graduates in the early 1960s had filled available jobs, and also because the cold war was not considered serious enough to create new jobs through lucrative defense contracts. In fact, by the late 1960s, many Americans were suspicious of the so-called "military-industrial complex" for carving too much out of the tax dollar to support projects that were wasteful in times of peace. The primary need was to solve the problems of social unrest rather than to prop up our defense technology. Many would-be scientists and engineers began to realize that these professions attracted neither the prestige nor occupational rewards that would have been

---

24. Philip L. Bereano, "The Scientific Community and the Crisis of Belief," *American Scientist* 57 (1969): 484-501.

25. Barry Commoner, *Science and Survival* (New York: The Viking Press, 1966), p. 104.

1. INTERVENTION

guaranteed only a few years earlier. Unfortunately, however, the supply of scientific talent did not slow down in accordance with the reduced demand, and as a result of the imbalance, many highly trained personnel found themselves either unemployed or working at unskilled jobs outside their fields.

The 1970s: A Renewed Interest

The decline of attention to the gifted in the 1960s is evident in the contrasting number of professional publications on that subject at the beginning and end of the decade. The number of entries under "Gifted Children" in the 1970 volume of *Education Index* was less than half the number in the 1960 volume. Nevertheless, by the outset of the present decade, there were unmistakable signs of a revival of interest. Probably the biggest boost came from a 1970 congressional mandate that added Section 806, "Provisions Related to Gifted and Talented Children," to the Elementary and Secondary Education Amendments of 1969 (Public Law 91-230). This document expressed a legislative interest in the gifted that eventually led to federal support of program initiatives throughout the country.

As a result of federal encouragement and some public and private initiative, the gifted have been exposed to an increasing number of special educational experiences in the 1970s. While as late as 1973 fewer than 4 percent of the nation's gifted children were receiving satisfactory attention at school, and most of the fortunate ones were concentrated in ten states, by 1977 every state in the union demonstrated at least some interest in the ablest.

Leadership at the federal level also grew much stronger in the first half of the decade. After being in existence for a brief three-year period as an understaffed, temporary unit in the U.S. Office of Education, Bureau of the Handicapped, the Office of the Gifted and Talented was given official status by legislation in 1974. The Special Projects Act resulted in a 1976 appropriation of $2.56 million for developing professional and program resources in the field. That allocation was renewed for 1977, and there is every reason to expect that federal support will be sustained at least for the years immediately ahead. There are also proposals for legislation that would change the Bureau of the Handicapped to the Bureau of Exceptional Persons, thus including gifted and talented individuals as eligible for sustained support of their education, along with the handicapped. If passed, such federal legislation will go a long way toward erasing the image of education for the gifted as being only a periodic fad in the schools. It is admittedly a way of forcing attention on the ablest by tying their fortunes to those of the handicapped, for whom funding rarely abates appreciably. The public may never feel equally sympathetic to both groups, but it could be forced to reduce some of its favoritism toward one over the other if they are combined rather than separate recipients of support through legislation.

The thrust of recent activity for the gifted has been mostly programmatic and promotional, with relatively little emphasis on research. Funding at all levels is invested in curriculum enrichment,

1. Pre-Sputnik

teacher education, and training for leadership in the field. As part of their work on curriculum, many educators are designing or adapting special instructional systems in order to offer the ablest students experiences that are uniquely appropriate for them, not just promising practices from which all children can derive benefits.

Present-day efforts to design distinctive curricula for the gifted may result in some lasting contributions to the field. Products that have already been developed and distributed in many localities incorporate large numbers of exercises in divergent thinking. This trend reflects the foundational work of several prolific educators whose writings fairly dominated the field during the 1960s. Among the most widely influential persons has been E. Paul Torrance, who alone and with the help of occasional collaborators was responsible for at least seven major books and monographs as well as a large number of professional papers on the subject of creativity from 1960 to 1970. The popularity of research and materials development pertaining to divergent thinking is also having its impact on the classroom more than ever before. "Values clarification" has made its debut in recent years and is gradually spreading in classes for the gifted. It introduced a new dimension in the curriculum by stimulating children to understand themselves better and to develop belief systems and behavior codes that they can justify as bases for some of the most important decisions of their lives.

Again, as in the post-Sputnik period, interest has been expressed in gifted children who have high social intelligence and in those especially talented in the visual and performing arts. It is hard to say whether educators today are paying more attention to the needs of such children than their predecessors did two decades ago. From all indications, it would seem that they are not as yet far beyond the lip-service level of commitment. Even less fortunate are the gifted among underprivileged minority populations who still remain largely neglected, except in the arts, but not deliberately so. There is no doubt that many educators would gladly initiate enrichment experiences for these children and that support could be obtained for such plans if they stood a chance of success. Yet, the profession is still stymied in its efforts to find a way of discerning high-level academic potential that is buried under a thick overlay of social and economic handicaps. In fact, it is no less difficult today than ever before to tease out and inspire the fulfillment of scholarly talent in the nation's underprivileged classes.

Generally, the enrichment programs initiated in the present decade have been impressive in their variety, inventiveness, the extent of their dissemination, and in the spirit and proficiency with which they are being implemented. The same cannot be said for research productivity. A review of the state of research for the years 1969-1974 revealed a fairly bleak picture;[26] only thirty-nine reports on the gifted and talented had been published in that period. Today, these efforts continue to be limited, but there are several major projects now underway that deal with the nature and nurture of talent at all age levels.

---

26. R. L. Spaulding, "Summary Report of Issues and Trends in Research on the Gifted and Talented," (undated manuscript).

1. INTERVENTION

What prompted the resurgence of activity in gifted education after nearly a decade of quiescence? A full answer probably will not come until future historians can view the 1970s in a proper time perspective. But the explanation that seems most obvious right now is America's backlash against awareness-oriented youth who turned excessively self-indulgent, and against campus revolutionaries who trashed some sacred scholarly traditions. Geoffrey Wagner has recently published a scathing indictment of universities for compromising academic standards, inflating grades, and diluting degree requirements in order to fend off unrest among students.[27] Perhaps these are signs that the pendulum is inevitably swinging away from extreme egalitarianism in the direction of excellence. It is hard to imagine that there would be a popular acceptance of the Consciousness III notion about brilliant minds not being better at thinking than anyone else and poor thinkers necessarily being excellent in their own ways. This kind of argument is too fantasy-ridden to flourish successfully even in an egalitarian-minded society. There are, however, legacies of the 1960s that are volatile enough today to have prevented the gifted from making a comeback. They include the following realities:

1. Few manpower shortages exist at the high-skill levels. The job market is glutted with Ph.D.'s who cannot find work in their fields of training. In 1976, the starting salary of college graduates was only 6 percent above that of the average American worker, whereas in 1969, a person with a college diploma could earn 24 percent more than the national mean.[28]

2. The cold war, while relentless, does not threaten any new surprises to shake our confidence in the nation's talent reservoir. There is even talk of moderating the confrontation between East and West through policies of detente and the SALT talks.

3. It is not much easier today than in the late 1960s to persuade our ablest students that they have to work hard at school in order to serve their country in ways that only they can. National policies in Viet Nam and in the civil rights movement had persuaded too many of them that the country was not worthy of such dedication. When the Viet Nam war came to an end, Watergate emerged to reinforce the cynicism and alienation of youth, including many gifted individuals among them.

4. Quality, integrated education is as much a dream today as it has ever been. A prodigious amount of work yet remains to be done before underprivileged children can begin to derive their rightful benefits from experiences at school. That kind of investment of effort in compensatory programs usually draws attention away from curricular enrichment for the gifted.

5. Science and scientists are still monitored critically for possible moral lapses. The most recent controversy concerning value judgments in the scientific community has revolved around experiments in genetic engineering. Some gifted children may choose to avoid fields of science in order to keep their consciences clear about possibly opening any kind of Pandora's box in scientific discovery.

---

27. Geoffrey Wagner, *The End of Education* (South Brunswick, N.J.: A. S. Barnes, 1976).

6. The 1970s have experienced hard times and drastic cutbacks in expenditures for education. Programs for the gifted are usually the most expendable ones when budgetary considerations force cutbacks in services to children.

Despite the aforementioned lingering influences of the 1960s, we are experiencing a drift toward excellence after indulging egalitarianism for awhile. This revival of interest, however, is no more a sign of pure historical inevitability than was its decline a decade ago. It is rather, in part at least, a sign of initiatives taken by people who believe in differentiated education at every ability level and who are participating in vigorous campaigns to save the schools.

Attention to individual competencies among the handicapped has dramatized the need to individualize education, with every child receiving a fair share of what is uniquely appropriate for him, regardless of how deficient or proficient he is in mastering curriculum content. It is logical, then, that the gifted also receive special attention to accommodate their unique learning strengths and thereby demonstrate the educator's attention to human differences. Eventually, PL 94-142 may include the gifted, which would take us a long way toward actualizing the belief that democracy in education means recognizing how children are unlike each other, and doing something about it. Protagonists for the gifted argue that the more sophisticated we become in discerning human individuality and the more inventive we are in providing for individual needs of the ablest, the more likely we are to achieve equality in the schools.

THE ROLE OF THE GIFTED IN "RESCUING" PUBLIC EDUCATION

It is no secret that educators are searching desperately for ways to maintain order in thousands of classrooms. This is especially true in big-city schools where more than 10 percent of the nation's pupil population is enrolled. The dismal picture is a familiar one: scholastic achievement levels are three, four, and even five years below norms; drugs, violence, vandalism, and truancy have reached epidemic proportions; and costs are climbing to such a height that there may soon be insufficient funds to pay the bills while maintaining an adequately staffed program.[29] Many middle-class families have fled the inner city or sought help from private schools in order to provide a meaningful educational experience for their children. This has further aggravated the situation in urban centers.

School administrators are aware that one way to bring back the middle classes to the schools is to initiate special programs for the gifted. They are, therefore, opening so-called "magnet schools" that offer enrichment activities in particular subject matter areas and are luring back to their classrooms sizable numbers of children who would otherwise be studying elsewhere. The presence of the ablest is beginning to make a difference in the total school atmosphere, which demonstrates that they are capable of enhancing all of education if their learning capacities are properly respected. This truism may turn out to be the most important lesson learned from our experience with gifted and talented children in the 1970s.

---

29. *Ibid.*, September 12, 1977.

Issues in Education for the Gifted

James J. Gallagher

In every field of endeavor each generation leaves a mixed legacy to the next. Along with the hard-won wisdom that comes from experience and the progressive accumulation of knowledge, collections of misinformation and misjudgments that can only be explained by understanding the temper and biases of the times are also passed along. As an antidote to any misplaced confidence that we at last have the tiger of education for the gifted by the tail, it may be useful to catalogue some unsolved issues or misguided efforts that have been created or accepted by the present generation and which we are in danger of turning over to the next generation.

A Definition of Giftedness

One splendid example of how the incorrect assumptions of past generations influence us today involves the acceptance of the concept that giftedness is entirely created by genetic forces. The early influential research by Terman et al. was based on this assumption.[1] Until the last decade, our major identification techniques and much of our program design have also been based on this assumption.

For example, a single intelligence test score was usually considered sufficient to define giftedness, thus implying that we did not expect major changes or modifications in measured ability in the child as a result of environmental intervention, except in the most seriously deprived situations. If changes in intelligence test scores occurred, they were accounted for on the basis that the children were finally free to show their "true" ability. The earlier score could then be dismissed as invalid because of the special conditions of the earlier examination.

Other variations in measured ability were explained as due to faults in the testing instrument or to errors in measurement. Few people suggested that those children who failed to achieve the cutoff scores required for eligibility for a gifted program should be retested, because few believed that the children could progress enough intellectually to meet the standards of eligibility for the program at some future time.

The acceptance of the purely genetic nature of intelligence led to some embarrassing and troubling results, such as the consistent racial and ethnic differences found in the proportions of children testing as gifted. Such results were not widely quoted or displayed, although there have been clear and consistent findings on the question.[2]

The accumulation of evidence from studies in child development suggests that there is a subtle and complex interaction between environment and native ability, the result of which is what is measured by a score on an intelligence test.[3] The full range of implica-

---

1. Lewis Terman et al., *Genetic Studies of Genius*, vol. 1, *Mental and Physical Traits of a Thousand Gifted Children* (Stanford, Calif.: Stanford University Press, 1926).

2. Mortimer Adler, "A Study of the Effects of Ethnic Origin on Giftedness," *Gifted Child Quarterly* 7 (1963): 98-101; Walter Barbe, "Characteristics of Gifted Children," *Education Administration and Supervision* 41 (1955): 207-17.

3. Helen L. Bee, "A Developmental Psychologist Looks at Educational Policy," (Paper given at the Aspen Institute Program on Education for a Changing Society, Aspen, Colo., 1976.

From *The Gifted and the Talented: Their Education and Development*, by the National Society for the Study of Education, reprinted with permission.

tions of this fact has not been fully grasped or acted upon by educators of the gifted, although some initial steps have been taken. These steps include the use of many different techniques to identify gifted children in minority groups. But we still have not fully accepted the interaction concept—the concept that we can create giftedness through designing enriched environments and opportunities, or that we can destroy it by failing to create those environments and opportunities. We have lived for so long with the single-dimension concept that genetic forces totally control intelligence (or with some disbelievers, that environment totally controls intelligence) that we have not yet adjusted to all the implications of the interaction paradigm.

A broadened concept of giftedness, designed to include more than those characteristics measured by intelligence tests, was given additional impetus by the extraordinarily influential study by Getzels and Jackson,[4] who attempted to differentiate between gifted and creative children, and by a decade of work by Torrance[5] focusing on the distinctive characteristics of creative children. Once the magic aura of the intelligence quotient was broken, it became possible to think of other dimensions that should be included in a general definition of giftedness. In addition, the increasing emphasis on the culturally different gifted children spurred the search for other valuable talents beyond the purely academic.

The effort to identify a variety of talents led to a broadened definition of the gifted child that appeared in a report on the status of the gifted child in the United States. That report, prepared for the U.S. Congress by Sidney P. Marland, Jr., then commissioner of education, provided a definition that was included in subsequently enacted federal legislation. The definition represented the first formal recognition, by name, at the federal level of the problems of education for gifted children. Since this definition has been so widely used, it is probably the one that should be discussed in terms of its virtues and faults. The definition reads as follows:

Gifted and talented children are those identified by professionally qualified persons [and] who by virtue of outstanding abilities are capable of high performance. These are children who require differentiated educational programs and services beyond those normally provided by the regular school program in order to realize their contribution to self and society.

Children capable of high performance include those with demonstrated achievement and/or potential ability in any of the following areas: (a) general intellectual ability, (b) specific academic aptitude, (c) creative or productive thinking, (d) leadership ability, (e) visual and performing arts, (f) psychomotor ability.[6]

Stating a definition is one thing and making it operational in an educational sense is quite another. What is leadership ability? Is it

---

4. Jacob Getzels and Philip Jackson, *Creativity and Intelligence* (New York: Wiley, 1962).

5. E. Paul Torrance, *Creativity* (Belmont, Calif.: Dimensions Publishing Co., 1969).

6. Sidney P. Marland, Jr., *Education of the Gifted and Talented*, vol. 1 Report to the Congress of the United States by the U.S. Commissioner of Education (Washington, D.C.: U.S. Government Printing Office, 1972), p. 2.

1. INTERVENTION

the same whether we think of the captain of a football team, of the leader of a debate team, or of the leader of a student protest movement? What is the test or means for identifying such leadership characteristics? If this trait can be trained, can we "create" gifted leaders with an appropriate educational program?

If we measure for general intellect and ability, how many who are gifted academically and in leadership will be intellectually gifted? There is now some suspicion that in our eagerness to specify these new dimensions we may have overestimated their separateness from high intellectual ability.[7] For example, the "High Creative—Low IQ" syndrome made popular by Getzels and Jackson was based on research on a group with extremely high IQs. The "Low IQ" students turned out to be "low" only relative to their comparison group. The "High Creative—Low IQ" group obtained a mean intelligence score of 127, a score that would qualify most of them for educational programs for the academically gifted in many cities and states.

What is psychomotor ability? If it includes basketball and football players, then we have had many more sophisticated talent searches and special programs for the gifted than most of us have realized. Do those who use the term "psychomotor ability" have in mind ballet dancers? If so, what is the link to the visual and performing arts? Who are included in the visual and performing arts anyway, and how are *they* identified?

In education, it is natural for us to respond to the question "Who are you talking about?" by trying to state a definition. Scientists know that the definition of a concept is not the first thing to be completed, but quite literally the last. We will not have a better definition until we find out more than we now know about the questions posed above. The inadequacies of the definition are merely symptoms pointing to our incomplete knowledge about the relevant concepts. If we are to pass along a more coherent statement to the next generation, then we will need not only better rhetoric but more sustained research and development as well.

There is also an increasing tendency to focus attention on special subgroups within the gifted category (for example, gifted women). Some of these subgroups are touched upon in other parts of this volume and will not be dealt with here.

Educational Programming for the Gifted

Attempts to modify the school program for gifted students must focus on one or a combination of three major dimensions: (a) the content, (b) special skills, and (c) a modified learning environment.[8]

CONTENT

By far the most common discussion of special programming for gifted children has focused upon possible changes in setting or learning environment. The literature is cluttered with discussions of acceleration, of whether special classes are better than regular

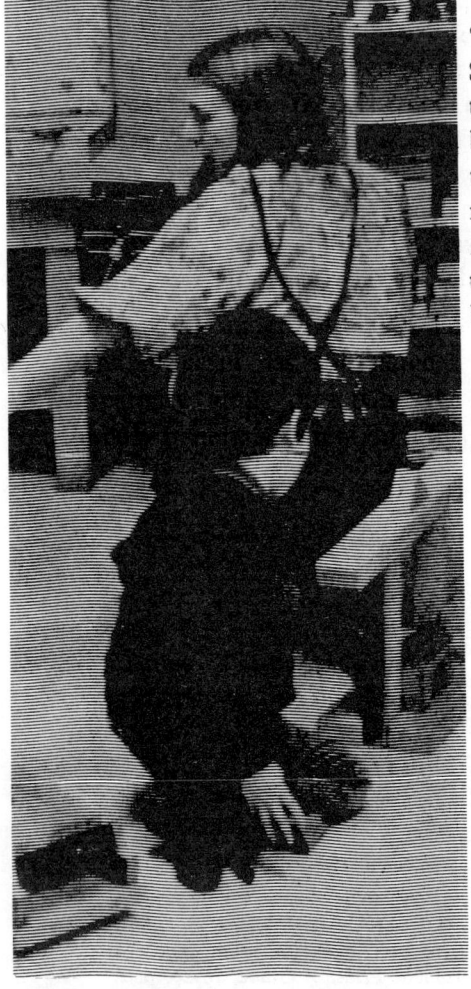

---

7. Michael Wallach, "Creativity," in *Carmichael's Manual of Child Psychology*, 3d ed. Paul H. Mussen (New York: John Wiley, 1970), vol. 1, pp. 1211-1272.

classes, or of whether resource room programs are as effective as other models of program design. Relatively little attention has been paid to the actual content that would make up the heart of any differentiated program, regardless of the particular learning environment in which it was delivered.

Renzulli has commented as follows on the lack of systematic and sophisticated content in programs for the gifted:

> In conducting evaluative studies, I have witnessed far too many programs for the gifted that are essentially collections of fun-and-games activities; such activities lack continuity and show little evidence of developing in a systematic fashion the mental processes that led these children to be identified as gifted.[9]

Elsewhere I have urged the development of more complex curriculum units and materials for the gifted based upon advanced conceptualization of a subject, to which Bruner has referred as the "structure of the discipline."[10] Such coordinated curriculum or self-contained units, however, are more easily discussed than created, and at the present time there are few visible attempts to generate differentiated curriculum in the content fields. It would be useful to develop curriculum units around central seminal ideas in a fashion similar to that used in Bronowski's television series, "The Ascent of Man." For example, Bronowski dealt with the concept of war as follows:

> War, organized war, is not a human instinct. It is a highly planned and cooperative theft. And that form of theft began ten thousand years ago when the harvesters of wheat accumulated a surplus and the nomads rose out of the desert to rob them of what they themselves could not provide.[11]

Kaplan has emphasized the importance of integrating content with additional attention to the learning process.[12] She stressed the use of topics that stimulate thinking, are action-oriented, and provide options for individual differences among gifted students. Renzulli recommended that one side of his "enrichment triad model" (individual and small-group investigations of real problems) was particularly relevant for gifted students, and developed ideas on how to stimulate such investigations.[13] Despite these and other suggestions, it is clear that the educational practitioner who must provide direct service to gifted students is essentially entering a difficult instructional situation almost totally unarmed because there are few, if any, organized curriculum resources to draw upon.

---

8. James J. Gallagher, *Teaching the Gifted Child*, 2d ed. (Boston: Allyn and Bacon, 1975).

9. Joseph S. Renzulli, *New Directions in Creativity* (New York: Harper and Row, 1973).

10. Jerome S. Bruner, *Toward a Theory of Instruction* (Cambridge, Mass.: Belknap Press, 1966).

11. Jacob Bronowski, *The Ascent of Man* (Boston: Little, Brown and Co., 1973), p. 88.

12. Sandra Kaplan, *Providing Programs for the Gifted and Talented: A Handbook* (Ventura, Calif.: Office of the Ventura County Superintendent of Schools, June, 1974).

13. Joseph S. Renzulli, *The Enrichment Triad Model: A Guide for Developing Defensible Programs for the Gifted and Talented* (Wethersfield, Conn.: Creative Learning Press, 1977).

1. INTERVENTION

SPECIAL SKILLS: CREATIVITY

Over the past decade, there has been no single topic that has been so well discussed and researched as the dimension of "creativity."[14] The reason for such interest is clear. In a rapidly changing and developing modern society, it is foolish to prepare students for the world of their parents. Gifted first graders today may not leave their advanced graduate programs or professional schools until the year 2000. How do we prepare those students for the year 2001?

As Silberman put it:

To be practical, an education should prepare a man for work that doesn't yet exist and whose nature cannot even be imagined. This can be done only by teaching children how to learn, and by giving them the kind of intellectual discipline that will enable them to apply man's accumulated wisdom to new problems.[15]

There are two dramatically different views of the fundamental nature of creativity itself. On one hand, it may be approached as if it were a set of teachable cognitive skills, and cognitive models, such as Bloom's taxonomy of objectives for the cognitive domain[16] or Guilford's "structure of intellect,"[17] are seen as ways of providing an analytic approach to creativity. There are key dimensions in each of these models that are especially concerned with creativity. In the Guilford model, for example, divergent production has been identified by a number of writers as closely equivalent to creativity. Many exercises and activities that would enhance these skills have been produced in the last decade.[18]

On the other hand, one school of thought suggests that creativity is associated with a distinctive set of personality traits that sets some individuals apart from their more unimaginative peers. Such a finding would result in some educational strategies very different from the cognitive exercises noted above. In reviewing the literature, Dellas and Gaier[19] and Dewing[20] suggested that an openness to stimuli, whether the stimuli were taboo in the society or not, is one of the key characteristics of the creative mind. Part of the reputation of creative persons for bizarre or unusual behavior undoubtedly stems from their ignoring taboos with regard to violence, sex, and so forth.[21] Another strong and consistent finding is

---

14. John C. Gowan, *Development of the Creative Individual* (San Diego, Calif.: Robert Knapp, 1972); Torrance, *Creativity*.

15. Charles Silberman, *Crisis in the Classroom* (New York: Random House, 1970), p. 114.

16. Benjamin Bloom, *Taxonomy of Educational Objectives: The Classification of Educational Goals, Handbook I: Cognitive Domain* (New York: Longman, 1956).

17. Joy P. Guilford, *The Nature of Human Intelligence* (New York, McGraw-Hill, 1967).

18. Mary N. Meeker, *The Structure of Intellect: Its Interpretation and Uses* (Columbus, Ohio: Charles Merrill, 1969).

19. Marie Dellas and Eugene Gaier, "Identification of Creativity: The Individual," *Psychological Bulletin* 73 (1970): 55-73.

20. Kathleen Dewing. "Family Influences on Creativity: A Review and Discussion," *Journal of Special Education* 4 (1970): 399-404.

21. Donald W. MacKinnon, "The Nature and Nurture of Creative Talent," *American Psychologist* 17 (1962): 484-95.

2. Issues

that gifted individuals are independent in attitude and social behavior.[22] They neither follow nor are swayed by the crowd. They have a strong self-concept and sense of personal identity. In this sense, they are sometimes viewed as unusual in a group, since they neither follow the social path set by the group nor do they repress antisocial or asocial feelings.

Torrance explored teacher attitudes toward the most desirable student characteristics.[23] In reviewing the attitudes of over a thousand teachers, he identified those characteristics that seemed most ideal to teachers in the United States. Among these were: consideration for others, determination, industriousness, sincerity, courtesy, doing work on time, and so forth. When these qualities were compared with a list of characteristics most highly rated by a panel of experts as important components of the productive and creative person, there were only two characteristics found in common—curiosity and independence in thinking.

Missing from the teachers' list were such creativity-related factors as intellectual courage, independence in judgment, being absorbed or preoccupied with tasks, intuitiveness, persistence, the willingness to take risks, and the unwillingness to accept the judgment of authorities. It should be obvious that characteristics widely desired as socially conforming may be antithetical to creative production. The paradox with which the educators must come to grips is that there are competing positive characteristics, all valued by our society, which may predispose the child to shun a life of creativity.

SPECIAL CASES: THE UNDERACHIEVERS AND THE CULTURALLY DIFFERENT

There are two groups of children about whom our knowledge has substantially increased over the last decade, but for whom that increase in knowledge has not been matched by appropriate modifications in the educational environment. These are the gifted underachievers and the gifted who are culturally different.

For gifted underachievers. There have been a variety of devices used to define the underachiever in terms of the gap between potential and performance. Some programs use the gap between achievement test scores and intelligence test scores for defining purposes. Others use the gap between academic grades and intelligence test scores. Regardless of the device used, the general portrait of the underachiever seems fairly consistent from study to study. A composite portrait of the gifted underachievers reveals a lack of self-confidence, the inability to persevere, a lack of a sense of purpose or drive, the presence of feelings of inferiority, and family conflict.[24]

A chicken-egg problem seems to be involved here. That is, are the children underachieving because of a low self-concept, or is their low self-concept the result of their chronic underachievement?

---

22. Frank Barron, *Creative Person and Creative Process* (New York: Holt, Rinehart and Winston, 1969).

23. E. Paul Torrance, *Rewarding Creative Behavior* (Englewood Cliffs, N.J.: Prentice-Hall, 1965).

24. Lewis Terman and Melita Oden, *Genetic Studies of Genius*, vol. 4, *The Gifted Child Grows Up: Twenty-five Years' Follow-up of a Superior Group* (Stanford, Calif.: Stanford University Press, 1947).

1. INTERVENTION

By the time the school becomes concerned with these issues in the upper-elementary school, the interactions have become so intertwined that they have to be dealt with as a combination of effects.

In the past, two different strategies have been used in attempts to eliminate or reduce the problems of underachievement. The first of these was personal counseling based upon the research findings of a low self-image and of feelings of inferiority among underachievers. The second strategy has been a shift in educational environment to create either a more permissive or a more demanding environment, either of which might tend to modify the destructive patterns of response of the underachievers. Raph, Goldberg, and Passow reported the experimental findings from both of these approaches and commented upon the lack of positive results in both instances.[25] Because the counseling that has been described in such evaluation studies has often been limited and short-term, it has apparently not had outstanding impact. The modifications in educational environment likewise appear to have had little effect.

It may well be that the schools have underestimated the powerful effects of the personality patterns involved and thus underrate the amount of modification required to make a major impact. At any rate, we currently seem to be waiting for the next generation to emerge with better and more effective techniques to deal with these underachieving children.

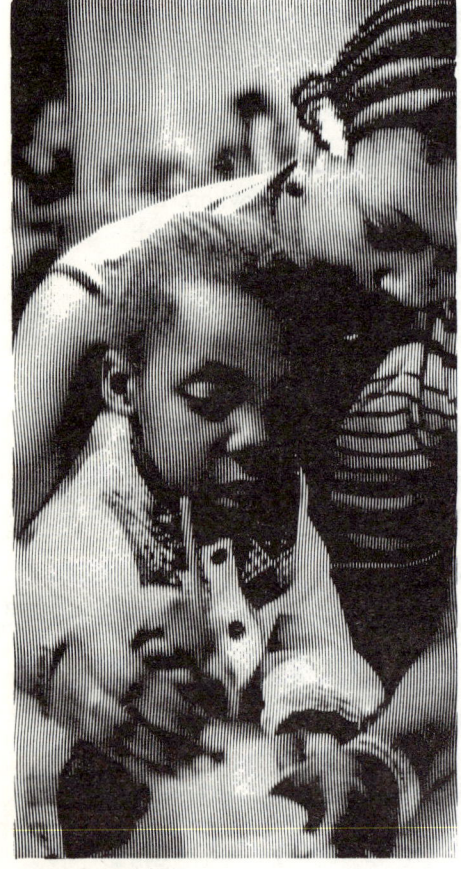

For the culturally different gifted. Another group consists of those children referred to as the "culturally different gifted." We can anticipate special educational problems for children who come from the multitude of diverse ethnic and racial backgrounds that comprise American society. Increasing attention has been paid to these children over the past decade. Unfortunately, attention appears to be focused more on how to identify and recognize outstanding talent from cultural subgroups rather than on the more educationally fruitful discussion of what special experiences, content, or skills should be provided for them.[26]

One of our incorrect assumptions has been that talent is essentially indestructable. This concept relates to the idea noted earlier that ability is entirely genetically determined. Following that assumption, we have tried to find methods to uncover the talent that would always be there, just as one would lift up a basket and find a lantern shining beneath it. An alternative explanation, however, is more in line with known facts. Since ability in young children is the product of an interaction of the environment and native ability, then a very bad environment, experienced over an extended period of time, can be expected to reduce substantially or even eliminate the high talent and ability that might have been present originally. The notion that superior talent can in fact be suppressed or destroyed should lend additional urgency to our attempts to provide stimulating and exciting educational experiences for the culturally different gifted.

---

25. Jane B. Raph, Miriam L. Goldberg, and A. Harry Passow, *Bright Underachievers* (New York: Teachers College Press, 1966).

26. Ruth Martinson, "The Identification of the Gifted and Talented," (Ventura, Calif.: National/State Leadership Training Institute on the Gifted and Talented, 1974).

2. Issues

Torrance and Torrance, as well as other authors, have emphasized that the culturally different child may come to school with a number of advantages as well as disadvantages, and that those advantages might provide the base for special educational programming.[27] Such advantages could be more freedom to explore, less inhibition, less commitment to established norms—all of which could provide a foundation for special program opportunities.

Gallagher and Kinney reported on a conference oriented to the culturally different gifted in which there was major participation of persons from a variety of culturally different backgrounds. Four major recommendations emerged from the conference:

1. The need for a curriculum stressing cultural pluralism;
2. Full use of community resources to supplement the school program;
3. The importance of recruitment and training of personnel who understand cultural pluralism and who may be members of the culturally different group themselves; and,
4. The need to impress on public decision makers at the state and federal levels that resources are needed to produce model programs and demonstrations that would illustrate good practices with the culturally different groups.[28]

It is clear that we have no organized strategy to deal with the diversity of needs and interests. As one thinks of the American Indian in the desert, the inner-city Puerto Ricans in New York, blacks living in poverty in the rural south, and the Chicanos in southern California, one realizes the foolishness of designing *one* alternative program to meet the needs of all these special groups. One of the major unsolved issues of our day, therefore, is that of determining the strategy for effective programming in these varied situations.

COST BENEFITS OF SPECIAL PROGRAMMING

One of the strongest and most influential movements in the past decade in American education has been the development of systematic program planning and evaluation.[29] Planning is an increasingly used device, if not a popular one, as resources become limited and problems intractable. The related issue of cost benefits has emerged, placing the educator under pressure to demonstrate that the extra cost of any special program is compensated for by the greater range of benefits that the program produces. These benefits are often defined by student output or other associated benefits. A compelling case can be made for the cost benefits of gifted programs. Even if we assume only modest benefits resulting from additional assistance to the gifted and the talented, the potential future impact of these students on the society makes any gains of substantial importance.

Nevertheless, we should be about the business of developing a

---

27. E. Paul Torrance and Pansy Torrance, "Combining Creative Problem Solving with Creative Expressive Activities in the Education of Disadvantaged Young People," *Journal of Creative Behavior* 6 (1972): 1-10.

28. *Talent Delayed—Talent Denied: A Conference Report*, ed. James Gallagher and Lucretia Kinney (Reston, Va.: Foundation for Exceptional Children, 1974).

29. *School Evaluation: The Politics and Process*, ed. Ernest R. House (Berkeley, Calif.: McCutchan Publishing Corp., 1973).

1. INTERVENTION

systematic methodology that can weigh the benefits of the programs for the gifted, even as procedures have been devised to provide similar evidence for the programs for the mentally retarded. The economic costs of a total educational program should include the cost of *not* having a special program for the gifted. Here the results could become dramatic. What is the cost of the medical discovery never made? Of the political compromise never reached to head off a war? Of the sonata that was never written?

The story of unrealized potential has been and will continue to be a strong, dramatic theme. Since all of us realize less than our own potential, it is easy for us to identify with such stories. In the field of medicine there have been startling new discoveries in immunization and in antibiotics, new and dramatic surgical techniques, and a wide variety of other contributions to better health. Who made these discoveries? It is clear that they were made by *gifted* scientists in various biomedical fields. What is the cost effectiveness of a special program for gifted students who may become, among many other possibilities, medical scientists and researchers? The cost of *not* having them is obviously a cause of grief.

The Future of Educational Programs for the Gifted

AMERICA'S LOVE-HATE RELATIONSHIP WITH THE GIFTED

The gifted scholars of tender years are often told by their elders that they are the future of the nation and that we are delighted with their academic performance and look eagerly to their forthcoming contributions to the society. These gifted students might well be confused by the conflicting messages they receive because even the most perceptive of them has a difficult time grasping the fundamental point that we adults do not say everything we mean, nor do we mean everything we say, about their talent.

A strong case can be made for the presence in the American society of a love-hate relationship with giftedness and talent. On one hand, we revere the gifted individual who has risen from humble background. We are proud to live in a society where talent can triumph over environment or family status. At the same time, since our origins came from battling an aristocratic elite, we are suspicious of attempts to subvert our commitment to egalitarianism. We do not wish a new elite class to develop, and as a result we seem to waver in our attitudes. We design our elementary and secondary programs for gifted students in ways that can be defended by careful administrators as giving no special favors, no tipping the scales in favor of the socially powerful or the specially endowed.[30]

Sometimes satire is the best way to illustrate the ambiguous positions in which we find ourselves. Kurt Vonnegut, Jr. has carried one of the common feelings about the gifted in our society to a logical conclusion in a short story entitled *Harrison Bergeron*, set in some future society:

The year was 2081, and everybody was finally equal. They weren't only

---

30. John Gardner, *Excellence: Can We Be Equal and Excellent Too?* (New York: Harper and Row, 1961).

equal before God and the law, they were equal in every which way. Nobody was smarter than anybody. No one was better looking than anybody else.[31]

The reason for this enforced equality was that people who were outstanding in various ways were given handicaps. Those that could dance well had to wear sandbags on their feet, those who were strikingly good looking would have to wear a mask so as not to embarrass those who did not have those characteristics. And those with high intellectual ability?

George, while his intelligence was way above normal, had a little mental handicap radio in his ear. He was required by law to wear it at all times. He was tuned into a government transmitter. Every twenty seconds or so, the transmitter would send out some noise to keep people like George from taking unfair advantage of their brains.[32]

The essentially destructive approach to "equality" does not really pass until we reach higher education when a miraculous transformation takes place. The United States has created the most complex and extensive higher education and professional school establishment in the world. We do not call the Stanford Medical School or the Harvard Law School a program for gifted students, but we know that they are and no apologies are made that only the "best" students should be allowed to attend. After all, some of us may need a good lawyer from time to time, others may need an excellent surgeon, and others would like to get some good advice from a competent psychiatrist.

As we view the needs of the society, the agenda of unsolved problems such as pollution, population, energy, and a lacking sense of national purpose, we feel the need for the best and the brightest to be well prepared and well motivated, not only to achieve their individual destiny, but also to aid the society as a whole.

At the local, state, and federal levels we vacillate in our public school program between the need to be "fair" and the need to be "effective." At times when the society seems to be threatened, such as in the Sputnik era and recently with the variety of problems surrounding energy shortages, we lean toward the productive use of all talent. In more placid eras such as the early 1950s, the post-World War II decade, when there seemed to be little to worry and threaten us, we sought "equality" as a more appropriate goal. At the very least, we need to make these conflicting values visible so that a more mature societal decision can be made.

Requirements of quality programs for the gifted. Since the bulk of education for the gifted will inevitably be focused on public education, which is funded and supported in part through legislative bodies, attention must be turned toward legislative action at both the state and federal levels to support innovative programs. It is this route that would provide the resources for the development of new programs, for training, and for innovation. But such action is quite recent. It was in the 1950s and 1960s that a number of states became specifically involved. It was only in 1974 that the gifted were first mentioned in federal legislation in P.L. 93-380.

---

31. Kurt Vonnegut, Jr., *Welcome to the Monkey House* (New York: Dell, 1950), p. 7.

32. Ibid.

1. INTERVENTION

Rossmiller, Hale, and Frohreich have catalogued the relative expenditures of programs for exceptional children from five states.[33] The excess cost, over and above the normal cost of schooling, ranges from $92 per child for the intellectually gifted to $1,729 per child for the physically and multiply handicapped. Of all exceptional children, the programs for the gifted cost the least, but these costs are often enough above the average to be significant in hindering the development of special programs.

There is no conceivable way in which the number of specialists needed for the gifted could be trained by existing training institutions under current assumptions and models for delivery of services.[34] Experimentation with a variety of other models that lie within the bounds of possibility is obviously called for.

MAJOR COMPONENTS OF AN EFFECTIVE SUPPORT SYSTEM

There are major components of an effective support system that would bring quality education to the gifted. These components could be provided by legislation not now on the books. As I have indicated elsewhere, the following components are essential elements in a support system for educational programs for the gifted:

1. *Continuous in-service training.* It is important that any such programmatic effort involve a continuous and systematic effort to upgrade the skills and knowledge of the teachers directly involved in the program. Workshops and institutes in content areas such as mathematics or social studies, or in stimulating productive thinking, would be examples of such training efforts.

2. *Leadership training.* It is important that a program of any considerable size have a staff person in a leadership position who has responsibility for systematic program development. Leadership personnel would organize and participate in in-service programs, coordinate content fields, bring in the best of what we know in fields such as mathematics or art from the rest of the educational staff or the community, and provide the administrative leadership for the program within the school system.

3. *Research and development.* There is a natural assumption that somewhere in some secluded laboratory or research center important research is being done that will produce new curriculum adventures for the gifted. Unfortunately, this is not true. What is urgently needed, particularly by those resource teachers who are working with the gifted children, is the development of self-contained units that have conceptual validity and that provide the kind of specialized experience and insight to the gifted students that they would not be capable of obtaining through the regular program.

4. *Technical assistance and communication.* It is important to establish a continuing program of technical assistance that would be available for program consultation to a school system that might wish specialized and individual help on its own program develop-

---

33. Richard A. Rossmiller, J. Hale, and L. Frohreich, *Educational Programs for Exceptional Children: Resource Configurations and Cost* (Washington, D.C.: National Education Finance Project, 1970).

34. James J. Gallagher, "Technical Assistance—A New Device for Quality Educational Services for the Gifted," *TAG Newsletter* 16 (1974): 5-8.

ment. Such a unit would provide help on a variety of needs, such as special curricula and the design and execution of evaluation programs, so that the local school system could assure itself that it is doing a creditable job.[35]

In education generally, state funds have traditionally been spent on activities in programs of direct service, with very limited funds set aside for research, demonstration, leadership training, or technical assistance. It therefore seems appropriate that some type of federal legislation could be developed to extend the current section in the Elementary and Secondary Education Act to provide resources for these support functions that are catalytic to good program development.

Summary

The field of gifted education has many unresolved issues that will be passed along to the next generation for more adequate resolution. Among the most important are the comprehension of the full implications of giftedness that is created by a mix of genetics and environment and of the broadened definition that is still far from operational.

In the special education dimension, there is a particular need for major curriculum materials to meet the needs of gifted students and of special educational adaptations proved successful for the gifted underachiever or the culturally different gifted.

Finally, we have yet to come to grips with the ambivalent feelings about giftedness that are abroad in modern American society. These feelings of pride and envy, of security and anxiety, of achievement and competition, shade all of the public actions related to education for the gifted and we have yet to be able to adapt our own planning and educational programs to that fundamental ambivalence.

---

35. James J. Gallagher, "Educational Support Systems for Gifted Students," *North Carolina Association for the Gifted and Talented Quarterly Journal* 1 (1975): 10-11.

THE GIFTED STUDENT: A RESEARCHER'S VIEW

Elizabeth Monroe Drews

THE gifted, in my view, can be simply defined as those who show themselves, in relation both to their age group and to all others, as more fully human. This means that they reach intellectual, aesthetic, and moral heights, and that they show insights and sensitivities in those areas which others do not. Ever since intelligence tests came into general usage, and particularly as a result of Terman's work, we have tended to use this narrow caliper as a means of selection, forgetting that artistic and ethical talents are every bit as important as intellectual talent, perhaps even more so. Fortunately, the present moral crisis was sensed by gifted students (as well as older philosopher generalists) in the Youth Revolution of the 1960's. Not only was the importance of art and nature, of truth and love reaffirmed, but searching questions were also asked about war and peace, prejudice and poverty. These questions are still being asked—and more seriously, if perhaps less shrilly.

At a time when the world could well be on the brink of disaster or, if we dramatically revise our lives, at the point of transformation, it is ridiculous to continue with single vision ways of selecting the gifted. To employ only one measure—and that of an essentially cognitive nature, the individual intelligence test (Stanford-Binet or Wechsler)—is inadequate. We must select for affective as well as individual growth. Although the individual test, including the nonverbal impressions obtained by the examiner, has many advantages over the group test, it is still a strictly limited instrument since it explores only that narrow segment of cognitive learning which is conscious.

Exploring a Broad Array of Talents

I am suggesting that we can use at least three ways to explore a broad array of artistic and empathic talents and sensitivities: by inquiring into interests, by judging performance, and by administering tests.

The first of these methods, discovering the talented children by their show of interest, can be used by any concerned and alert observer. As an example of the second method, practicing artists in the school can not only serve as models of excellence and inspiration, but will also detect the unusually talented children who work with them. Thirdly, there are measures of character development recently devised that could well be used in this way. Attitudes and behavior in such realms as cheating, comformity, and helping others can be ascertained by tests as a supplement to observation. There is rather general agreement on value hierarchies and the various stages of character development by those who have studied this area intensively. There is consensus as to which values are better (or higher), and who is at what stage.

It has been said that we are what we think, what we read, what we watch on television, even what we eat. In the book that Leslie Linson and I wrote, *Values and Humanity,* we made the point that we are what we value. It is by our values that others know us and that we recognize and discover ourselves.

Recognizing Self Images

Helping the students recognize their self images and values was among the objectives of the programs which I was able to initiate in the Public Schools of Lansing, Michigan, where I had been Director of Psychological Services.

In the course of this research the students were asked to describe themselves. Three types emerged

---

Elizabeth Monroe Drews is a professor at Portland State University and at the University of California at Berkeley. Her experiences with gifted students have led her from a one room schoolhouse to university campuses, and have included teaching, counseling, program development, research, and writing in Oregon, Michigan, California, China, and Denmark.

from their descriptions. Moving upward on the moral scale, they were (a) the *social leaders,* (b) the *studious,* and (c) the *creative intellectuals.*

The Social Leaders

Students, of course, are not pure types. In common with everyone else, they exhibit clusters of tendencies among which some are dominant or characteristic. When asked, they can tell you who and what they are, and this judgment about themselves has considerable validity. The avowed aim of the social leaders was to acquire money, power, and status. In this pursuit they were perfectly willing to be expedient and opportunistic. Valuing power, pleasure, and money, a majority of the boys did not "blame anyone for trying to grab all he can get in this world." By contrast, less than a third of the studious and creative intellectuals felt this way.

The social leaders did well enough academically, often helped by their charm, but their social interests came first. While the studious were preparing for examinations and the creative intellectuals were reading about existentialism, the social leaders were generally out electing someone to office or, better yet, getting themselves elected. Choosing to see people as connivers and managers, their effort was to be the masters in that game.

The Studious

At a middle level of development were the studious high achievers. These were conformists whose behavior was standard-traditional and far from rebellious. They did their assignments and they did them well, although perhaps not always joyfully. Although they studied more hours per week than any other group, they tended to lack imagination and intellectual initiative. In fact, they seemed all too willing to fit into the conventional academic norm of following instructions, taking examinations, and solving the problems set forth by teacher and textbook.

Many of the studious high achievers wanted to know what to do and how, but rarely asked why. However, their feeling for logic was good; their sense of organization, superb. Learning for learning's sake might lead them astray. Above all they wanted to be "good boys" and "good girls" and follow the conventional wisdom. They were not often school leaders, but they did their work and they turned it in on time. Seldom creative and original, many were highly productive in terms of such things as the number of problems completed or the number of words in a theme. In their future lives, they wanted to be hard working and conscientious, to help others, and to live by the rules. They liked a schedule that was "set" and a life that was "ordered." They tended to be deadly serious and sometimes they took themselves that way.

The Creative Intellectuals

The most gifted intellectually and certainly the most imaginative of the three types were the creative intellectuals. These were nonconformists, but not in the amoral sense. Instead, they were highly moral individuals who followed their own consciences. They would not automatically conform to their teachers' standards or those set by other students. Like Thoreau they were born protesters who interrogated every custom. Trusting their own perceptions, they were unwilling to accept authority or authoritarian statements without critical examination. Frequently, they reported, they disagreed with classmates and teachers, preferring to listen to "people who hold ideas that are unpopular." In their attitudes to life, they were would-be movers and changers. Their approach was essentially intellectual, in the sense that it involved ideas and a willingness to use reason in rebuilding a world nearer to the heart's desire. In addition, their style was creative, in the sense that imagination was given full play. They were inventors, not copiers.

In this group of creative intellectuals were large numbers of our future scientists (but not the engineers and technicians), artists, writers, musicians, and philosophers-at-large. As adolescents, many of the creative intellectuals had interests in all these areas as well as being the ones who delved into ESP and similar topics on the outer fringes of knowledge. They also did in-depth studies of a scholarly nature. One student apologized for remaining a low achiever despite group counseling help, saying, "I've read all of Freud and all of Shakespeare this term and Maslow besides—and I've been so busy educating myself that I just didn't have time to do more than B work in school." Reflection normally preceded action. They did not always study the text or do their assignments, but they read a great deal at every opportunity—often reading while the teacher was teaching, not an endearing practice.

The creative intellectuals' behavior was open and seeking. They often reveled in "being" and aesthetic awareness, enjoying touch and taste, sight and sound. But this in no way denied their sense of becoming. Many translated their idealism into action, espousing principles and declaring dedications.. The girls particularly were concerned with humane and altruistic causes.

If we agree with John R. Platt, the biophysicist, that the world is too dangerous for anything short of utopia—that we must radically improve our present life styles or risk destruction—then we must all work toward personal change and plan for the emergence of a new human nature, a new person, a new image of humanity. What I am speaking of is reaching out for joy, not merely adjustment. The latter can mean tranquillized inertia, a willingness

1. INTERVENTION

to accept things as they are even when the situation is dangerous and harmful.

Developing and Recognizing Human Capacities

The point of all this is that we have great potentialities that are only slightly developed. As Thoreau said, "But our capacities have never been measured; nor are we to judge what we can do by any precedents, so little has been tried." It was Emerson's view that the proportion of our ability that we use is only equal to the tip of the little finger. Paul Goodman mentioned that perhaps we make use of only 2% of our potentialities, while William James said, "Compared to what we might be we are only half awake."

How many of our young have capacities comparable to those of a Leo Tolstoy or a Marie Curie is not known, but their numbers, in my view, are far greater than is generally acknowledged. Unfortunately, few find ways to emerge, and only a few of those who do are recognized or encouraged. Until very recently a majority of gifted youth has rather resolutely kept their originality within acceptable bounds.

Along with this great reservoir of undeveloped human capacities, we must recognize that each person is unique and differs from every other one. Indeed, it would appear that those differences increase as people become more developed and more fully human. The most highly individual of all, i.e., those whose unique traits can be most clearly discerned and who are most differentiated from others, are the ones whom Abraham Maslow called the self actualizing. (These individuals are often highly gifted intellectually, but even more important, they have a high ethical concern for the good of others along with insight into and acceptance of themselves.) And the occasions when they reveal their unusual gifts and sensitivities are the moments that Maslow referred to as peak experiences. He believed they were "more purely different" from others at these times when they rose above the ordinary level and transcended themselves. Interestingly enough, these brief interludes which have been likened to mystic experiences are also moments when the individual feels a profound unity with others.

Whether our diversity will save us, as some claim, or whether it will destroy us, as others aver, depends on how we think about it and how the culture exploits it. All of us, and particularly the gifted, must recognize and develop the psychic bond which unites all humanity in a common kinship. If there is to be a unification of the world, our gifted children must understand this unity of each with all, rather than acquiesce in continued conquest and exploitation of the poor by the rich and of the weak by the strong. A "pecking order" in the schools which contributes to an arrogance in the gifted and a humiliation of the slow will not lead to a better world.

Our competitive culture is pitilessly destructive in many ways and our schools reflect this. Yet we can look at things differently. Even in a society of conspicuous consumption, it is still true that the best things in life are free. As George Leonard pointed out, the Myth of Limited Good does not apply to such aspects of life as love and friendship, health, respect, security, even spiritual well being.

Generally in the past the gifted child has been selected and the adult creative geniuses lauded on the basis of intellectual or artistic superiority. The virtuoso did not have to be virtuous, nor the genius generous. But I feel the fate of the world and the needs of humanity dictate a reconsideration of all this. In my view, as I mentioned earlier, the gifted are those whose ethical qualities are comparable to their other talents.

A Desire to Deal with Moral Issues

Early in their lives most gifted children want to deal with moral issues and large human problems. Often they are appalled that the adults whom they know are not concerned about the things that bother them. We are morally irresponsible if we shrug off these concerns.

Before he had entered school, the prodigy Mike Grost had read extensively in mathematics and astronomy. By age 9, he tested in the top 10% in all the usual areas of knowledge when compared with graduating high school seniors. He was allowed to attend honors classes at the university in the morning, while he continued in elementary school in the afternoon. It was at this time that he began his efforts to understand the relationship between science and religion. When asked what books he would take with him to a desert island, he replied that he would choose only two books: Russell and Whitehead's *Principia Mathematics* and Thomas Aquinas' *Summa Theologia*.

It was Mike's opinion that St. Thomas had been working in a situation that put him under a great handicap. "The Dead Sea scrolls had not yet been discovered, and the translations of Aristotle were in many ways inaccurate." Mike also reported that St. Thomas was further hampered in his insights by the fact that the major theological innovations of his time were occurring in England, not in France where he lived. Thus, it was Mike's conclusion that he personally could make a great contribution to knowledge by rewriting St. Thomas in terms of 20th century insights, particularly those of Russell and Whitehead.

Perhaps it is, as Wordsworth said, that the infant (at least the fortunate, unimpaired one) is born trailing clouds of glory and that it is only the adult world which causes "shades of the prison house... to close" upon the growing boy. Similar ideas about our innate potentialities were also expressed by the 19th century New England transcendentalists.

It may be that most education tends to dim and obscure this early mental and moral clarity, and that the more gifted children are those who retain the vision longer than others. Certainly there is unlimited evidence that gifted children can do amazing things with their minds, and that their interests lead them to ask profound and searching questions.

It is important that the gifted have an opportunity to develop their potentialities. As e. e. cummings said, "Youth's one need is to transcend itself." Growth, positive development, evolution are the urge of each organism. "Capacities clamor to be used," Maslow believed, "capacities are needs." Since we have varied talents—mental and physical, aesthetic and spiritual—we enjoy life more, feel less thwarted, if we cultivate them and let them bloom. Growth—intellectual, artistic, empathic—can continue throughout life. Studies have shown that intelligence can and does increase, people can "find" themselves.

Gifted people, however, especially those whose "capacities clamor to be used," can easily become embittered. Girls early show talent, particularly in verbal, aesthetic, and empathic skills and sensitivities. In fact, the tests in our research studies showed girls to be superior to boys in the aesthetic and altruistic realms and certainly as creative as boys in many other areas.

Women have found it difficult in the past to develop their talents. The routine tasks of doing housework and herding the children were considered appropriate for all young women, even those with great scientific talents, artistic flair, genius in the use of words or the leadership of people. Encouragement for their writing, scholarship, or social leadership was usually lacking. Mental health studies in the 1960's showed far fewer girls than boys in guidance clinics as children or adolescents, but more women than men neurotic at age 40. Talents stultified are reflected in a deterioration of mental health.

In all this I am not only concerned with the lack of self realization, but also with the loss to the society of the talents of the highly gifted and morally mature. The world today is in particularly short supply of people with humane concerns who are in administrative positions. Far too many of those who "run things" do so because they want power and like to throw their weight around, not because they wish to help others. In a country of private affluence and public squalor there can be no question but that the artist's touch and guidance are needed. And in a land where the great beauties

3. Researcher's

of nature are threatened and destroyed at every hand, the dedicated naturalist is essential.

There has been, as we all know, a great proliferation of new facts and theories in this century. As with fact, the boundaries of subject matter and disciplines change continually. Based as these boundaries are on assumptions about the nature of the discipline (or matter or the world), these boundaries change with new discoveries. As Thomas Kuhn has shown in *The Structure of Scientific Revolutions*, it is by these new insights or intuitive leaps that the great "revolutions" or changes occur in science. Suddenly someone produces a new idea, a novel way of tying things together, another point of view, and the "paradigm" (as Kuhn refers to it), if accepted, can transform the world view. Gifted students must learn to be comfortable with such ambiguity and incompleteness, to know and accept that nothing is ever finished and much remains incoherent.

The Purpose of Education

Some think the essential work of the school is to disseminate knowledge. Their view is that children, and especially the gifted ones who might be expected to become leaders, should learn the major theories and "facts" of their time. The second view, one which I share, holds that the primary purpose of education is to help young people to become better human beings. A third position, that schools should teach students to learn to learn, is concerned more with the process than with knowledge itself. This premise recognizes the ephemeral quality of much knowledge and emphasizes the limitations of the mind as a storage receptacle.

As intelligent beings, we all need to have a store of information about the past and about our contemporary world. But there is an obvious limitation to this approach. As we have seen, much of what is regarded as factual knowledge is fluid rather than solid, transitory rather than permanent.

Although I feel that the heart of a good education is personal growth, there is a way of thinking about and defining knowledge that does not separate knowing from being and becoming. I refer to the concept of *superior knowledge*. It is defined by Michael Polanyi as that which is coherently believed "to be right and excellent."

Superior knowledge is not an endless proliferation of facts and ideas. Unlike science it does not double every 10 years. Instead it is comprised of certain underlying themes which could be called rules to live by. They are found in all the major philosophies and religions of the world, in the great classics and the scriptures. Timeless and eternal, such knowledge conveys the essential truths

1. INTERVENTION

of the human condition. In Thoreau's view all wise men have asked the same questions we ask and "each has answered them. . . by his words and his life." Thus gifted students should study what the saints and sages have to say and how they have lived their lives.

Where education can help is in presenting and clarifying this knowledge and encouraging students to act accordingly. Everyone has some knowledge, conscious or unconscious, of what is good and what is bad. Superior knowledge is not necessarily the property of the educated. Emerson stated, "There is a certain wisdom of humanity which our ordinary education often labors to silence and obstruct."

It is not that the lessons of the past have been neglected as a teaching source. Many would say they have been overemphasized. Yet, too often these studies were conducted as scholastic exercises. Students were not advised to apply their knowledge of the good to their own lives.

There are many ways that even young gifted children can make this world a better place. But they are rarely encouraged to do so. How often do we suggest that they live by, and take action in terms of, higher values and superior knowledge? Nevertheless, all who try such approaches find youngsters most inventive when the challenge is held out and doors are opened for them. Without such opportunities they are apt to feel powerless and defeated before they are over the threshold of their lives.

Not only can we place an emphasis on superior knowledge and thus help students better understand themselves and the world, but learning can itself become more humane and satisfying. The objectivity required of the data collector, the mesmerized memory work that is the lot of the student, would both change if the view of knowledge changed. In Emerson's words, "[Schools] can only save us when they aim not to drill, but to create."

The work involved in study or scholarship can be meaningful in its own right and can also serve as a way of discovering oneself and bringing meaning into one's life. For example, ecology, sometimes called the "subversive science," is not only rewarding intellectually, but also gives us the added satisfaction of knowing that we are improving our environment and preserving nature's harmony. Virtues such as gentleness and mutual aid are central to the discipline, and its study can suggest how we might apply these qualities in our own lives.

The third purpose of education, helping students "learn to learn," was widely discussed in the 1960's. Under this general rubric we can include study skills, learning to do experiments, and using reference libraries. However, the most important aspect of learning to learn is learning to think critically and creatively.

An Experimental Curriculum for the Gifted

I would like to share with you the development of an experimental curriculum for the gifted in the Lansing Public Schools in which we tried to use some of the ideas about knowledge and self understanding I have just discussed. We wanted to determine whether we could teach critical thinking and produce changes in student thought patterns. These did not occur in the conventional classes that used textbooks with tunnel vision and a bland point of view.

The students and their teachers (who were also trained as counselors) were involved in every aspect of the planning and production. I feel that much of the success of the program was due to this involvement. It was their program, not one developed by an outside agency and arbitrarily imposed as a teacher-proof package.

Our first concern was that the students grow in moral and ethical ways, and that they learn to think and to care. Thus our curriculum focused on studies both of the self and of others; broadly speaking, the world. For many years, students had been complaining to me about social studies:

> We study American History in the 5th grade, the 8th grade, and the 11th grade. Every year the pilgrims come in but we only get to about World War I; then we have the last 50 years in the last 50 minutes. When are we ever going to study about the world we're living in right now?

To answer that complaint we began the new course with a study of the world as it is. However, we were careful not to give just the negative views common in the media. We made an effort throughout to share prospects as well as problems. We wanted to present positive images of humanity—as potentially good or transcendental, as well as negative ones—man as a caged beast or a programed robot.

We felt that it was essential to reinstate hope and optimism, to show that there is much beauty and love in the world within everyone's reach. The best things in life are free: a baby's smile, the early morning dew on the grass, the sharing of exciting ideas with friends. And other great goods—philosophy, religion, and the arts—cost very little money.

The problems that we discussed in our course were overpopulation, technology and ecology, war and peace, large versus small organization, and materialism and conspicuous consumption, to name a few. None of these had a simple answer and most could indeed be looked at more than one way. In this program the students did not deal with just one topic but with a number of significant questions, and they came to see how all were interrelated.

The world which we finally presented was in a loose-leaf, open ended form: the *Four World Textbook*. The four worlds were the natural, the technological, the aesthetic, and the human. Each consisted of about 30 multilithed pages which were made up of a variety of clippings, drawings, and typed excerpts. Students could make of these worlds what they would, adding and subtracting pages and, in effect, developing personal anthologies.

To bring students back to the person and to human potentialities, to give them passports to their own territory, we had produced 30 minute style-of-life films of 10 creative, philosophical, and socially concerned men and women. We wanted students to meet adults who were more "fully human," both in terms of philosophical depth and in the joy that they derived from their work.

The Being and Becoming Film Series and the *Four Worlds Textbook* were the core materials for the new program. Both the text and the films were used in the context of class discussion. Students were encouraged to present their viewpoints orally, a new experience for many, and to engage in confrontations and dialogues with their peers and teachers, using as subject matter the issues raised in text or films or by the students themselves. The talk was never dull and never teacher dominated. Ideas ranged from the concrete and personal to the abstract and philosophical. We felt that education can and must be concerned with issues of crucial importance to the world. It must assist the developing self as it struggles to find a personal identity and a place in a meaningful world.

Perhaps due to the heated discussions, the lack of final or absolute answers, the continual involvement of the students, the total front approach, the fine preparation and dedication of the teachers, and the persuasiveness of the people who were the film models, we were able to achieve significant gains in critical thinking as well as in many other areas when the new course was tested experimentally.

In Search of the Ideal Learning Environment

I have had a series of recurring dreams about the ideal learning environment for the gifted. Over the years I have written designs for a "learning center," and in my homes in East Lansing, Michigan, in Portland, Oregon, and now in Berkeley, California, I have built extra rooms for seminar use. From my experience I would say the furnishings must be comfortable and attractive with food preparation facilities near at hand and with nature visible at the window and accessible at the door, available for a stroll or sunning. Many teachers have had the experience of taking students into a beautiful setting, particularly one redolent with nature, and finding even the bored and the unruly transformed.

In *Learning Together* I described the "new community" which selects a section of a city (Portland, Oregon) as a learning mall and involves people of all ages and a variety of occupations. Particular use is made of the forest areas, parks, gardens, zoo, science museum, city library, the art museum and school, and the historical museum. Gifted students who have long since met their academic requirements often do not need to attend classes on a regular basis, although they may eagerly participate in philosophy seminars or enroll in university classes or apprentice themselves to artists or artisans.

Continually I search for alternatives to the 2 x 4 classroom, the child incarcerated between the two covers of a textbook and the four walls of a single room. The two most exciting elementary schools, involving students of a variety of ages, that I have seen recently are located in very different settings. One is in a suburb of Copenhagen, the Bagsvaerd School, and the other, The Old Green School, is in Canby, a small town in Oregon. Both accept children from about 6 to 14 years, although the Oregon school has some older ones.

At the Bagsvaerd School, children were self selected by their own interest or because the philosophy of the school appealed to their parents. Although the educators of Denmark say little about "gifted children," many of these obviously were just that. With five teachers and sixty-some children there was leeway for individual help. Students were encouraged to read, do science experiments, create art, make music, and work together in a variety of ways.

Given freedom, the teachers found that children could work through their problems. At the beginning many students reverted to behavior that has been common in schools through the centuries. Some of the big boys, aggressive and egocentric, fought with each other and lorded it over the other children. There were about 500 brilliant green enamelled boxes (donated by Tuborg Beer) which were to be used for partitions in the large room. At first the older boys made two competing castles and then proceeded to wage war. The smaller children—not yet wise to the ways of the world—objected to this behavior, sent emissaries to the strongholds, and finally talked the malefactors into helping them make a ship which schoolmates clambered into and where all began playing and working together.

1. INTERVENTION

Many of the customary problems that teachers usually confront simply did not exist in the free situation. The young children profited especially, taking responsibility for many things, including running the school food program. There was no great pressure to learn, but it was found that, with excellent teachers as consultants, the students became deeply involved in many projects. They rarely used textbooks; instead they read all manner of current materials, including newspapers. Those who enjoyed reading requested a quiet room just for that. Almost everyone demanded that a soundproof room be provided for the musicians.

The Old Green School had ten or twelve fewer children than Bagsvaerd and two teachers rather than five, but the pattern was similar. At first they inhabited the basement of an old school building complete with nooks and crannies—reading alcoves and hobby closets. In the spring of 1974 this building was destroyed by fire and the school is now housed in a vacated symposium. But excitement for learning is unimpaired. All ages and kinds of children work together with boundless enthusiasm. Even the youngest take on projects of enormous scope.

Young children read adult books without fear of criticism. And there were always, in both schools, enough adult volunteers to supply talented conversational partners for many of the more intellectually adventurous children. In Canby as well as in Copenhagen children wrote books of imposing length, did large scale art projects, and conducted impressive science experiments. Several of the Bagsvaerd children had typed and duplicated novels. But more important than any of this was the sense of community that prevailed and the fact that there was in each situation far more cooperation than competition.

An alternative high school of outstanding quality, one that truly "works," is the Off-Campus School in Bellevue, Washington. Populated solely by drop-outs from the conventional schools and housed in a beautiful modern building (a former church) in a parklike setting, this school has been open for a little over four years. Despite the basis for student selection (they must have been dropped or have dropped out willingly), an urbane and gifted teacher, Glenn Holden, assured us that this was in many ways the most intellectually demanding of the Bellevue high schools.

Most of the work is accomplished outside the school after the student and the teacher have decided which direction the reading and the other activities will take. Such freedom in allotting their time allows students to fit in studies with work schedules. Creative dramatics, yoga, physical education, and hiking are done in groups. But the academic subjects are taught in a series of individual tutorials which consist of discussion and evaluation. Students never fail to show up for these and rarely forget their assignments, because it is they who help choose what work they will do and who will call in for their appointments. In contrast with the normal load of six classes in conventional high schools, a student at the off-campus school generally concentrates on one or two courses at a time. These are often finished in a short period of three to six weeks.

Student attitudes were good. They could work at their own rate, put questions directly to their teachers and expect to get answers. Integration of subject areas as well as of work with study were possible. For example, a unit in genetics has been used to lead into a mathematics unit on probability. In general, the aim was to encourage individuality and to enlist the students' own interests. The school accepts as its theme Thoreau's dictum, "If a man does not keep pace with his companions, perhaps it is because he hears a different drummer. Let him step to the music which he hears, however measured or far away."

There are a number of qualities that must be present in a good learning environment, but they cannot be established by fiat. The teacher as conductor—in both the sense of conduit for an electrical charge and as a maestro—is the vital factor. A good environment is one that helps all to feel accepted and free to be their best selves. As William Jennings Bryan said, "People should be allowed to make their own mistakes." Gifted students should be given enough rope, not hang themselves, but so that through exploration they will see the range of possibilities. Love is vital to acceptance, the central ingredient.

The environment should be more than free and accepting; it must also be responsive. Where bright students ask questions—and they ask many, that's one way to identify them—the responses should whet their desires to learn more and continue with their queries.

For the gifted, responsiveness in the environment is still not enough. There should be memorable ideas and things to contemplate, and what Whitehead called "vivid" people. We learn best, Emerson felt, not by "instruction, but [by] provocation."

The Role of the Teacher

The teacher's role, I believe, is more that of a facilitator and source of inspiration than of a fount of knowledge. Max Lerner has spoken of the incandescent teacher, and there is an old saying that to kindle another you must yourself glow. We all know that there are people we feel warmed by and others who leave us cold; some who kindle our imaginations, others who dampen our enthusiasm. Perhaps it is, as Goethe believed, that we only learn through those we love.

As you probably have gathered, I believe that kindness is a more important quality than intellectual sharpness. Certainly a teacher needs both emotional and ethical maturity, along with intellectual depth. The film models, as well as the teachers in the *Being and Becoming* program, all talked about what they believed in and cared about. The students responded by saying they had never heard an adult discuss a philosophy of life before and this was a very meaningful experience.

Carl Rogers has written movingly on the point that no one can teach another; we can only learn together. This is the "letting be" of Lao-Tzu. My view is that in all education we need a combination of this Eastern nonintervention and Western challenge. *To lead out* is the literal meaning of the Latin verb *educere*, from which the word education is derived.

Despite what I have said about the importance of kindness, the need for the teacher to be the students' friend, to be on their side, if necessary to be their advocate, I also believe teachers should know something. They should like to learn; they should be expert in at least one area; and the most gifted should become philosopher generalists. Taking a student by the hand and saying "let's go look it up together" is not enough. And the negative function of getting out of the learners' way while they look up things for themselves is not the proper role for the teacher. Gifted students need to find their intellectual kin, those who also care deeply about ideas. The teacher who can ask the trenchant question or point to a new way of looking at a problem is needed by the gifted at all ages. But this must be done in the manner of a Whitehead whose friend Lucien Price reported, "There was not a grain of ill will anywhere in him; for all his formidable armament, never a wounding word."

It would follow that teachers not only need to like gifted children, but they should also revel in their minds rather than being threatened by them. Basic to liking the gifted is having a positive image about human beings. I tend to believe that thinking well of others and of yourself are of a piece.

I feel strongly that teachers need opportunity to keep abreast of their subjects and their times. To do an adequate job of teaching I believe no teacher should be asked to be on the firing line in classroom teaching more than half a day, perhaps only 10 to 15 hours a week. Teachers need time to think about their students, to do research on their subjects, to renew themselves. If they are to be models for the gifted, the writers need to write, the musicians to play, the scientists to experiment. How can teachers have the excited minds found among the creative if they are dead tired?

The first two chapters of *Learning Together* are about the problems of a gifted young creative intellectual, Don Saxon. He had some excellent teachers and some very poor ones and his record fluctuated like a yo-yo in these various settings. As with many of the more sensitive gifted young people, he would refuse to learn if sufficiently at odds with a teacher. But Don thought teachers were very important and knew what he would like them to be:

What we need is people who vibrate knowledge—teacher philosophers. People who create things! Capital E—Empathy; Capital T—Truth; Capital L—Love.

Educational Non-acceleration: An International Tragedy

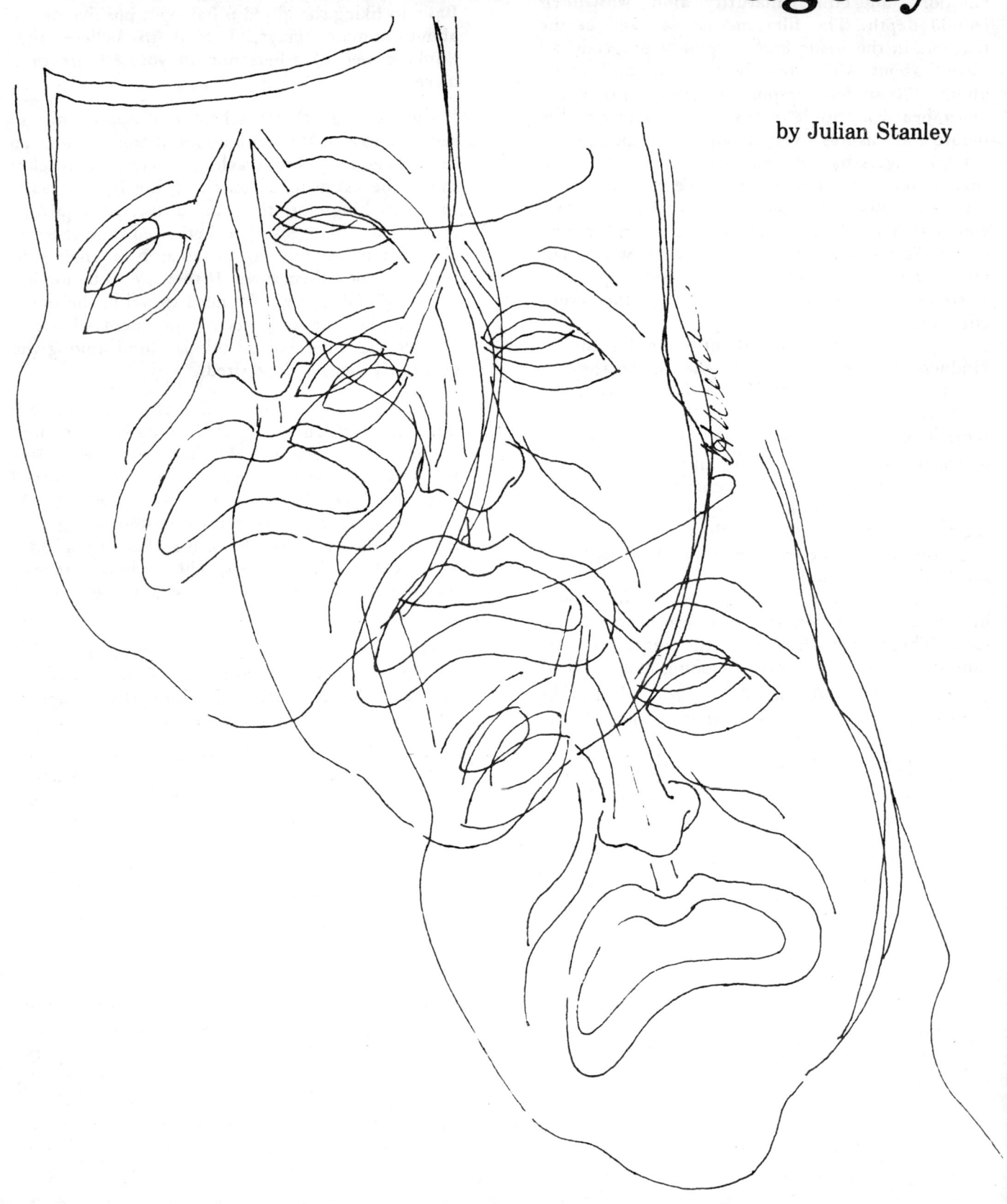

by Julian Stanley

(This article represents an updated version of Dr. Stanley's invited address to the Second World Conference on Gifted and Talented Children held at the University of San Francisco, August 2, 1977.

Let me begin by sharing with you a portion of a letter I received from a highly gifted Chinese-American girl who had recently completed the ninth grade. It is, unfortunately, a rather typical example of how educators often frustrate the gifted, especially before senior high school.

Dear Professor Stanley:

Thank you very much for your encouraging letter.

In June 1973, at the end of my 5th grade school year, I took the New York State Algebra I Regents, and scored 98%. In September of the same year, I moved to Maryland. _____ County Public Schools chose not to acknowledge this fact (i.e., the high test score), and I was placed in a 6th grade math class. Having finished the 6th grade text in 1½ months, I was told to "do it over again for a review." I then spent the rest of the year reading books placed between the covers of my math book. Finally, at the end of much frustration, I was placed in an accelerated math class for gifted children, at the beginning of 8th grade. Even then, I had to re-take Algebra I. However, the pace was much faster, and I enjoyed it, especially during the past year, when we covered Algebra II-Trig. with _____ (a teacher trained under the auspices of the Study of Mathematically Precocious Youth (SMPY).

I have been accepted to the _____ Academy. I want to set up a challenging schedule, using your letter as a reference.

Should I need any further guidance, I shall be in touch, but I believe the frustrating, wasted years are ending, and the future looks brighter.

Thank you for taking the time and consideration to show that someone does care.

Sincerely,

_____

Many intellectually brilliant youths eager to proceed faster educationally have been prevented from doing so by their parents, educators, or psychologists. The United States is a serious offender in this respect, but I know from personal observation that the situation is even worse in a number of other countries. This brings to mind the horrible Greek legend about Procrustes, who forced his guests to lie on a very long or a very short bed and fitted them to it by stretching them if the bed was too long or by cutting off part of their legs if the bed was too short. The age-in-grade lockstep is a Procrustean solution endorsed by all but a few.

Yet a vast amount of substantial evidence accumulated for more than half a century shows that highly able youths who want to quicken their educational pace in a number

4. International

of ways would be well advised to break the lockstep. As Daurio (1978) set forth in a long review, there is no substantial evidence to the contrary. The oft-sounded fears that educational acceleration will hurt the social and emotional development of intellectually highly talented youths in the United States who want to move ahead faster than their agemates are groundless. On the contrary, frustrating the natural pace of highly apt students can cause serious academic and emotional damage.

How did this false "social and emotional development" shibboleth become so ingrained that it caused educational acceleration, common and successful in the past when tutors prepared youths for higher education, to be replaced by often vacuous or irrelevant so-called educational "enrichment?" At a superficial level it is obvious that the word "enrichment" has a wonderful sound, akin to some of the other catchwords of which educators are fond--for example, "creativity" and "whole child"--whereas the term "educational acceleration" lacks glamour. But I suspect that the main causes of resistance to acceleration are much deeper than a euphemism for busywork, fun-and-games, and whatever special subject matter the school wants to offer its many varieties of talent. The almost rabid egalitarianism of my countrymen plays a strong part, as do considerations of scheduling convenience and simple ignorance about the research literature. Envy and distrust of the intellectually talented, who make excellent grades in school without half trying, are not new phenomena.

41

1. INTERVENTION

Most harmful of all seems to be the "I knew a person who . . ." way of substituting anecdotes, often untrue, and outright rumors for more careful consideration of the issues. Like all kinds of prejudice, this is reinforced by making unreasonable demands of the object against which one is prejudiced. For example, if a student enters college full-time at age 15 or 16 and does not achieve magnificently, he or she is considered a failure ascribable to under-agedness. If, however, the same student enters college at the "regular age" of 17 or 18 and does poorly, causes other than being age-in-grade are sought. To prove that beginning college work younger than the norm is not harmful, the critic of educational acceleration demands that every such youth be highly successful academically, whereas no such lofty expectations are entertained for the age-in-grade undergraduates.

The situation is even more no-win than that, because no matter how well the young college student does academically the critics will usually assume that he or she would have developed better socially and emotionally by not moving ahead educationally faster than one school year at a time. This dogmatic stance will be maintained in the face of all contrary evidence, including the youth's own protestations that he or she is much happier being accelerated. This unreasoned assumption that only one's agemates are one's social and emotional peers is a gross denial of individual differences and of the great adjustive capacities of many intellectually highly talented youths. More than perhaps anything else, it is frustrating the fulfillment of the intellectual and personal needs of brilliant students.

Many parents join wholeheartedly with educators in this conspiracy to restrain their well-qualified, eager children from moving ahead at the accelerated paces natural for them. Often, too, even when acceleration is recommended by school personnel, parents are reluctant or obstructive. Many parents let golden opportunities for acceleration pass by, either by cautious inaction or outright refusal. Few parents of intellectually talented children seem excellently qualified for that demanding role. Most of them do not realize how hard and ingeniously they must work with educators and others in order that their children will develop appropriately.

Closely related to this is failure of most parents to get their intellectually talented offspring deeply involved in the educational decision-making process nearly early enough. For example, a youth not yet seven years old who, according to a standardized test, has the reading ability of an average twelfth-grader (as one of our proteges indeed did) should already be helping to make educational choices for himself. In this connection it is important to fit the student's choice-making responsibilities more to his or her mental age than chronological age.

In our work with 6400 students of both sexes who reason extremely well mathematically, we at SMPY and our colleagues from Dr. Lynn Fox's Intellectually Gifted Child Study Group (IGCSG) at The Johns Hopkins University have encountered all types of parents. A particularly overwhelming variety is the authoritarian, aggressive, dominating mother or father--especially of a son--who wants to plan everything for the child right through four years of college. Despite our best efforts, such parents give their children little say in the educational process. Often the youngster grows resistant to the parents' suggestions and to ours. Information from us conveyed to him or her via the parents proves much less effective than if the youth were directly involved.

Another type of parent that seems not ideal for intellectually talented youths might be termed "laissez-faire." This mother or father makes remarks such as "I don't want to push my children," "I just want my child to be normal," "I want my child to be well-rounded," and especially "I'm more interested in my child's social and emotional development than in his becoming a genius." Often these statements reflect the parents' unwillingness to work hard on their child's behalf. Sometimes they indicate a family so strongly oriented toward activities such as sports, music, and church that special educational opportunities have low priority.

Many families seem confused about distinctions among the following three things: inspiring a brilliant youth to *want* to excel educationally, pushing the child beyond his or her own desires, and adopting a hands-off attitude. Long-term educational stimulation by parents is virtually essential, but to be effective it must be done via love and hard work rather than coercion and exploitation. Helping parents to become better facilitators of their intellectually talented children's education pays rich dividends for those youths and for society. This is why, at SMPY, we correspond and interact directly with the mathematically precocious youth themselves to the greatest extent possible.

AN INDIVIDUAL DIFFERENCES MODEL FOR EDUCATIONAL ACCELERATION

Perhaps current pressures against letting eager youths move ahead educationally at their preferred rates can be illustrated well by an analogy. Suppose that in some remote country, two persons can each run 1600 meters (about a mile) in less than four minutes, but no one else can do so under six minutes. We might wonder about the human physiology, training, and restrictions in such a country, because it is well known that in other countries a more even distribution of running times accords with the natural abilities of the runners. Given freedom of expression and of training, some persons should be running between four and four and one-half minutes, more at four and one-half to five, still more in the five-minute interval, and the most at whatever the mode of the running population is. Aptitude for running, opportunities to train well, and motivation to run fast are important, individually and interactively. We would not expect running times to be distributed normally, because the absolute lower limit is less than four minutes below the best times, whereas the worst running time is plus infinity. If every member of some group, say 16-year-old males, were required to run the 1600-meter distance regularly we would expect considerable continuity along the time dimension, but a somewhat positively skewed distribution of times. It is easier to run slow than to run extremely fast, but quite a few of the runners would be equipped by aptitude and motivation to run much faster than the average of the group. If they did not do so we would be surprised and puzzled.

The 1600-meter runners of that strange country are like our intellectually highly talented students. Occasionally, such a student breaks the bonds of the age-in-grade educational lockstep and streaks ahead to an early baccalaureate or doctor's degree, but the best that most manage is to complete college at the "standard" age. They spend 17 years traversing the 17-year period from the beginning of kindergarten through the end of the fourth year of college. A few save a year or even two years along the way--that is, as much as 12% of the time. Many take longer or don't ever earn the bachelor's degree.

The gap between the youngest recipients of the initial college degree and the age of most of the recipients is at least eight years. We know, for example, that Merrill Kenneth Wolf received his B.A. degree from Yale University in 1945 when he was barely 14 years old. Norbert Weiner received his from Tufts University (then Tufts College) before his 15th birthday. Yet 73% of the recipients of baccalaureates at Johns Hopkins in 1971, the year that SMPY began, were age-in-grade by the strict criterion of becoming 22 years old during the calendar year

4. International

in which one was graduated. (Actually, some whom we considered a year over-age because they became 23 years old in 1971 were actually right on their own schools' schedules, so the correct percent is appreciably greater than 73). Only three of the 447 graduates were still 20 years old on 31 December 1971, which by our criterion means just two years of acceleration. None was younger.

Thus it would seem that a chasm yawns between the 14-year-old fast-movers and the norm of progress. The 8-year gap is 47 percent of the 17 years of schooling. Were Lewis Terman alive today he would probably point out that a well-motivated, highly facilitated student with an IQ over 200 should be able to complete his or her schooling in about half the usual time. He had deplored the lack of educational speed in his gifted group.

But, someone would argue, Wolf and Wiener are great exceptions, virtually unique; almost no one else among the more than 3,000,000 children born in the United States each year could match their feats. Evidence, both from the past and more recently, does not support this argument. With only moderate facilitation in mathematics for three years Eric Robert Jablow was found by SMPY to be ready to become a full-time student at Brooklyn College at age 11½, after completing the sixth grade of a public school. Though he accelerated no more, Eric was graduated with a major in mathematics, *summa cum laude*, this June less than three months after his 15th birthday. In September of 1972 he became a student

43

1. INTERVENTION

at Princeton University, working toward the Ph.D. degree in mathematics under a three-year graduate fellowship that he had won from the National Science Foundation. Eric could easily have saved another if he and his parents had wanted him to do so. He is extremely able, well adjusted, and splendidly motivated, of course, but each year or so in the New York City area or in the vicinity of any large city there are likely to be several other students as academically promising as he. They could readily complete the bachelor's degree with distinction at a selective college by age 14, 15, or 16.

Among the more than 1000 high-IQ youths in Terman's classic study of gifted children only one earned a bachelor's degree as young as age 16. He was graduated from Columbia University, having majored in chemistry and having been elected to membership in Phi Beta Kappa. Only two of the group finished college while still 17. One who completed college at barely age 18 is a famed psychometrician, well known--at least by professional reputation-to nearly all of you. At an extremely early age he was elected president of the American Psychological Association. Keep in Mind that Terman made no direct effort to help any of his group move ahead faster in school.

SMPY's intent is strongly interventional. We aim to foster as much educational acceleration among our large number of proteges *as they are eager to try*. Because SMPY began only recently, in September 1971, chiefly with seventh and eighth graders, there has not yet been time for many of our participants to complete their baccalaureates early, much less their doctorates. Amazingly, though, even from the chiefly Baltimore area talent search we conducted in March of the 1972 that had only 450 contestants in mathematics and/or general science have already come four under-age graduates of Johns Hopkins.

In May of 1977 one of these finished his Bachelor of Engineering Science degree in electrical engineering, Phi Beta Kappa and with a National Science Foundation three-year graduate fellowship, three months before his 18th birthday. How did this young man move so fast? As a seventh grader he had entered SMPY's March 1972 talent search in both mathematics and college-level general science. He was the top scorer of all 192 science contestants (many of them eighth or even under-age ninth graders) and had ranked third among the 396 who took two difficult mathematics tests.

During the summer of 1972 this youth and four other of SMPY's male participants took college courses in mathematics at Towson State College. He enrolled for college algebra and trigonometry and for analytic geometry concurrently and made final grades of "A" in both.[1] Then he skipped the eighth, eleventh, and twelfth grades and completed his work at Johns Hopkins in three years. In the fall of 1977 he began work toward the Ph.D. degree in computer science at Cornell University.

Another of the original talent--search group was also graduated from Johns Hopkins in May of 1977 at age 17, two months before his 18th birthday. He, too, won a National Science Foundation three-year graduate fellowship, which he is now using in electrical engineering at the Massachusetts Institute of Technology. He had skipped the second, eleventh, and twelfth grades and entered with 39 semester-hour credits already earned by means of college courses taken part-time from the middle of the eighth grade onward. Thus it was convenient for him to earn his degree in three years.

Each of the other two young men from the original talent search earned his degree "only" three years early. One did so by skipping grades 10, 11, and 12. Graduated at 18, Phi Beta Kappa, with a *summa cum laude* record and a three-year National Science Foundation graduate fellowship,[2] he is now working toward a Ph.D. degree in theoretical physics at Princeton University.

---

[1] All five boys earned "A" in college algebra and trigonometry, and three of the four who took analytic geometry earned "A" in it, too. The other earned a "B", chiefly because he had transportation difficulties. For further discussion of this class, see Keating, Wiegand, and Fox (1974).

[2] Lest it begin to seem that most of graduates of Johns Hopkins receive three-year NSF graduate fellowships, let me point out that these three young men won half of all such awards at Johns Hopkins in 1977 and 3/550ths of all such awards in all eligible fields of science for the entire country. Because SMPY's proteges at Brooklyn College (already mentioned) and George Washington University also won NSF graduate fellowships in 1977, the members of our relatively small group got nearly 1 percent of all the NSF fellowships anywhere. That is a truly remarkable achievement, especially when one considers that these graduates were accelerated in grade placement from 3 to 7 years.

The other one of the four accelerants, who finished at age 19, majored in mathematics and earned good grades. He is working full-time as a data analyst and pursuing his hobby, the playing of bridge.

Besides the extreme prodigy at Brooklyn College who has already been discussed, it is worthwhile to consider four other early graduates under SMPY's auspices. One of these came from SMPY's January 1973 talent search. He skipped the seventh, ninth, tenth, and twelfth grades and completed college in five semesters. He became 17 years old in December of 1976 and finished his college work that month. Currently, he is attending the University of Chicago and working toward the Master of Business Administration and Ph.D. in economics degrees.

A boy who did not come through one of our contests but whom we helped decide to start college early was graduated, Phi Beta Kappa, from George Washington University in June of 1977 at age 18 with a baccalaureate in mathematical statistics and an NSF fellowship. In the fall of 1977 he became a doctoral student in mathematical statistics at Stanford University.[3]

Two years before SMPY began, Joseph Louis Bates entered Johns Hopkins as a regular freshman at age 13. Four years later, at age 17 years 7 months, he received a B.A. degree in quantitative studies. By the end of that summer, at age 17 years 10 months, he had a master's degree in electrical engineering. Then he went to Cornell University to work toward a Ph.D. degree in computer science.

The final example was a young man who entered Johns Hopkins in the fall of 1972 after the tenth grade of a public school, transferred to Princeton University the next fall, and was graduated there in mathematics, *summa cum laude* and Phi Beta Kappa, in June of 1976. He, too, won a three-year NSF graduate fellowship. In the fall of 1976 he began work toward the Ph.D. degree in mathematics at the University of California (Berkeley). Within nine months he had earned a Master's degree in mathematics and continued toward the doctorate.

To recapitulate, the SMPY's college graduates as of May 1977 totaled nine. Six of these took the baccalaureate at Johns Hopkins, four of them in two and one-half to three years. One took a master's degree concurrently with his bachelor's. They ranged in age from barely 17 to 19. The three others took their bachelor's degrees elsewhere at ages 15 to barely 20. Four were elected to Phi Beta Kappa, and another had a 3.96 average (where 4.00 is straight A) but seemed not to meet the Phi Beta Kappa requirements of his college because he took a Bachelor of Science degree. Six of the nine won NSF three-year graduate fellowships. All reported being quite glad that they had come to college early. All seemed satisfied with their social development and emotional stability. Several of them began research and writing careers as undergraduates.

4. International

All but two of the nine had come from public schools in Baltimore, Baltimore County, or nearby Howard County. If in this new endeavor SMPY with its small resources, working in a geographical area not especially noted for concentration of intellectual talent, can help produce this much acceleration, think of how much more would have resulted from a larger effort! Instead of being proud that at the 1977 commencement it had five graduates younger than anyone in a usual class of about 500, perhaps those who make policy at Johns Hopkins should have been chagrined that there were not at least 25. It is probable, though, that even in its small graduating class Johns Hopkins had more graduates in 1977 who were accelerated at least three years than did any other university in the country. According to Alexander W. Astin's annual reports for the American Council on Education, only about one freshman in 1000 is still 16 years old on December 31 of the year in which he or she enters college--that is, only one-tenth of 1 percent are even two years accelerated when they begin.

We at SMPY consider this a serious failure to provide adequately for intellectually brilliant youths eager to move fast through college and to an early doctorate so that they will have more time and energy for creative work postdoctorally. Indeed, as the title to this paper indicates, educational non-acceleration may well be an international tragedy, wasting the talents of many youths. We make no argument that any student should be urged ahead at a pace or in a manner about which he or she is unenthu-

---
[3] For further information concerning the seven early graduates discussed thus far see *Time* (1977) and Nevin (1977). Some of their characteristics are also discussed in Stanley (1976, pp. 19-21).

1. INTERVENTION

siastic, but only that the best-motivated should have a clear field.

THE SUCCESS OF RADICAL ACCELERANTS

At this point many may object and say it is well known that the typical intellectual prodigy does not amount to much in the long run. A great deal of this inaccurate feeling probably derives from the enormous amount of unfavorable publicity that the sad case of William James Sidis received during the first half of this century. Montour (1977) has researched that story carefully and reported her findings in a perceptive fashion. Her article is essential reading for all persons seriously interested in the welfare of intellectually talented youths. In this and a number of other studies (Montour 1976 a-k and 1978 a, b) she shows that nearly all intellectually brilliant persons who manage to move through school fast lead happy, successful lives, especially if interpreted in terms of their own goals rather than of the stereotypes that society has about success.

For example, most educated persons in many countries have heard about how Norbert Wiener coined the word "cybernetics" ("the theoretical study of control processes in electronic, mechanical, and biological systems, especially the mathematical analysis of the flow of information in such systems"--*American Heritage Dictionary of the English Language*) and contributed much to it. He was one of the most important applied mathematicians and electrical engineers from about 1919 onward for 45 years. That was a great deal of success for one who received his baccalaureate at age 14 and his Ph.D. degree at 18. Wiener did this despite--or perhaps partically because of--an extremely demanding father. For details, see his two interesting autobiographical volumes, *Ex-prodigy* (1953) and *I Am A Mathematician* (1956).

How well did Merrill Kenneth Wolf, the youngest college graduate of whom we are aware, do after completing his B.A. degree in music theory under Paul Hindemith at Yale in 1945 when he was barely 14 years old? For some seven years thereafter he studied keyboard instruments such as the piano, organ, and harpsichord under Arthur Schnabel and others before entering medical school at age 21. Today he is a professor of (neuro) anatomy at the University of Massachusetts Medical School after formerly having been associate professor at the Harvard Medical School. By any reasonable standards Dr. Wolf is quite successful. His music is still a source of pleasure to him, especially during summers. (See Keating, 1976, name index).

Another highly successful prodigy (Ph.D. degree from MIT at age 20) is the Harvard University Nobel Laureate chemist, Robert Burns Woodward (See Feinstein, 1977). Perhaps the most prominent young mathematician in the country is Charles Louis Fefferman, who completed his bachelor's degree in mathematics and physics at the University of Maryland at age 17 and his doctorate in mathematics at age 20. By age 22 he was a full professor of mathematics at the University of Chicago, the youngest professor that distinguished institution has ever had. At age 24 he moved to Princeton University and became its youngest professor ever, also. Three years later he was the first recipient of the $150,000 Alan Waterman Award of the National Academy of Sciences. In 1977 he became 28 years old, about the age at which many first-rate persons receive their Ph.D. degrees. It is clear that the years of schooling he saved (at least five) have proved invaluable thus far.

Of course, it would be unreasonable to expect the typical early graduate from college to become as successful as Wiener, Woodward, Fefferman, or even Wolf. To us at SMPY it seems sufficient that youths who reason extremely well mathematically and who are strongly motivated to plunge ahead educationally be helped to attend excellent colleges and get first-rate doctorates at an early age, rather than marking time in high school and then perhaps being unwilling to face the stiff competition of the top institutions of higher education. We are content to see our proteges use their talents appreciably better than they might have done otherwise.

Nevertheless, there are already strong signs of research creativity in most of the nine graduates thus far. At age 17 one found the solution to a previously unsolved computer problem. Another had an article published when he was 16. One worked during part of two summers as a research assistant at two major research institutions before he became 17. At 18 another gave an invited paper at a conference on theoretical physics. One's honors thesis for the bachelor's degree was so excellent that he was immediately elected to membership in Sigma Zi, the graduate honorary scientific society. One is developing a computer device that has excellent commercial possibilities. Several other remarkable achievements in addition to getting the initial degree early could be cited.

These activities are occurring even sooner in the school career of the early graduates than for the typical brilliant age-in-grade student. Instead of being postponed until the last year or two of graduate school or beyond, they have been moved back to the undergraduate years. As undergraduates the early graduates were even more professional and research-oriented than were their equally able but considerably older classmates. We consider this a favorable sign indeed.

Only the years will reveal how scientifically creative these young men will become. We have no carefully matched control group with which to compare them. Compared with the substantial but lesser attainments of other youths in our study, however, the radical accelerants seem thus far to be the most promising subgroup of the talent-search participants. This is not due to factors in parental backgrounds favoring the accelerants, because our youths from strongly professional homes seem less likely to accelerate their educational progress drastically than are the children of persons somewhat lower in the socioeconomic scale.

Occupations of the fathers of the nine early graduates when the latter were college seniors are revealing: certified public accountant, district sales manager of a large company, engineer, owner-operator of an ice-cream shop, owner-operator of a pest-control service, paper salesman, part owner of a home-improvement company, retired FBI agent, and teacher of mathematics. None was the child of a physician, lawyer, male college professor (one mother was then an associate professor), or wealthy business man. Both parents are alive and living together. So far as we are aware, there has not been a divorce in any of these nine families. Apparently, it takes a great deal of parental stability and encouragement to produce successful accelerants, but not excellent parental educations or high incomes.

SMPY MOVES ALONG

I am tempted to give you a great deal of technical information about SMPY, but that would limit our time for discussion here. It is unnecessary, because SMPY's work thus far has been reported extensively in a number of easily available books and articles. Suffice it to reiterate that our efforts are resolutely interventional, longitudinal, and accelerative. We are proud of our strong emphasis on trying to help these youths improve their educational opportunities over the years until they enter an outstanding college or university as full-time undergraduates, preferably with sophomore standing. Many persons talk enthusiastically about the needs of the gifted, but during the years since Terman began his monumental follow-up study in 1921 all too few educators and psychologists have actually done much educationally for intellectually talented youths that is really substantial. Quite a few have

4. International

spent most of their time seeking large amounts of money, despite the fact that the provisions SMPY discusses require mainly initiative and actually save the student's parents and the schools money. (Some of these provisions will be discussed below.)

We are especially proud of SMPY's almost unique stress on educational acceleration as one of the prime methods for helping brilliant youths who want to escape the age-in-grade lockstep. We owe a great debt to Terman and our still-alive but aged friends Sidney Pressey (1949), Dean Worcester (1956), and James Hobson (1963), three who almost singlehandedly contradicted the common "wisdom" which said that most educational acceleration was undesirable. We owe much to persons at the University of Chicago during the 1930's, such as Robert Hutchins and Ralph Tyler, who made that fine institution the country's haven for early entrants and early graduates then. We thank Hutchins and the Fund for the Advancement of Education of the Ford Foundation for their highly successful early-entrance experiment of the 1950's (see FAE 1953, 1957).

We have taken over with great energy and zeal the difficult and highly unpopular task of making avenues to educational accelearation much more accessible than they were almost anywhere. Our work in Maryland and adjoining areas is prototypal. We develop principles, practices, techniques, and programs that are widely applicable. If we can do that in a short while with great success in a typical state of the Union, so can others elsewhere--and all the more so if

1. INTERVENTION

they have a larger percentage of extremely talented youths with whom to work than we do. Let us consider briefly some of the main means by which SMPY has striven to improve the educational opportunities of those students who, when in junior high school, reason at least as well mathematically as the upper 2 or 3 percent of their age group in the country do.

VARIOUS WAYS TO ACCELERATE

The following possibilities are not listed in order of importance, but instead somewhat chronologically:

1. Enter school early, especially if the child is intellectually quite precocious and would otherwise be "old in grade." For example, if according to school-board rules the child must become 5 years old by December 31 of the year in which he or she would enter kindergarten but misses this deadline by only a month or two, enrollment in kindergarten "a year early" should be considered carefully if the child's mental age will exceed that of the average kindergarten in the group to be entered. Some consideration should also be given to the child's size and presumed social and emotional development, but the decision must be based on long-term considerations. Of extreme importance for this decision is the Stanford-Binet-type IQ. Beginning kindergarten early will often be preferable to skipping a later grade (especially the first or second) where friendship cliques have already been formed. See Worcester (1956) and Hobson (1963).

2. Skip the last grade before moving from one level of school to another school at the next level, such as the last grade of elementary, middle, or junior high school. Then the student will be with a group making new friendships and will not be as conspicuous as if a grade were skipped within a school. For any grade-skipping, high ability and personal eagerness to move ahead are essential. For some skips, tutoring in certain subjects during either the year before the skip or in the grade to which skipped may be desirable. Sensible election of subjects is essential, of course. For example, one would not ordinarily take French II without adequate background in first-year French, or Algebra II without knowing Algebra I. This does not mean that a full year of French I or Algebra I will be needed, but just that equivalent knowledge of the prerequisite material, however gained, is important.

3. Skip the last year or two of senior high school and go on to college fulltime. Of course, one must plan ahead in order to do this effectively and efficiently. A number of SMPY participants have found early entrance to college an ideal way to avoid "senior rot," as some of them term the boredom resulting from the last year in high school. Usually, after one year of successful course work in college they are given diplomas from the high schools previously attended. See Stanley (1976a).

4. Plan carefully in order to be graduated from high school a year early, perhaps by taking required senior-class courses during the tenth and eleventh grades.

5. Enter a certain course, such as Algebra I, a year or more early. Quite a few seventh graders can do well in the first year or algebra, even though it may be scheduled primarily for eighth or ninth graders. An occasional student even younger can.

6. Complete two or more years of a subject in one year. For example, do Algebra I and II or Algebra II and plane geometry in a single school year. A variety of fast-mathematics classes pioneered by SMPY accomplish this objective well. Some highly able, well motivated seventh-graders learned Algebra I-III, plane geometry, trigonometry, and analytic geometry--which usually take about four and one-half years in school--by studying on Saturday mornings for 13 months (late June through next early August) with a special teacher. They were then ready for the calculus. See Fox (1974), George and Denhan (1976), George (1976), Stanley (1976b), and Stanley (1977).

7. Have a special "mentor" pace, stimulate, and tutor the brilliant student rapidly through various mathematics courses. We at SMPY have found that when this is done properly it can be more effective than any other procedure yet tried. For example, seventh graders who reason extremely well mathematically can learn first-year high-school algebra with a skilled mentor excellently in anywhere from nearly zero to about 15 hours. Such students can be worked with in two- or three-hour sessions once weekly and do a great deal of well-designed homework between sessions. Success should be judged by performance on a

standardized Algebra I test such as that of the Cooperative Achievement Tests series or on a suitably broad-based test prepared within the student's school system. If the latter is to be taken, of course the mentor will use instructional materials appropriate for its objectives. Participants in SMPY's talent searches who score extremely high on the mathematical part of the Scholastic Aptitude Test of the College Board, which SMPY uses, are offered the opportunity to work with mentors in flexible groups of 1-5 students per mentor that are homogeneous with respect to current level of mathematics.

8. Take regular college courses for credit on a parttime basis while still enrolled in junior or senior high school. This can be done during the school day on released time, and/or during late afternoons, evenings, Saturdays, and summers. No special provisions are made for the student. He or she simply registers, pays the usual fees, and does the work of the course. It is better not to point out to the instructor that the student is younger than the average of the class. Amazingly, instructors of college classes usually are not aware that a student who makes A's and seems brilliant is young, even though that person may be only 12 years old and quite short. For example, a highly experienced, middle-aged college math teacher called such a youth to her desk after the third class of a college algebra and trigonometry course and said to him, not "You seem young for this course," but instead "You seem overqualified for this course." He then signed up for her analytic geometry course, also, and was the best student in both classes. See Keating, Wiegand, and Fox (1974).

Taking college courses this way has many advantages that make it popular with SMPY's proteges and others:

- No special preparations are needed. No one has to organize a special class or find ways to finance special arrangements at school.

- Of course, parents must pay the required fees, but probably the credits earned can be used later to reduce time in college. Thus the expense can be considered advance payment of college tuition.

- Taking college courses early can provide orientation toward later fulltime college attendance, especially if the college attended is somewhat comparable in level to the subsequent institution. The less stringent the college at which courses are taken on a part-time basis, the earlier a student of a given ability level can do well there. Even though the college courses may not seem high-level enough for the student, still to him or her they may be preferable to the analogous high-school course.

We at SMPY have, for example, seen a ten-year-old be the best student in an introductory computer science course at a state college. He was competing with seven of our youths who were older than he and with 12 adults. While still ten he began a second-level computer course in the Johns Hopkins summer session and made an "A" on it, also. Of course, this is a truly brilliant youth, with a Stanford-Binet IQ of 190, but he dramatically illustrates the fallacy of assuming that one must be of the usual college age in order to take a college course.

Two other youths, one 12 and the other 13 years old (both of them eighth-graders), took the introductory computer science course with regular day students at Johns Hopkins and made A's. It can hardly be coincidental that both of them went on to be graduated from Johns Hopkins at age 17.

- Often, arrangements can be made to substitute certain college courses for the equivalent high-school ones. Also, some college courses such as computer science or economics may be acceptable as electives in high school, thereby hastening graduation. One of our youths took no mathematics below the college level beyond the first-year algebra in junior high school. During the summer after the eighth grade he made "B" in a college algebra and trigonometry course at Johns Hopkins. During each of the next four semesters of school he took a mathematics course at nearby Goucher College, thus completing a year of calculus and a course in linear algebra by the end of the tenth grade. Meanwhile, during each of the two summers he took two semesters of college chemistry at Goucher. In the fall after the tenth grade he became a full-time sophomore at

1. INTERVENTION

Johns Hopkins because of the 39 credits of college work he had earned from the last half of the eighth grade onward with all A's except for the one B in his first college math course. You will not be surprised to learn that he easily won his baccalaureate with distinction at age 17 in six semesters rather than the usual eight and went on to another great university to study for a Ph.D. degree in electrical engineering. Would you be surprised five or ten years hence to find that he is well embarked on an outstanding postdoctoral career?

9. Credit by examination is an excellent way to move ahead while avoiding repetitive course material. In high school or college one may be allowed to "challenge" courses--that is, to study for them privately and then take an examination. One may be able to get credit for college courses by means of the Advanced Placement Program (APP) examinations or the College Level Examination Program (CLEP) of the College Board. APP is especially useful for getting the first year of college calculus out of the way early. Many other first-year-of-college courses may also be waived, usually with credit, in the same way. If one does not go the APP or CLEP route, it may still be possible to get credit at the college one enters by taking departmental exams there, but this is a less reliable procedure than are the external exams. Much depends, however, on the college's policies regarding advanced standing.

We have seen a young, accelerated student earn 47 college credits by APP examinations in two years. This is the equivalent of 1.6 years of college, enabling the student to earn a degree in five or even four semesters. Two tenth-graders each earned 24 credits (80 percent of a year) by taking APP exams in such subjects as biology, calculus, chemistry, and physics. One of these scored high in two subjects he had not even studied formally, biology and chemistry! Also, credit outside of science and mathematics is common among the SMPY participants. Truly, APP exams are a wonderful opportunity to accelerate educationally and to save substantial or even large percentages of the costs of attending college. This may enable a student to attend a more expensive institution than his parents could afford otherwise.

Eager youths who are in the upper one-half of one percent of their age group nationally with respect to mathematical reasoning ability and who also have excellent general intelligence can readily enter college at age 15 or 16 with sophomore standing. Usually, they will be better off academically, and probably socially and emotionally also, for having done so, especially if during the first year or two they can commute to the college from home.

10. Taking correspondence courses at the high school or college level from a major university such as California or Wisconsin is a possibility, but it requires so much self-discipline from the student that we have not found it very satisfactory. Feedback from the homework-grader at the other end of the line comes too slowly for most youths. If this approach to acceleration is used, some suitable support system at home or school such as a mentor is needed, or else the student is likely to lose interest.

11. We at SMPY do not endorse the usual type of so-called self-paced instruction, including programmed instruction. In our experience, mathematically precocious youths work much more quickly and better when they are paced fast and at a high level of rigor by excellent instructors or mentors and, except for the one-to-one tutoring situation, by their equally able classmates. We have seen plane geometry take ten two-hour sessions in a fast-math class, one school year in a regular class, and considerably more than one school year by self-paced instruction. There are exceptions, of course. A few brilliant students prefer to work almost entirely on their own and do so effectively, but this is typical.

12. Some private elementary and secondary schools may have distinct academic social, or athletic advantages over public ones and may therefore be worth their substantial costs to parents who can afford them. We at SMPY are convinced, however, that they are no panacea for intellectually talented youths. The best of such schools often take care of the academic needs of youths with IQ's between about 120 and 140 well, but few of them have strong advantages over the better public schools for students brighter than that or with extremely high special aptitudes. Being small, they usually lack scheduling flexibility. Having an intimate atmosphere, they are often more resistant to the various kinds of educational acceleration than public

schools are. Sometimes they are not even as responsive to the pleas of parents on behalf of their intellectually talented children as public schools are.

Sending their brilliant child to a parochial or independent school does not free parents from the need to supplement the curriculum considerably. Each family must decide carefully whether, in terms of its total resources, the amount of money is better spent for private-school costs, or, instead, for educational supplementation and augmentation. It is important to have a clear agreement with the private school, in writing, as to what will actually be done for the child that will be decidedly superior to the opportunities of the best public school in which he or she might be enrolled. *Vague promises are not adequate.*

IN CONCLUSION

If some of the many strictures in this paper seem harsh, keep in mind how long overdue they are. There have never been many advocates of educational acceleration, whereas so-called enrichment has long dominated the gifted-child scene. When one considers how little objective support there is for the various and often nebulously defined activities called enrichment (see Daurio 1978 and Stanley 1976c) and how much there is for acceleration this seems bizarre. Among educators, educational psychologists, parents, and the general public matters of opinion are likely to overshadow those of fact, so perhaps resistance to acceleration is not surprising. At least and at last, however, educational acceleration deserves careful consideration on its own merits as a major set of ways to improve the education of the intellectually talented, rather than being derided or ignored.

Were our educational system not so wedded to the age-in-grade and Carnegie-unit locksteps and if it catered far better to individual differences of all kinds in intellect, ameliorative programs such as SMPY's might not be needed. In a sense, they are stopgap procedures. Because there seems little hope for major changes in the structure of formal education in the foreseeable future, however, there is no likelihood that the dire need for many SMPY-type programs will disappear soon.

Two caveats are in order. First, it should be obvious that most of my experience with intellectually talented youths has been in the United States, and therefore my remarks are directed chiefly at coordinators of the education of gifted children and at their parents in this country. Educators and parents from other countries may find much in this paper that speaks to their condition, but they will realize the necessity for making the modifications that natural differences dictate.

Secondly, we at SMPY work almost exclusively with youths who reason exceptionally well mathematically, among the top 1 to 3 percent of their age groups nationally. Our findings and recommendations relate directly to them. We are far less confident that certain of our procedures are as applicable to youths whose intellectual talents are great but not in the area of mathematics, the mathematical sciences, and the physical sciences. Nevertheless, although all participants in our annual talent searches must exhibit mathematical aptitude equal to that of at least the top 1 in 33 of their age group, they are an excellent group from the standpoint of reading comprehension and knowledge of general vocabulary, too. Some of them are, indeed, far more gifted verbally than mathematically. Some (especially among the girls) who reason extremely well mathematically prefer the social sciences or the humanities. Because of this diversity of interest we have seen many types of response to the various ways to accelerate one's educational progress. These give us some confidence, as does the research literature, that educational acceleration is not useful merely for the mathematically and scientifically brilliant, but also for most other brilliant youths who crave it.

4. International

Mathematics is, however, a closed system that draws far less on life experiences than do the social sciences and humanities. One does not need to have lived, loved, suffered, and lost in order to understand algebra. Thus a high SAT-M score, accompanied by a moderately good SAT-V score, tells us rather reliably what subjects the student can probably learn earlier than most of his or her agemates.

We feel that this is also true of an exceptionally high SAT-V score. The SAT-V score seems to reflect fairly accurately the assimilation of life experiences in the verbal area that would be useful in a college course in the social sciences or humanities. We have seen some of our participants take economics, political science, sociology, psychology,

1. INTERVENTION

intensive Russian, and the like quite successfully at an early age. Specialists in the gifted need to explore various special-ability areas more fully.

So I leave you with the thought that educational acceleration is not the ogre educators and others have alleged. Instead, we at SMPY have found it to be *the* method of choice for those youths who reason extremely well mathematically and are eager to move ahead educationally. For other gifted children it should be a far-more-considered set of alternatives than at present. I invite you to examine the evidence closely and then to act accordingly.

> Dr. Stanley is Professor of Psychology and Director of the Study of Mathematically Precocious Youth (SMPY), The Johns Hopkins University, Baltimore, Maryland.

ARE WE EDUCATING ONLY HALF OF THE BRAIN?

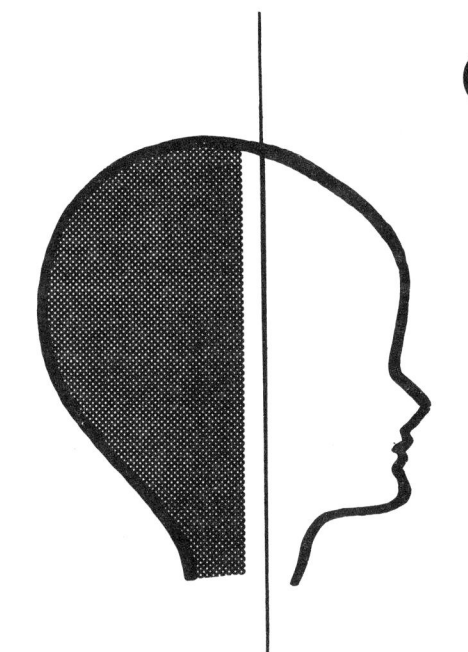

Over half a century ago, Graham Wallas (1926) defined the four components of creativity of preparation, incubation, illumination, and verification. By incubation he meant a relaxing by reverie or diversion so that deeper processes in the mind could bring the "aha" or creative illumination. Preparation, (Intellectual discipline), had to proceed this stage, and verification, another cognitive operation, had to follow. In view of this early pointer, it is surprising how little attention has been paid to incubation since then until very recently. Indeed, all the prescription of both Guilford and Osborn, has been focused on cognitive preparation.

First, we need to review a bit of physiology. The quotation is from Gowan 1975:261:

The brain is composed of two cerebral hemispheres, each of which governs the motor activities of the other side of the body. The two hemispheres appear to work as dual controls, being joined by a massive conduit of nerves known as the *corpus callosum*. About 1950 Myers and Sperry discovered that if the *corpus callosum* were cut, each hemisphere could function independently as if it were a complete brain. This discovery led to a number of itriguing questions such as what are patients like who have had this operation? and are there differential hemisphere functions?

Sperry and Gazzaniga (Gazzaniga, 1957) conducted tests to show the differential function in split brain patients. These showed that for some reason, the left side of the brain quickly assumed the normal functions of speech and writing, and that the right side was unable to speak and write. The right side, however, is not without intelligence. When a patient feels fruit with his left hand in a photographer's change muff in which there are (for example) two apples and an orange, he cannot say what the fruit is, but he can signal that the two apples are alike and the orange is different. The right hemisphere of such patients also handled spatial relations better than the left. It also appears from other research to handle holistic concepts and creative imagination better.

Right hemisphere imagery is the vehicle through which incubation produces creativity. In his famous paradigm of creative process,

1. INTERVENTION

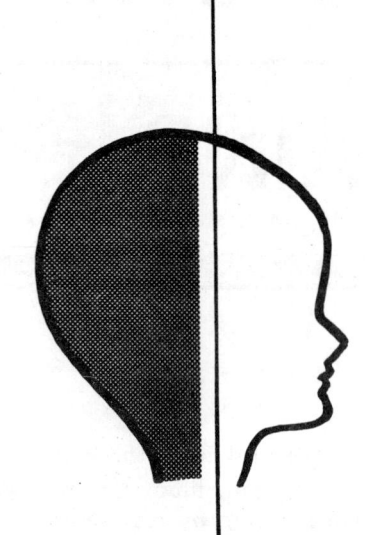

Graham Wallas (1926) identified four components: preparation, incubation, illumination, verification. By incubation, he meant any technique of relaxation of the conscious cognition (left cerebral hemisphere function), such as, but not confined to dreams, daydreams, fantasy, hypnosis, meditation, diversion, play, etc., which allows subliminal processes (right hemisphere functions) to operate. He saw preparation (academic discipline), as the necessary, and incubation (relaxation), as the sufficient condition for creative insights to emerge.

We shall assume the definition of mental imagery as essentially nonverbal (in the Guilford Structure of intellect parlance -- nonsymbolic) material occurring in consciousness not immediately preceded by perceptual intake. By creativity, we shall mean the production of material or relationships new to the culture. To open up the discussion, we follow our initial statement with further elaboration: Whereas most functions of the left hemisphere are concerned with convergent production as described by Guilford, functions of the right hemisphere are principally concerned with divergent production. These functions involve imagery through which incubation produces creativity.

Growing awareness that right hemisphere imagery is the source of creativity is an interdisciplinary phenomenon. Says prestigious M.I.T. Engineer, Prof. Stanley West, (1975:221):

With support from recent research in the neurosciences I speculate that minor scientific creativity is likely to be mainly left hemisphere cognitive excitation, while major scientific creativity is likely to involve the excitation and intercommunication of both cerebral hemispheres...... In other words, some kind of altered state of awareness...... may be essential to creativity...... Creativity in many extraordinarily gifted individuals depends in part upon temporary dominance of the right cerebral hemisphere.

West then quotes his colleague M.I.T. professor Weizenbaum: (in press: 169-70);

Ths history of man's creativity is filled with stories of artists and scientis who after working hard and long on some difficult problem, consciously decide to "forget" it, to, in effect, turn it over to their unconscious, i.e., to their RH (right hemisphere). After some time, often with great suddenness and totally unexpectedly, the solution to their problem announces itself to them in almost complete form. The RH appears to have been able to overcome the most difficult logical and systematic problems by, we would conjecture, relaxing the rigid standards of thought of th LH (left hemisphere). Given the looser standards the RH employs, it was perhaps able to design thought experiments which the LH simply could not, because of its rigidity, conceive. The RH is thus able to hit upon solutions which could then, of course, be recast into strictly logical terms by the LH

West, then goes on to conclude (1975:223):

> Visual imagery is but one segment of right hemispheric mental processes. Indeed, images in the right cerebral hemisphere need not be restricted to spatial relationships among physical objects. This imagery may consist of concepts, theories, or other cultural categories as elements of a system as well as notions such as causation or precedence - the relationships among the elements - but one should also note that neither the elements nor the relationships are linguistic artifacts, and, furthermore, imagery of this sort is essential for both cognitive resynthesis and scientific synthesis.

Shepard (1978:125-6) also writing on imagery in scientists marvels at the intuitive imagery of Michael Faraday who "was able to find a large number of results" without mathematical analysis. He operated:

--"by a kind of intuition, with the security of instinct, without the help of a single mathematical formula" (quoted in Kendall, 1955). What kind of intuition" or "instinct" was this? A clue may be discerned in the claim that the invisible lines of force, which Faraday visualized as narrow tubes curving throughout space, "rose up before him like things" (Koestler, 1964; Tyndall, 1868).

The culmination of classical electromagnetic theory was achieved by Faraday's towering successor, James Clerk Maxwell, who brilliantly crystallized the fundamental relationships governing electric and magnetic fields, and the propagation of electromagnetic waves, in the form of a beautifully symmetrical set of equations universally known simply as "Maxwell's equations." What is significant here is that although Maxwell has been regarded as a prime example of an abstract theoretician, he is reported to have "developed the habit of making a mental picture of every problem" (Beveridge, 1957, p. 76). He, in fact, arrived at his formal equations only at the end of a long series of more and more elaborately visualized concrete hydrodynamic and mechanical models of the underlying "ether" - models that he ultimately discarded, as Sir Edmund Whittaker once put it, in much the same way that one might discard a temporary "scaffolding" used in the erection of a permanent edifice (Newman, 1955).

The present-day relativistic reformulation of electromagnetic theory had its inception when Albert Einstein performed his epochal Gedanken experiment of imagining himself traveling alongside a beam of light (at 186,000 miles per second). It was then that he confronted the paradox that the stationary spatial oscillation that he mentally "saw" corresponded neither to anything that could be perceptually experienced as light nor to anything described by Maxwell's equations (Einstein, 1949; Holton, 1972). As is well known, Einstein later stated quite explicitly that he "very rarely" thought in words at all (Wertheimer, 1945, p. 184). Indeed, he explained that his "particular ability" did not lie in mathematical calculation either, but rather in "*visualizing . . . effects, consequences, and possibilities*"

such as the "Eureka" of Archimedes) in the mathematicians, comes in dreams to scientists, and some (like Newton and Faraday) are susceptible to a kind of "sleepwalking fantasy" and are considered eccentric as a result.

For those who wish to go beyond the cautious statements of scientists into further extrapolations of the relations between creativity, the right hemisphere and consciousness in general, there is the recent work of Jaynes (1976) and Wilber (1977).

Conditions Favoring Right-Hemisphere Imagery

"Under what conditions does imagery occur?" It is now quite obvious that, while imagery occurs spontaneously under hypnosis, and in trance, dreams, hypnogogic and hypnopompic states, as well as in other natural and induced altered states of consciousness, it can be found also in the more normal states, such as, daydreaming, fantasy, meditation, creative spells, relaxation, sensory deprivation, and the like, where the go and full memorability are present. The key elements in the situation appear to be a) lowering the sensory input and b) stopping the internal verbal chatter; both of these point to allying the overriding function of the left hemisphere. From the above it appears that right hemisphere imagery goes on all the time and that it is merely necessary to pay attention to it. Learning of how to do this is obviously a new educational challenge, if we are to educate both halves of the brain and hence stimulate creativity in young people.

If the function of incubation is to allay the activity of the left hemisphere so that right-hemisphere imagery can be consciously observed, how better can we learn about this process than through the testimony of geniuses? We shall see that, whereas the left hemisphere seems to act as a problem solver, the right seems to act as a radio receiver. Thus, when the static of the left hemisphere has been abated, some type of resonance phenomenon is set up, of which the first evidence is *vibrations*. Consider what the composer Brahms told Arthur Abell (Abell, 1964, pp. 19-21):

> I immediately feel vibrations which thrill my whole being... In this exalted state I see clearly what is obscure in my ordinary moods, and I feel capable of drawing inspiration from above, as Beethoven did... Those vibrations assume the form of distinct mental images.... Straightaway the ideas flow upon me... and not only do I see distinct themes,... but they are clothed in the right forms.... I have to be in a semi-trance condition to get such results - a condition when the conscious mind is in temporary abeyance, and the subconscious is in control.

Similar statements by Puccini and Wagner will be found in a discussion of the discrete steps in the creativity of musical composers (Gowan, 1976, pp. 378-86) from which is quoted:

> For most, it will be seen that the process of such high creativity consists of three phases: 1) the prelude ritual... 2) the altered state of consciousness or creative spell, during which the creative idea is born, starting with vibrations, then mental images, then the flow of ideas which are finally clothed in forms. This syndrome often proceeds with extreme and uncanny

1. INTERVENTION

rapidity in what is always referred to as a trance, dream, revery, somnambulistic state, or similar altered condition, and 3) the postlude in which positive emotions about the experience suffuse the participant.

What genius does naturally by intuition, education can help the less able to learn by accretion, but the mechanics of the process must be understood, which is precisely the reason for this article. We now possess enough facts and hunches regarding right-hemisphere functions to be able to put this knowledge to practical use. Admittedly in this article we have looked at the forest rather than the trees, brushing with broad strokes over a wide canvas. What has been said, for example, must be qualified as applying only to left-hemisphere dominance (right-handedness), and any sophisticated reader will at once recognize other exceptions and singularities which later will have to be dealt with separately. But the broad pattern leading from incubation, through imagery to creativity is clear, and if we wish to produce a more creative tomorrow, we should act on it in education today. The civilization we save thereby may be our own.

Conclusion

Putting together elements discussed previously, as well as information presented elsewhere, (Gowan, 1967, 1972, 1974, 1975, 1976, 1977, 1978; Gowan, Khatena, & Torrance, 1978) we may summarize the metamorphosis characteristic of incubation in which nonverbal imagery plays a central part, as follows:

There has previously been intense left-hemisphere study and analysis of the problem/situation, whose apparent function is to prepare a matrix of vocabulary and verbal description so that the ultimate creative solution can be "intellectually negotiated" and hence shared with society.

1) Through accidental or contrived means, the protagonist is placed in an environment which triggers emotion, where he is alone and undisturbed and, under ardent desire and fixed purpose, finds himself in the altered state of consciousness of right-hemisphere process in a creative spell, fantasy, dream, vision, revery (which are probably mere names for the uncanny feeling which goes with allying left-hemisphere function).

2) With left-hemisphere function allayed, and right-hemisphere function active, some sort of resonance effect takes place often accompanied by somatic feelings of vibration; and all takes place in condensed time.

3) Out of the vibrations come images, which may be indistinct or virtual images which appear superimposed on the visual field. The images are not passive, but, partaking of the function of archetypes, have a certain generating and heuristic effect, in that they lead to discovery and action.

4) This process is accompanied by intense positive emotions of awe joy, content, satisfaction, completion, somewhat similar to, but often greater and more sublime than sexual orgasm and remarkably like the "peak experience" described by Maslow. In obedience to the

James-Lange theory this condition persists for a time after the experience.

5) In the case of all save artistic creativity, there now ensues intense left-hemisphere activity to notate, verbalize, describe, and operate this imagery into "intellectually negotiable" form, so that it can be "consensually validated" by others. This activity which is part of the Wallas "evaluation", may go on for a long time. It requires the precursor "preparatory" stage so that the matrix is ready to clothe the images in verbal or numerical form. While this element is termed "creative," it is probable that the true "Wallas Illumination" occurs with imagery. If the matrix has not been prepared, the right-hemisphere activity will merely evoke a pleasant emotion, and no lasting social creative product will emerge.

Incubation is the mental analog of physical gestation in which an ovum is developed into a baby. Incubation is the process of metamorphosis, and right-hemisphere imagery is the vehicle through which incubation produces creativity.

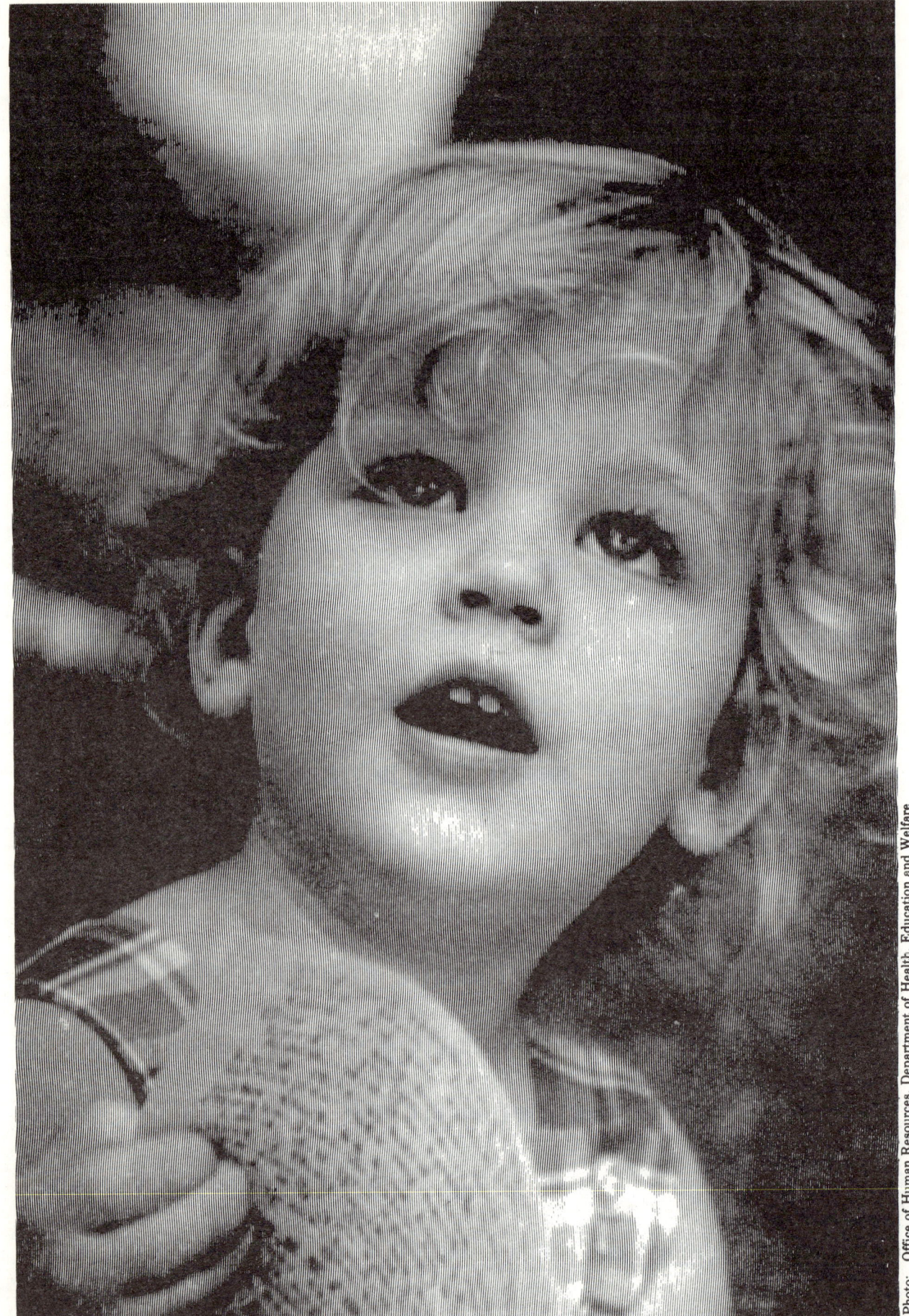

Photo: Office of Human Resources, Department of Health, Education and Welfare

FOCUS...

Does Intelligence Have a Genetic Basis?

One hundred years of arguments over the meaning and value of intelligence testing are cataloged in *The IQ Controversy*, edited by Ned J. Block and Gerald Dworkin. The four-part book contains essays by various scholars covering both sides of the question, closing with an enlightening discussion of the controversy by the two editors. This book was reviewed in the April *Mensa Bulletin, International Section* by Philip M. Powell, Assistant Professor, Department of Educational Psychology, University of Texas.

The first part of *The IQ Controversy* includes the debate between Lewis Terman and Walter Lippman in the 1920s. Some of Lippman's arguments against IQ testing were (1) IQ should not be confused with intelligence, (2) IQ test results only predict school success, (3) IQ measures were not based on an adequate theory of intelligence, and (4) IQ test results may rationalize social prejudice.

"Terman's counter-arguments were weak," Powell said. "They consisted basically of appeals to highly-esteemed psychological authorities who agreed with Terman, and a fascination with the whiz kid performance of those with very high IQs compared against those with low IQs. Terman also clearly believed that IQ tests measured innate intelligence."

David McCelland, in his chapter in the book, "Testing for Competence Rather than for Intelligence," argues that behaviors critical to a job should be well defined. "Those who can do these criterion behaviors should be given the job and the devil with their IQs," Powell reported as McCelland's point of view. "This approach is so obviously sound that one again wonders why so much fuss is made about IQ in this society."

Addressing that question, Arthur B. Jensen wrote the *Harvard Educational Review* article, "How Much Can We Boost IQ and Scholastic Achievement?" Powell comments as follows:

Jensen's purpose was to provoke discussion of the reasons for the "failure" of Headstart and other compensatory education programs to upgrade the IQs and educational achievements of the Black and the poor. To explain these "poor results," Jensen argues that (1) IQ tests measure innate intelligence; (2) Intelligence is a highly hereditable trait; (3) Therefore, if two populations differ significantly in mean IQ then they probably differ in genotypic intelligence. To comprehend Jensen's argument and his mistakes, a definition of hereditability and some other remarks are necessary; "Hereditability... is defined as the ratio of the variance due to the differences between the genotypes to the total variance in the population." (Lewontin, p. 85 of "Race and Intelligence" in The IQ Controversy*). Also, hereditability estimates are valid only for a set of existing environments; hence phenotypic differences in the manifestations of a common trait between two populations may be increased in one set of existing environments and decreased in another set.*

Consequently, using Lewontin's definition of hereditability and my above sentence, one can define two problems with Jensen's argument as Lewontin himself pointed out in one of his essays in The IQ Controversy*. One problem is that Jensen confuses hereditability within a population for a given trait with hereditability of a difference across populations on a common trait. In short, Jensen pools within–and between–group hereditability which does not allow him to compare the relative effects of heredity and environment for a common trait which occurs in two different populations. Also, the hereditability evidence Jensen uses to make his argument in the first place is based on the white population. Thus premise (2) in Jensen's argument stated earlier is quite specious. Worse yet, many of the studies from which Jensen obtained the hereditability estimate of 0.80 for intelligence for the white population have been recently found to be untrustworthy. In short, the 0.80 hereditability estimate is probably a gross overestimation with 0.40 or thereabouts being more likely.*

Also it is a logical error, on Jensen's part, to reason that since whites have a high hereditability for intelligence, Blacks must also. At best, all Jensen is able to talk about with any confidence, given variable research, is the hereditability of intelligence (IQ?) in the white population, within the context of a set of existing environments. Thus, Jensen's entire argument is suspect since it may be true; a) that IQ tests are confounded by social class and hence are not "pure" measures of the full range of variables that define intelligence (premise 1); b) that intelligence, as indexed by IQ tests, is a "trait" with high hereditability may itself be a questionable assumption (premise 2); and c) that, therefore, it may be false to conclude that if two populations differ in mean IQ based on tests devised by one of them, it necessarily follows that these same populations differ in genotypic intelligence (premise 3).

Thus, Jensen is not entitled to make his conclusion that minorities (read Blacks) should be taught to develop rote memory skills, where there are negligible phenotypic differences in performance between the races, instead of being taught to develop abstract reasoning skills where there are significant phenotypic differences in performance between the races. One might even have occasion to wonder how Jensen's article ever got published in the Harvard Educational Review, given the precise negative criticisms levelled by eminent scholars against Jensen's arguments. In fact, without a lot of scurrying about, one can see such criticisms detailed in The IQ Controversy.

Anyhow, at the conclusion of part two, one could not help noticing the ringing similarities between Jensen's point of view and that of Terman in the 1920s. It was becoming clearer to me that, whatever Jensen's purposes were, he was propounding similar ideas to those used to rationalize American anti-immigration quotas in 1924 because Southern and Eastern Europeans had "low IQs." Well, obviously, the effects of Jensen's arguments are explosive in a democracy....

After reading this book, I guess I can answer the question raised earlier about the virulence of the IQ controversy. The answer is simple. In a democracy, it is hard to rationalize social privilege and social frustration. Further, people who have been taught to be materialistic, individualistic, competitive yet democratic, christian and charitable need "scientific theories" to rationalize their prejudices, their social class strivings, and their outer-directed existences. In short, until we all learn to value people as people, regardless of their possessions whether physical or psychological, we will always generate (IQ) controversies to divide our country, especially in hard times, instead of motivations to construct a better society consistent with our most profound historical declarations.

In giving permission to reprint excerpts from his review, Powell added the following comment for teachers and administrators: "Teach the gifted to value and develop themselves as total human beings, with an integrated mind and heart. Such people will free the human race so that it can begin to actualize itself."

Photo: Office of Human Resources, Department of Health, Education and Welfare

IDENTIFICATION OF THE GIFTED

No single test has been found to be an adequate basis for identifying a gifted population. Rather, researchers and practitioners alike have come to the use of multi-phase and multi-process methods. Often a screening phase precedes final identification. Also, a recognition has grown of the relation between identification and program goals. Clearly, identification criteria for a program for those talented in the performing arts will differ sharply from those employed in selecting participants for a program for those with advanced mathematical skills. Further significant differences may be seen in the methods employed in selecting special populations, such as the very young, the handicapped, the black, and the adolescent age group. Specific operational means have been developed for each of these cases.

The following section contains articles that suggest and illustrate current methods in identification of the gifted and talented, and realistic program goals. Dr. Joseph Renzulli offers a common starting ground for all personnel to work from with his article "What Makes Giftedness? Reexamining a Definition." A graphic definition of giftedness is presented that illustrate the integration of skills, and general and specific performance areas.

One segment of the gifted population that has greatly been ignored is the handicapped gifted child. These children that are defined as those whose full devlopment is impaired through physical, sensory, social-emotional and/or learning deficits, and who also show evidence of outstanding abilities in one or more areas of talent. Personnel trained to serve the handicapped in the past have demonstrated little interest in developing and programming that emphasize abilities. "Young Handicapped Children can be Gifted and Talented" describes a program sponsored by the Bureau of Education for the Handicapped that is developing procedures for identifying and programming for the gifted/handicapped child. As in all articles contained here, the emphasis is on a positive approach towards identification and programming.

What Makes Giftedness?
Reexamining a Definition

Mr. Renzulli offers a new research-based definition of the gifted and talented. It is an operational definition intended to help the practitioner.

by Joseph S. Renzulli

JOSEPH S. RENZULLI (University of Virginia Chapter) is associate director of the Bureau of Educational Research, University of Connecticut, Storrs. © 1978 by Joseph S. Renzulli.

Throughout recorded history and undoubtedly even before records were kept, people have always been interested in men and women who display superior ability. As early as 2200 B.C. the Chinese had developed an elaborate system of competitive examinations to select outstanding persons for government positions,[1] and down through the ages almost every culture has been fascinated by its most able citizens. Although the areas of performance in which one might be recognized as a gifted person are determined by the needs and values of the prevailing culture, scholars and laypersons alike have debated (and continue to debate) the age-old question: What makes giftedness?

The purpose of this article is therefore threefold. First, I shall analyze some past and current definitions of giftedness. Second, I shall review studies that deal with characteristics of gifted individuals. Finally, I shall present a new definition of giftedness that is operational, i.e., useful to school personnel, and defensible in terms of research findings.

The Definition Continuum

Numerous conceptions and countless definitions of giftedness have been put forth over the years. One way of analyzing existing definitions is to view them along a continuum ranging from "conservative" to "liberal," i.e., according to the degree of restrictiveness used in determining who is eligible for special programs and services.

Restrictiveness can be expressed in two

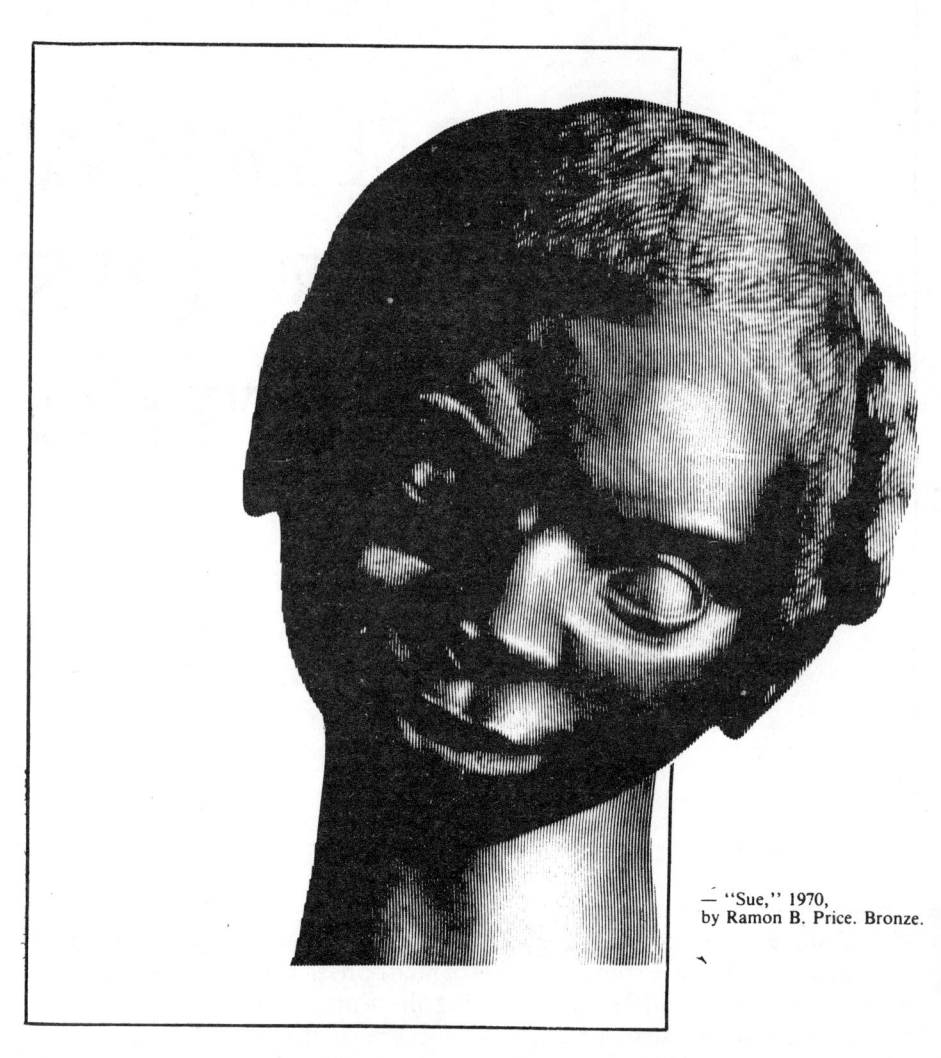

— "Sue," 1970, by Ramon B. Price. Bronze.

ways. First, a definition can limit the number of performance areas that are considered in determining eligibility for special programs. A conservative definition, for example, might limit eligibility to academic performance only and exclude other areas such as music, art, drama, leadership, public speaking, social service, and creative writing. Second, a definition may specify the degree or level of excellence one must attain to be considered gifted.

At the conservative end of the continuum is Lewis Terman's definition of giftedness, "the top 1% level in general intellectual ability, as measured by the Stanford-Binet Intelligence Scale or a comparable instrument."[2]

In this definition restrictiveness is present in terms of both the type of performance specified (i.e., how well one scores on an intelligence test) and the level of performance one must attain to be considered gifted (top 1%). At the other end of the continuum may be found more liberal definitions, such as the following one by Paul Witty:

There are children whose outstanding potentialities in art, in writing, or in social leadership can be recognized largely by their performance. Hence, we have recommended that the definition of giftedness be expanded and that we consider any child gifted whose performance, in a potentially valuable line of human activity, is consistently remarkable.[3]

Although liberal definitions have the obvious advantage of expanding the conception of giftedness, they also open up two "cans of worms" by introducing the values issue (What are the potentially valuable lines of human activity?) and the age-old problem of subjectivity in measurement.

In recent years the values issue has been largely resolved. There are very few educators who cling to a "straight IQ" or purely academic definition of giftedness. "Multiple talent" and "multiple criteria" are almost the bywords of the present-day gifted student movement, and most educators would have little difficulty in accepting a definition that includes almost every area of human activity that manifests itself in a socially useful form.

The problem of subjectivity in measurement is not as easily resolved. As the definition of giftedness is extended beyond those abilities clearly reflected in tests of intelligence, achievement, and academic aptitude, it becomes necessary to put less emphasis on precise estimates of performance and potential and more emphasis on the opinions of qualified human judges in making decisions about admission to special programs. The issue boils down to a simple and yet very important question: How much of a trade-off are we willing to make on the objective/subjective continuum in order to allow recognition of a broader spectrum of human abilities? If some degree of subjectivity cannot be tolerated, then our definition of giftedness and the resulting programs will logically be limited to abilities that can only be measured by objective tests.

The USOE Definition

In recent years the following definition set forth by the U.S. Office of Education (USOE) has grown in popularity, and numerous states and school districts throughout the nation have adopted it for their programs:

> Gifted and talented children are those . . . who by virtue of outstanding abilities are capable of high performance. These . . . children . . . require differentiated educational programs and/or services beyond those normally provided by the regular school program in order to realize their [potential] contribution to self and society.
>
> Children capable of high performance include those who have demonstrated any of the following abilities or aptitudes, singly or in combination: 1) general intellectual ability, 2) specific academic aptitude, 3) creative or productive thinking, 4) leadership ability, 5) visual and performing arts aptitude, 6) psychomotor ability.[4]

The USOE definition has served the very useful purpose of calling attention to a wider variety of abilities that should be included in a definition of giftedness, but at the same time it has presented some major problems. The first lies in its failure to include nonintellective (motivational) factors. That these factors are important is borne out by an overwhelming body of research, which I shall consider later.

A second and equally important problem relates to the nonparallel nature of the six categories included in the definition. Two of the six categories (specific academic aptitude and visual and performing arts aptitude) call attention to fields of human endeavor or general performance areas in which talents and abilities are manifested. The remaining four categories are more nearly processes that may be brought to bear on performance areas. For example, a person may bring the process of creativity to bear on a specific aptitude (e.g., chemistry) or a visual art (e.g., photography). Or the processes of leadership and general intelligence might be applied to a performance area such as choreography or the management of a high school yearbook. In fact, it can be said that processes such as creativity and leadership do not exist apart from a performance area to which they can be applied.

A third problem with the definition is that it tends to be misinterpreted and misused by practitioners. It is not uncommon to find educators developing entire identification systems based on the six USOE categories and in the process treating them as if they were mutually exclusive. What is equally distressing is that many people "talk a good game" about the six categories but continue to use a relatively high intelligence or aptitude score as a minimum requirement for entrance into a special program. Although both of these problems result from misapplication rather than from the definition itself, the definition is not entirely without fault, because it fails to give the kind of guidance necessary for practitioners to avoid such pitfalls.

The Three-Ring Conception

Research on creative/productive people has consistently shown that although no single criterion should be used to identify giftedness, persons who have achieved recognition because of their unique accomplishments and creative contributions possess a relatively well-defined set of three interlocking clusters of traits. These clusters consist of above-average though not necessarily superior general ability, task commitment, and creativity (see Figure 1). It is important to point out that no single cluster "makes giftedness." Rather, it is the interaction among the three clusters that research has shown to be the necessary ingredient for creative/productive accomplishment. This interaction is represented by the shaded portion of Figure 1. It is also important to point out that each cluster is an "equal partner" in contributing to giftedness. This point is important. One of the major errors that continues to be made in identification procedures is overemphasis on superior abilities at the expense of the other two clusters of traits.

Figure 1. The Ingredients Of Giftedness

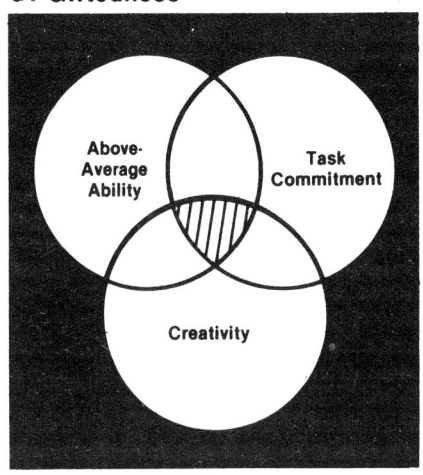

Above-Average General Ability

Although the influence of intelligence, as traditionally measured, quite obviously varies with areas of achievement, many researchers have found that creative accomplishment is not necessarily a function of measured intelligence. In a review of several research studies dealing with the relationship between academic aptitude tests and professional achievement, M. A. Wallach has concluded that:

> Above intermediate score levels, academic skills assessments are found to show so little criterion validity as to be a questionable basis on which to make consequential decisions about students' futures. What the academic tests do predict are the results a person will obtain on other tests of the same kind.[5]

Wallach goes on to point out that academic test scores at the upper ranges — precisely the score levels that are most often used for selecting persons for entrance into special programs — do not necessarily reflect the potential for creative/productive accomplishment. He suggests that test scores be used to screen out persons who score in the lower ranges and that beyond this point decisions be based on other indicators of potential for superior performance.

Numerous research studies support

2. IDENTIFICATION

Wallach's finding that there is little relationship between test scores and school grades on the one hand and real world accomplishments on the other.[6] In fact, a study dealing with the prediction of various dimensions of achievement among college students, made by J. L. Holland and A. W. Astin, found that

> ... getting good grades in college has little connection with more remote and more socially relevant kinds of achievement; indeed, in some colleges, the higher the student's grades, the less likely it is that he is a person with creative potential. So it seems desirable to extend our criteria of talented performance.[7]

A study by the American College Testing Program titled "Varieties of Accomplishment After College: Perspectives on the Meaning of Academic Talent" concluded:

> The adult accomplishments were found to be uncorrelated with academic talent, including test scores, high school grades, and college grades. However, the adult accomplishments were related to comparable high school nonacademic (extracurricular) accomplishments. This suggests that there are many kinds of talents related to later success which might be identified and nurtured by educational institutions.[8]

The pervasiveness of this general finding is demonstrated by D. P. Hoyt, who reviewed 46 studies dealing with the relationship between traditional indications of academic success and post-college performance in the fields of business, teaching, engineering, medicine, scientific research, and other areas such as the ministry, journalism, government, and miscellaneous professions.[9] From this extensive review, Hoyt concluded that traditional indications of academic success have no more than a very modest correlation with various indicators of success in the adult world. He observes, "There is good reason to believe that academic achievement (knowledge) and other types of educational growth and development are relatively independent of each other."

These studies raise some basic questions about the use of tests in making selection decisions. The studies clearly indicate that vast numbers *and* proportions of our most productive persons are *not* those who scored at the ninety-fifth or above percentile on standardized tests, nor were they necessarily straight-A students who discovered early how to play the lesson-learning game. In other words, more creative/productive persons come from below the ninety-fifth percentile than above it, and if such cut-off scores are needed to determine entrance into special programs, we may be guilty of actually discriminating against persons who have the greatest potential for high levels of accomplishment.

States Define Giftedness

Twenty-six states now define children who are exceptional by virtue of giftedness either in statutes or in state department of education regulations.* Pennsylvania, Idaho, Florida, and North Carolina require the same formal IEP (individualized education program) for the gifted as is mandated for the handicapped in the federal Education for All Handicapped Children Act (P.L. 94-142).

This information comes from Christine Lewis, the Montgomery County Intermediate Unit IEP facilitator for the gifted in Norristown, Pennsylvania.

*F. A. Karnes and E. C. Collins, "State Definitions of Gifted and Talented: A Report and Analysis," *Journal of the Education of the Gifted*, February, 1978, pp. 44-62.

Task Commitment

A second cluster of traits that are consistently found in creative/productive persons constitutes a refined or focused form of motivation known as task commitment. Whereas motivation is usually defined in terms of a general energizing process that triggers responses in organisms, task commitment represents energy brought to bear on a particular problem (task) or specific performance area.

The argument for including this nonintellective cluster of traits in a definition of giftedness is nothing short of overwhelming. From popular maxims and autobiographical accounts to hard-core research findings, one of the key ingredients that has characterized the work of gifted persons is the ability to involve oneself totally in a problem or area for an extended period of time.

The legacy of both Sir Francis Galton and Lewis Terman clearly indicates that task commitment is an important part of the making of a gifted person. Although Galton was a strong proponent of the hereditary basis for what he called "natural ability," he nevertheless subscribed strongly to the belief that hard work was part and parcel of giftedness:

> By natural ability I mean those qualities of intellect and disposition which urge and qualify a man to perform acts that lead to reputation. I do not mean capacity without zeal, nor zeal without capacity, nor even a combination of both of them, without an adequate power of doing a great deal of very laborious work. But I mean a nature which, when left to itself, will, urged by an inherent stimulus, climb the path that leads to eminence and has strength to reach the summit — on which, if hindered or thwarted, it will fret and strive until the hindrance is overcome, and it is again free to follow its laboring instinct.[10]

Terman's monumental studies undoubtedly represent the most widely recognized and frequently quoted research on the characteristics of gifted persons. Terman's studies, however, have unintentionally left a mixed legacy, because most persons have dwelt (and continue to dwell) on "early Terman" rather than on the conclusions he reached after several decades of intensive research. Therefore it is important to consider the following conclusion, reached after 30 years of follow-up studies on his initial population:

> ... [A] detailed analysis was made of the 150 most successful and 150 least successful men among the gifted subjects in an attempt to identify some of the nonintellectual factors that affect life success. ... Since the less successful subjects do not differ to any extent in intelligence as measured by tests, it is clear that notable achievement calls for more than a high order of intelligence.
>
> The results [of the follow-up] indicated that personality factors are extremely important determiners of achievement. ... The four traits on which [the most and least successful groups] differed most widely were *persistence in the accomplishment of ends, integration toward goals, self-confidence,* and *freedom from inferiority feelings.* In the total picture the greatest contrast between the two groups was in all-round emotional and social adjustment and in *drive to achieve*.[11] (Emphasis added)

Although Terman never suggested that task commitment should replace intelligence in our conception of giftedness, he did state that "intellect and achievement are far from perfectly correlated."

Several more recent studies support the findings of Galton and Terman and have shown that creative/productive persons are far more task oriented and involved in their work than are people in the general population. Perhaps the best known of these studies is the work of A. Roe and D.

6. Definition

> **Kohlberg's Level Six**
> by Jessica Maxwell
>
> Oh cursed be it that bade me see
> oh inefficient clarity
> oh clarion clarinet's reedy wheeze
> which, while on pitch,
> is still unclear
> is still some distant other's tune
> rising still
> so faint I can't quite catch the beat
> can't march in time my tapping feet feel but the rhythms of the moon
> which rises even in the midst
> oh sweet oblivion
> thou kissed but fools and left me crutches clutched and falling
> to this half-heard song
> this ill-reared imp
> who peeks from ferns
> now here, now where
> what frolicking fiendish flutist thou
> won't let me hear
> won't let me be
> who keeps me but a helpless mute
> who hears yet can't return a phrase
> what cryptic crippling arias raise
> this ambered ant
> this muscle frozen in mid-reach
> each to each
> it calls, it calls
> that tortuous truth that won't be good
> or understood
> it falls.
> Would that I could rest,
> nay fall asleep
> that it would fall on canceled ears
> or veiled eyes, inert to weep
> the silent cold and running wine
> an opiate
> a tonic weed
> in anesthetic healing art
> pretends, complete, the pauper's peace.
>
> ---
> *JESSICA MAXWELL is one of 69 gifted children whose careers are being followed by Mary Mecker, president of the Soi Institute in El Segundo, Calif. A former* Mademoiselle *editor, Ms. Maxwell is now a* Los Angeles Times *columnist.*

W. MacKinnon. Roe conducted an intensive study of the characteristics of 64 eminent scientists and found that *all* of her subjects had a high level of commitment to their work.[12] MacKinnon pointed out traits that were important in creative accomplishments: "It is clear that creative architects more often stress their inventiveness, independence, and individuality, their *enthusiasm, determination,* and *industry*"[13] (emphasis added).

Extensive reviews of research carried out by J. C. Nicholls[14] and H. G. McCurdy[15] found patterns of characteristics that were consistently similar to the findings reported by Roe and MacKinnon. Although the researchers cited thus far used different procedures and dealt with a variety of populations, there is a striking similarity in their major conclusions. First, academic ability (as traditionally measured by tests or grade-point averages) showed limited relationships to creative/productive accomplishment. Second, nonintellectual factors, and especially those that relate to task commitment, consistently played an important part in the cluster of traits that characterize highly productive people. Although this second cluster of traits is not as easily and objectively identifiable as are general cognitive abilities, they are nevertheless a major component of giftedness and should therefore be reflected in our definition.

Creativity

The third cluster of traits that characterize gifted persons consists of factors that have usually been lumped together under the general heading of "creativity." As one reviews the literature in this area, it becomes readily apparent that the words "gifted," "genius," and "eminent creators" or "highly creative persons" are used synonymously. In many of the research projects discussed above, the persons ultimately selected for intensive study were in fact recognized *because* of their creative accomplishments. In MacKinnon's study, for example, panels of qualified judges (professors of architecture and editors of major American architectural journals) were asked first to nominate and later to rate an initial pool of nominees, using the following dimensions of creativity: 1) originality of thinking and freshness of approaches to architectural problems, 2) constructive ingenuity, 3) ability to set aside established conventions and procedures when appropriate, and 4) a flair for devising effective and original fulfillments of the major demands of architecture: namely, technology (firmness), visual form (delight), planning (commodity), and human awareness and social purpose.[16]

When discussing creativity, it is important to consider the problems researchers have encountered in establishing relationships between scores on creativity tests and other more substantial accomplishments. A major issue that has been raised by several investigators deals with whether or not tests of divergent thinking actually measure "true" creativity. Although some validation studies have reported limited relationships between measures of divergent thinking and creative performance criteria,[17] the research evidence for the predictive validity of such tests has been limited. Unfortunately, very few tests have been validated against real-life criteria of creative accomplishment, and in cases where such studies have been conducted the creativity tests have done poorly.[18] Thus, although divergent thinking is indeed a characteristic of highly creative persons, caution should be exercised in the use and interpretation of tests designed to measure this capacity.

Given the inherent limitations of creativity tests, a number of writers have focused attention on alternative methods for assessing creativity. Among others, Nicholls suggests that an analysis of creative products is preferable to the trait-based approach in making predictions about creative potential,[19] and Wallach proposes that student self-reports about creative accomplishment are sufficiently accurate to provide a usable source of data.[20]

Although few persons would argue against the importance of including creativity in a definition of giftedness, the conclusions and recommendations discussed above raise the haunting issue of

2. IDENTIFICATION

Figure 2. A Graphic Definition of Giftedness

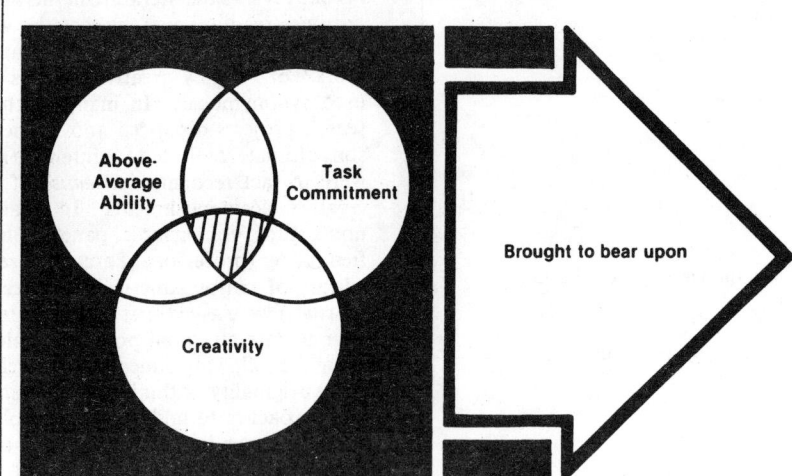

Above-Average Ability • Task Commitment • Creativity

Brought to bear upon

GENERAL PERFORMANCE AREAS

Mathematics • Visual Arts • Physical Sciences • Philosophy • Social Sciences • Law • Religion • Language Arts • Music • Life Sciences • Movement Arts

SPECIFIC PERFORMANCE AREAS

Cartooning • Astronomy • Public Opinion Polling • Jewelry Design • Map Making • Choreography • Biography • Film Making • Statistics • Local History • Electronics • Musical Composition • Landscape Architecture • Chemistry • Demography • Microphotography • City Planning • Pollution Control • Poetry • Fashion Design • Weaving • Play Writing • Advertising • Costume Design • Meteorology • Puppetry • Marketing • Game Design • Journalism • Electronic Music • Child Care • Consumer Protection • Cooking • Ornithology • Furniture Design • Navigation • Genealogy • Sculpture • Wildlife Management • Set Design • Agricultural Research • Animal Learning • Film Criticism • Etc. • Etc. • Etc.

---

subjectivity in measurement. In view of what the research suggests about the questionable value of more objective measures of divergent thinking, perhaps the time has come for persons in all areas of endeavor to develop more careful procedures for evaluating the products of candidates for special programs.

Discussion and Generalizations

The studies reviewed above lend support to a small number of basic generalizations that can be used to develop an operational definition of giftedness. The first is that giftedness consists of an interaction among three clusters of traits — above-average but not necessarily superior general abilities, task commitment, and creativity. Any definition or set of identification procedures that does not give equal attention to all three clusters is simply ignoring the results of the best available research dealing with this topic.

Related to this generalization is the need to make a distinction between traditional indicators of academic proficiency and creative productivity. A sad but true fact is that special programs have favored proficient lesson learners and test takers at the expense of persons who may score somewhat lower on tests but who more than compensate for such scores by having high levels of task commitment and creativity. Research has shown that members of this group ultimately make the most creative/productive contributions to their respective fields of endeavor.

A second generalization is that an operational definition should be applicable to all socially useful performance areas. The one thing that the three clusters discussed above have in common is that each can be brought to bear on a multitude of specific performance areas. As was indicated earlier, the interaction or overlap among the clusters "makes giftedness," but giftedness does not exist in a vacuum. Our definition must, therefore, reflect yet another interaction; but in this case it is the interaction between the overlap of the clusters and any performance area to which the overlap might be applied. This interaction is represented by the large arrow in Figure 2.

A third and final generalization is concerned with the types of information that should be used to identify superior performance in specific areas. Although it is a relatively easy task to include specific performance areas in a definition, developing identification procedures that will enable us to recognize specific areas of superior performance is more difficult. Test developers have thus far devoted most of their energy to producing measures of general ability, and this emphasis is undoubtedly why these tests are relied upon so heavily in identification. However, an operational definition should give direction to needed research and development, especially as these activities relate to instruments and procedures for student selection. A defensible definition can thus become a model that will generate vast amounts of appropriate research in the years ahead.

A Definition of Giftedness

Although no single statement can effectively integrate the many ramifications of the research studies described above, the following definition of giftedness attempts to summarize the major conclusions and generalizations resulting from this review of research:

> Giftedness consists of an interaction among three basic clusters of human traits — these clusters being above-average general abilities, high levels of task commitment, and high levels of creativity. Gifted and talented children are those possessing or capable of developing this composite set of traits and applying them to any potentially valuable area of human performance. Children who manifest or are capable of developing an interaction among the three clusters require a wide variety of educational opportunities and services that are not ordinarily provided through regular instructional programs.

A graphic representation of this definition is presented in Figure 2. The definition is an operational one because it meets three important criteria. First, it is derived from the best available research studies dealing with characteristics of gifted and talented individuals. Second, it provides guidance for the selection and/or development of instruments and procedures that can be used to design defensible identification systems. And finally, the definition provides direction for programming practices that will capitalize upon the characteristics that bring gifted youngsters to our attention as learners with special needs.

---

1. P. H. DuBois, *A History of Psychological Testing* (Boston: Allyn & Bacon, 1970).

2. L. M. Terman et al., *Genetic Studies of Genius: Mental and Physical Traits of a Thousand Gifted Children* (Stanford, Calif.: Stanford University Press, 1926), p. 43.

3. P.A. Witty, "Who Are the Gifted?" in N. B. Henry, ed., *Education of the Gifted*, Fifty-seventh Yearbook of the National Society for the Study of Education, Part II (Chicago: University of Chicago Press, 1958), p. 62.

4. S. P. Marland, *Education of the Gifted and Talented*, Report to the Congress of the United States by the U.S. Commissioner of Education and Background Papers Submitted to the U.S. Office of Education (Washington, D.C.: U.S. Government Printing Office, 1972). (Definition edited for clarity.)

5. M. A. Wallach, "Tests Tell Us Little About Talent," *American Scientist*, vol. 64, 1976, p. 57.

6. M. B. Parloff et al., "Personality Characteristics Which Differentiate Creative Male Adolescents and Adults," *Journal of Personality*, vol. 36, 1968, pp. 528-52; M. T. Mednick, "Research Creativity in Psychology Graduate Students," *Journal of Consulting Psychology*, vol. 27, 1963, pp. 265, 266; M. A. Wallach and C. W. Wing, Jr., *The Talented Students: A Validation of the Creativity Intelligence Distinction* (New York: Holt, Rinehart and Winston, 1969); J. M. Richards, Jr. et al., "Prediction of Student Accomplishment in College," *Journal of Educational Psychology*, vol. 58, 1967, pp. 343-55; L. R. Harmon, "The Development of a Criterion of Scientific Competence," in C. W. Taylor and F. Barron, eds., *Scientific Creativity: Its Recognition and Development* (New York: John Wiley and Sons, 1963), pp. 44-52; B. S. Bloom, "Report on Creativity Research by the Examiner's Office of the University of Chicago," in Taylor and Barron, op. cit.; and L. Hudson, "Degree Class and Attainment in Scientific Research," *British Journal of Psychology*, vol. 51, 1960, pp. 67-73.

7. J. L. Holland and A. W. Astin, "The Prediction of the Academic, Artistic, Scientific, and Social Achievement of Undergraduates of Superior Scholastic Aptitude," *Journal of Educational Psychology*, vol. 53, 1962, pp. 132, 133.

8. L. A. Munday and J. C. Davis, *Varieties of Accomplishment After College: Perspectives on the Meaning of Academic Talent*, Research Report No. 62 (Iowa City, Ia.: American College Testing Program, 1974), p. 2.

9. D. P. Hoyt, *The Relationship Between College Grades and Adult Achievement: A Review of the Literature*, Research Report No. 7 (Iowa City, Ia.: American College Testing Program, 1965).

10. Francis Galton, as quoted in R. S. Albert, "Toward a Behavioral Definition of Genius," *American Psychologist*, vol. 30, 1975, p. 142.

11. L. M. Terman, *Genetic Studies of Genius: The Gifted Group at Mid-Life* (Stanford, Calif.: Stanford University Press, 1959), p. 148.

12. A. Roe, *The Making of a Scientist* (New York: Dodd, Mead, 1952).

13. D. W. MacKinnon, "Personality and the Realization of Creative Potential," *American Psychologist*, vol. 20, 1965, p. 365.

14. J. C. Nicholls, "Creativity in the Person Who Will Never Produce Anything Original and Useful: The Concept of Creativity as a Normally Distributed Trait," *American Psychologist*, vol. 27, 1972, pp. 717-27.

15. H. G. McCurdy, "The Childhood Pattern of Genius," *Horizon*, vol. 2, 1960, pp. 33-38.

16. D. W. MacKinnon, "The Creativity of Architects," in C. W. Taylor, ed., *Widening Horizons in Creativity* (New York: John Wiley and Sons, 1964), p. 360.

17. E. P. Torrance, "Prediction of Adult Creative Achievement Among High School Seniors," *Gifted Child Quarterly*, vol. 13, 1969, pp. 223-29; R. J. Shapiro, "Creative Research Scientists," *Psychologia Africana*, 1968, Supplement No. 4; M. Dellas and E. L. Gaier, "Identification of Creativity: The Individual," *Psychological Bulletin*, vol. 73, 1970, pp. 55-73; and J. P. Guilford, "Some New Looks at the Nature of Creative Processes," in M. Frederickson and H. Gilliksen, eds., *Contributions to Mathematical Psychology* (New York: Holt, Rinehart and Winston, 1964).

18. S. B. Crockenburg, "Creativity Tests: A Boon or Boondoggle for Education?" *Review of Educational Research*, vol. 42, 1972, pp. 27-45.

19. Nicholls, op. cit., p. 721.

20. Wallach, op. cit.

FOCUS...

Creative People Need Freedom

The Eight Processes of Creativity

Researching the creative process, aesthetic components of predictive lines of action in particular, psychology researcher Franco Zambon advises creative people to "free themselves of society-imposed 'rules' " in order to produce creative ideas. In his doctorate research, Zambon has also developed a list of steps leading to creativity which describe processes that produce new ideas.

"New ideas are generally viewed as creative rearrangements of familiar ideas," he explains. "I believe that the human brain continually rearranges the information that the senses report to it. Actually, the sensory systems themselves probably rearrange and censor this information prior to transmitting it to the brain. In this context, it might be said that the brain deals with perceptions rather than true sensations."

Our preceptions include lines, angles, colors, odors, tactile impressions, and more. We then convert these essentials into corresponding perceptual data and respond to "definite patterns of stimulation." Zambon, who lectures at a New Orleans college and teaches math at Destrehan High School, says that some of our patterns lead to specific reactions. "A man may look at a beautiful woman," he adds, "and perceive the intense meaning that her form communicates. An individual, however, sometimes instinctively or automatically adds information to that which he receives."

Perceiving individuals are creating ideas when they fill in an incomplete picture or uncompleted sentences. These are instinctive and automatic acts of perception resulting in new arrangements of the original information. "In my own investigative work on creativity I conclude that some eight processes describe the creative experience," Zambon explains. "I like to call these 'aesthetic processes' in that a number of ancient artists and philosophers either talked about them or hinted at them. These aesthetic processes help to restructure information into new forms. In brief, they are:

1. Adhering to convention
2. Establishing order
3. Constructing a pure and single theme
4. Gathering essentials
5. Avoiding interruptions
6. Establishing symmetry
7. Producing graceful situations
8. Conforming to the requirements of fitness."

Zambon believes the eight lines of action listed

From the *Bulletin of the National/State Leadership Training Institute for the Gifted and Talented*, June 1979, Barbara Johnson, Editor

above are independent processes; he admits there may be other processes that influence or supplant them. While every person is capable of perception, the individual is strongly influenced by society. "Thus, we find that not all individuals are truly creative," he says. "Society can so change an individual's perception that he or she will report interpretations that are objectively foolish. Important experiments in 1956 reveal and verify the power of an immediate group to distort the individual member's perception. It follows that in order to produce creative ideas, people must remove or at least insulate themselves from society."

An example of a person who found creativity in freedom is Newton who developed his calculus while isolated at his mother's country home. "Albert Speer, who is known internationally for his ability to successfully manage industry," Zambon continues, "flatly stated that the more important people are, the more free time they need. Management courses stress the dictum: for people to produce creative ideas they must be left alone."

Studying the relationship between creativity and social change, the New Orleans researcher concludes: "Society accepts members' new perceptions only if they restructure explanations into linear form. On the other hand, society fails to accept a new perception from individuals if their perception can be justified only through synchronous thinking. Furthermore, a society fails to act on novel proposals which violate its aesthetic requirements. Indeed, society by its very nature in many cases can and does distort individuals' perceptions of the things around them. Consequently, it inhibits creativity.

"As a result, every individual in a society has a great chance of eventually feeling alienated from participation in its development. I believe that this frustrating situation amounts to what some call the 'existential dilemma.' Nevertheless, healthy individuals are creative and consequently able to 'self-actualize.' To do so, they must distinguish between communicative tools such as logic, and novel problem-solving processes such as insight. To encourage creativity, the individual must value some solitude, daydreaming, and recreational pursuits, such as travel and study of language, which American society discourages.

"A person should seek free spirits for companionship. Public schools in no way cooperate in this creativity dilemma. Perhaps, as educators and parents begin to value and understand the creative process, the possibilities for creative students will improve."

Young Handicapped Children Can Be Gifted and Talented

Over the last 10 years programs for young handicapped children have emerged in large numbers across the country. There has been concern, however, that there are gifted/talented in these programs who are underserved. The project reported here is funded by the Bureau of Education for the Handicapped. The project known as RAPYHT (Retrieval and Acceleration of Promising Young Handicapped and Talented) was charged in the development/demonstration stage with developing procedures for identifying and appropriately programming for these children. These procedures and procedures for providing technical services in the outreach stage of the project are delineated.

MERLE B. KARNES, ED.D.
Professor of Special Education
Institute for Child Behavior and Development
University of Illinois
Urbana-Champaign Campus

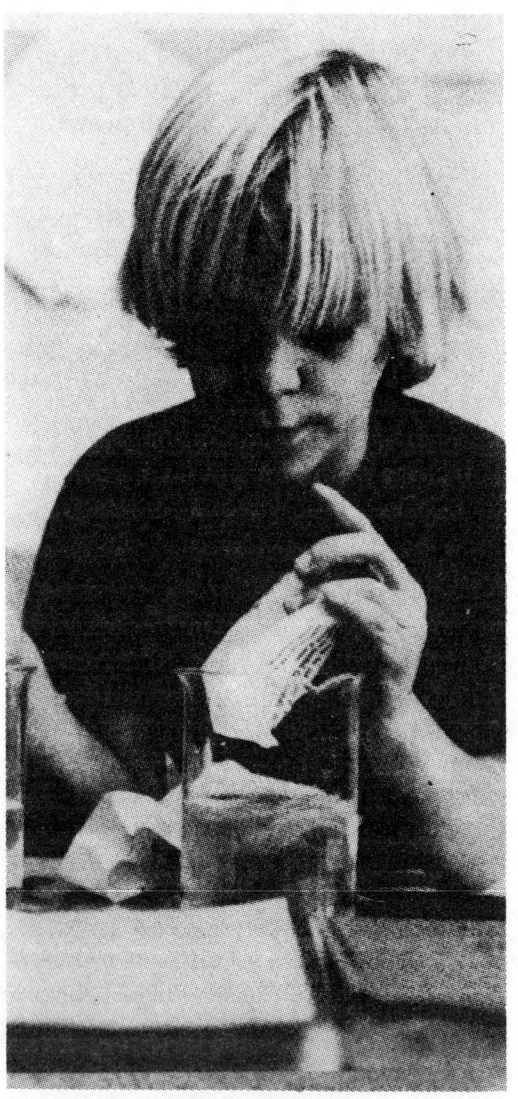

Over the past ten years programs for young handicapped children have emerged in large numbers across the country. An awareness of the needs of these children and more refined procedures for identification and programming can largely be attributed to the leadership and funding provided by the Bureau of Education for the Handicapped (BEH). In 1968 the Early Childhood Assistance Act was passed with a funding level of a million dollars. Currently BEH has been allocated 22 million dollars for identification, programming, and the study of critical problems in the field. Every state in the Union has at least one First Chance program, the name frequently used to refer to the network of preschool demonstration projects for handicapped children funded by BEH, and some have as many as ten. Programs deemed worthy of dissemination are funded to help others in replication and are referred to as Outreach Projects. The goal of BEH is to program for all young handicapped children by the year 1980. This is indeed an ambitious goal, but the progress made in recent years leads one to believe that the goal may be actualized.

As programs developed across the country, BEH staff became concerned about the failure to identify gifted/talented children in preschool classes for the handicapped. In fact, it appeared that special educators failed to identify the gifts and talents of handicapped children and focused instead on the weaknesses and deficits. This tendency is understanable since few special educators have had formal training in the identification of the gifted. On the other hand, consultants for and teachers of the gifted have rarely had an opportunity to work with handicapped children; rarely have they had training which would help them to understand handicapping conditions and the impact of handicaps on the development of the young child.

In 1975 the University of Illinois submitted a proposal to BEH which outlined procedures for identifying, diagnosing and programming for gifted/talented handicapped children ages three to

7. Handicapped

five. This project, RAPYHT (The Retrieval and Acceleration of Promising Young Handicapped and Talented), is one of two such demonstration projects funded by BEH. The other is located in the public schools of Chapel Hill, North Carolina. Currently, both projects are funded at Outreach level, which means that funds are allocated to help others replicate the two models. Each project, however, maintains a demonstration of its model at the original site.

This article focuses on the RAPYHT Project at the University of Illinois.

RAPYHT: Major Accomplishments During the Three-Year Development/ Demonstration Period

RAPYHT is part of a larger program at Colonel Wolfe School, University of Illinois, which serves young handicapped children ages three through five from fifteen rural Champaign County schools. A joint agreement among the fifteen school districts, the Champaign County Educational Service Region Office, and the University of Illinois is known as JEEPH (Joint Early Education of the Preschool Handicapped) and is administered by the University of Illinois.

Prior to a discussion of RAPYHT, it seems important to define the subjects with whom the project has concerned itself. First, the terms *gifted* and *talented* in this project are compatible with the definitions of the Office of Gifted and Talented in the Federal government and with the definitions used in the state of Illinois. Thus, the definition of the gifted/talented includes children who manifest talent in the following areas: (1) intellectual, (2) academic, (3) creative, (4) leadership, (5) visual and performing arts, (6) psychomotor. On the other hand, handicapped children are defined as those whose full development is impaired through sensory, social-emotional, and/or learning deficits. Typical *sensory deficits* occur in the areas of vision, hearing, and orthopedically handicapped. Children with *social-emotional deficits* are those who manifest problems in the areas of interpersonal relationships, are hyperactive and/or excessively aggressive, have withdrawal tendencies, and display lack of control. Children with *learning deficits* are those who display behavior indicating intraindividual growth and development patterns that differ significantly and importantly from area to area.

Screening and Identification of Subjects

The first goal of the project was to develop procedures for identifying gifted/talented handicapped children. Location of children to be screened has relied on a variety of techniques including lists generated by local school principals, media announcements, flyers sent home with children in school, and a telephone census. Location activities in any one school district vary according to the size of the district, the mobility of its population, and the wishes of the administration.

The first step in locating gifted/talented but handicapped children is to identify those with handicaps. Therefore, a Comprehensive Identification Process (CIP) is used to identify the young handicapped child in one or more of eight areas—cognitive,

2. IDENTIFICATION

speech and language, fine motor, gross motor, vision, hearing, medical history and socio-affective (Zehrbach, 1975a). While the primary screening objective is to select children likely to be handicapped, note is made of information gained from the parent report or from observation of child behavior during the screening activities that suggests talent.

Diagnostic procedures to determine handicaps include assessment of the child's performance on a battery of standardized instruments administered by members of an interdisciplinary team. Team members are trained to note characteristics which may indicate talent in one or more of the six areas listed previously. Information gathered by the diagnostic team is then summarized and presented at a staffing where placement eligibility is determined. Consensus as to whether each handicapped child is potententially or functionally talented is also determined at this time. A more detailed explanation of the process for identifying the handicapped (CIP) appears in an article written by its developer, Richard Reid Zehrbach (1975b).

The Preschool Talent Assessment Guide (PTAG) by Karnes and Taylor (1978) delineates the process of assessing talents in some detail. PTAG procedures are used after an initial talent screening using the Preschool Talent Checklists (PTC) developed by Karnes and Associates (1978) or some other appropriate device for screening talented children. The Preschool Talent Checklists include six checklists as well as instructions on how to score and interpret observations and criteria for selecting children for follow up. Items from one of the six Talent Checklists used to screen gifted/talented handicapped children are listed below:

1. Adapts readily to new situations
2. Is frequently sought out by other children as a play and work companion
3. Is self-confident around others
4. Tends to direct activities in which he/she is involved
5. Interacts easily with other children and adults
6. Generates ideas for activities and solutions to problems
7. Takes initiative with peers
8. Shows an awareness of the needs of others
9. Assumes responsibility beyond what is expected for his/her age
10. Is often used as a resource by other children

The Preschool Talent Assessment Guide reflects the changing views on the identification of the gifted and talented, and RAPYHT personnel hold that these views are particularly relevant to the preschool handicapped population. Karnes and Taylor (1978) state the basic assumptions upon which PTAG is based:

"1. *Talent identification should be a multi-faceted process which incorporates a variety of methods and resources and which includes identification criteria which are broad and flexible.*

2. *The assessment process should allow for identification of both functionally talented and potentially talented chil-*

dren. Functional talent is defined as performance at least 1½ standard deviations above the mean on an appropriate quantitative measure of abilities and/or demonstration of strong qualitative evidence of talent. The potential talent category includes the child who is judged to be capable of high level performance with further remediation of a handicapping condition and/or educational stimulation in the area of potential talent.

3. *Talent assessment should not be limited to administration of a set of short-term identification procedures but should include on-going evaluation of target children. Quite often a handicapped child will need to experience prolonged periods of stimulation in the classroom which provide opportunities for the expression of potential talents. Thus, exposure to a nurturant environment and continuous observation of child progress are essential components of the identification process."* Karnes and Taylor, 1978, pp. 2-3.

Three steps are followed after a child has been referred as a candidate for talent programming. Each child receives a more comprehensive talent assessment to determine if indeed he/she is gifted/talented in one or more areas in the following manner:

"PHASE I: Initial Follow-up. This preliminary phase of assessment involves collecting information about the child from parents, teachers, and relevant others through interviews, questionnaires, and/or review of documentary records. If this phase provides sufficient data for decision-making, the second phase of assessment may be omitted.

PHASE II: Individual Child Assessment. This phase consists of a more direct and in-depth evaluation of the child using one or more of the following kinds of procedures: a) standardized tests, b) rating scales, c) systematic observations, d) criterion tasks. The specific methods and instruments to be used will vary depending upon the talent area being assessed.

PHASE III: Decision-Making. The final phase involves reviewing and evaluating all assessment information during a formal talent staffing and making a final eligibility decision and program recommendations. The flowchart in Figure 1 presents an overview of the main steps in the talent screening and assessment process." (Karnes and Taylor 1978, p. 4)

Because handicap(s) may obscure expression of talent, and individual methods may not fully reveal a child's abilities, talent programming and prolonged observation are often necessary before a definite diagnosis can be made. Teachers are provided with ongoing inservice training regarding the use of talent development activities in their classrooms to provide optimum opportunities for selected children to express potential talents.

It is interesting to note that of the 575 children between the ages of 3 to 5 who were located and screened in the JEEPH Program in 1977-1978, 79 were selected to receive an in-depth diagnostic study to determine eligibility for one of the preschool classes for the handicapped. Of this number, 7 children were screened

2. IDENTIFICATION

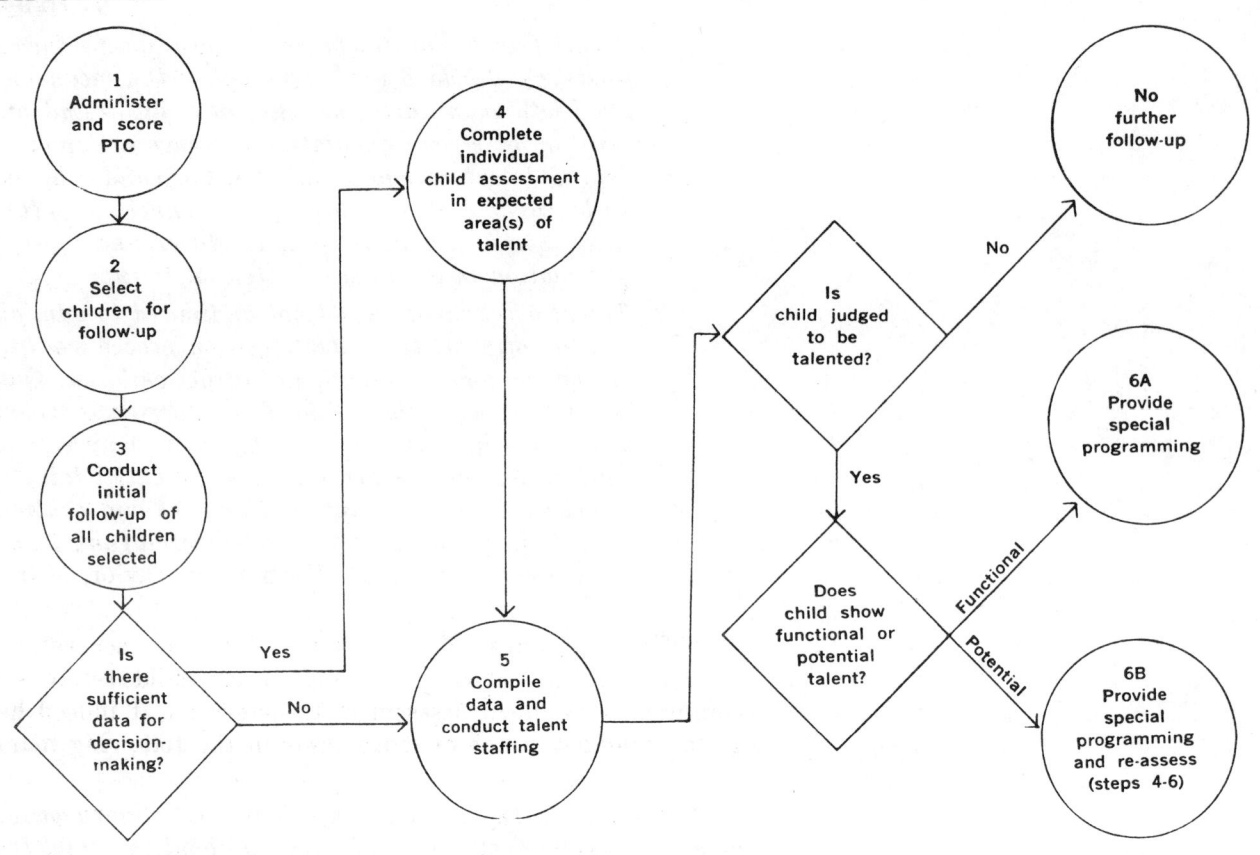

Figure 1. Flowchart of the Preschool Talent Screening Assessment Process (Karnes and Taylor, 1978, p. 5)

and after further study were identified as potentially talented; these children were subsequently placed in the RAPYHT Project. Six distal sites in five different special education programs in Illinois also participated in the project during the last two years of the demonstration phase. They were included in the demonstration program in order to locate a sufficient number of potentially or functionally gifted/talented handicapped children to test procedures under development.

Procedures for Programming for the Potentially or Functionally Gifted/Talented Handicapped Child

Identification of handicapped children who are also gifted/talented is an important first step, but even more important is programming for such children to nurture their unique talents. Project staff have from the beginning been committed to both acceleration and enrichment. As is the case in most preschool programs for the handicapped, developmental guidelines are used to rank the child in important areas of development. These data assist the teacher in programming for the child. A child might be only four yet beginning to read. The teacher must program for this child in such a way that he/she will acquire skills as needed.

To enable others to program more effectively for their gifted/talented handicapped children, procedures found to be useful in nurturing talent in the six areas were recorded from the inception of the project. The procedures suggested in the manuals have been found to be applicable to non-handicapped children who are gifted talented and to all children to some degree. To reiterate, young children do not always manifest their talents at an early age unless they are encouraged to do so. Programming and identification of the gifted talented is therefore a never ending process.

Procedures developed in RAPYHT can be incorporated into any good preschool program for the handicapped. At the University of Illinois two approaches which represent diverse points on a continuum (so far as the variable of teacher directions is concerned) were used. One was the informal, open classroom approach and the other a teacher-directed approach based on Guilford's Structure of the Intellect (SOI). A more detailed account of these two approaches is presented by Karnes and Bertschi (1978).

Procedures for Involving Families in the Identification of and Programming for Their Gifted/Talented Handicapped Children

Parent and family participation is an important component of RAPYHT, and an effort is made to provide families with alternative activities designed to achieve program and family goals. Family and staff work together to plan for the individualized involvement of each family member. Most often, the family members involved are the child's mother and father, but grandparents, brothers and sisters, and aunts have also participated in certain activities. The tactics employed are based on a positive, flexible, and individual orientation. Accountability and a humanistic stance are also stressed.

Oftentimes, families are so preoccupied with the handicap(s) of the young child that they overlook gifts/talents and, therefore, fail to encourage full development. It is encouraging to family members to recognize that the handicapped child has assets, and this knowledge helps them to adjust to the child's handicapping condition. Family members need training and understanding if they are to nurture the child's talents, and they have a right to expect the help of the professionals working with the child. Following the guidelines of Public Law 94-142, RAPYHT parents help to develop an individual educational plan (IEP) for their child in his area(s) of handicap as well as in his areas of talent. A variety of alternatives are available—observation in the classroom, direct teaching in the home and/or the classroom, participation in large or small group meetings, individual conferences, reading selected materials on the gifted from the parents' library, participation in case conferences, and participation on the Advisory Board.

One of the products developed in the project is a needs assessment interview which helps parents identify their needs so that professionals can more readily assist members of the family in acquiring the skills to interact more effectively with and to promote the talents of their handicapped child.

When parents are encouraged to focus attention upon their handicapped child's strengths and not merely his weakness, they may be led to consider alternative roles for their child. The result of this positive perspective can be that the parents' behavior changes to provide opportunities for the child to make his/her best skills even better rather than to maintain an exclusive focus upon trying to remediate the child's deficiencies.

Materials for Increasing Public Awareness

There is a need for more awareness on the part of profes-

2. IDENTIFICATION

sionals and legislators that handicapped children can also be gifted/talented.

Project staff felt that one effective way of communicating the concept was to develop a slide tape presentation that would document the handicaps as well as the gifts of these children. Included in these audio-visual case studies was information about the long-range goals and the specific programming for each child. The primary purpose of the presentation is to motivate viewers to support and promote the development of programs for young gifted/talented handicapped children.

In addition to audio-visual presentations, brochures were developed to highlight the need for identification and programming. Project personnel have welcomed opportunities to present the project to professionals and parents.

Procedures for Assessing Child Progress and Family Involvement

A major RAPYHT component is the individualized assessment of each child's educational needs so that individualized educational plans may be written. RAPYHT places priority upon determining the learning and/or developmental status of each child in the following skills: gross motor, fine motor, self-help, social-emotional, language, and mathematics. Areas of talent are also reviewed. After classroom assessments have been carried out and individualized plans written, each child's progress is monitored on a monthly basis through recording the number of behavioral objectives and goals achieved for each child in the six areas previously mentioned and in two talent areas which vary according to the child's identified strengths.

A battery of standardized tests is administered on a pre-post basis and provides information on the progress of each child in important areas of development. Exceptions are made, however, and other instruments are used when, due to handicapping conditions, one or more of the instruments in the battery do not provide a valid measure of a child's abilities.

Procedures for determining the effectiveness of parent involvement were developed during the first three years and include a system of recording the types of activities in which family members engaged and the amount of time they participated in the program. In addition, a questionnaire was developed which provides such information as parental rating of the degree of success of family involvement activities, parental attitude toward staff, parental attitude toward their own gains in knowledge/skill, parental attitude toward child progress, and parental attitude about the program in general, and finally evaluate information about how parents/family members perceive the value of their involvement as well as its impact upon the child.

Procedures for Inservice Training of Personnel

Three major sets of materials have been developed during the demonstration phase of the project. The first has to do with screening to identify children who may be potentially or functionally gifted/talented. A Preschool Talent Checklists Manual (Karnes and Associates, 1978a, 1978b) can be used to train personnel to use the Preschool Talent Checklists. This manual includes procedures for scoring and interpreting the scores and for using the information for instructional planning. The second set

7. Handicapped

includes the Preschool Talent Assessment Guide that delineates procedures for assessing talent in the six areas and suggests standardized tests and other methods of talent assessment. The third set of materials includes six manuals for nurturing talent in the six areas of concern (Karnes and Strong, 1978a, 1978b; Karnes et al 1978a, 1978b, 1978c, 1978d). Each manual provides a discussion of a single talent, lists the common characteristics of children with that talent, offers suggestions for methods to stimulate that talent, and delineates goals and activities for nurturing that talent. The last section of each manual is an annotated list of resources helpful to teacher, paraprofessional, ancillary personnel, or parent who is trying to nurture a given talent. Through discussions and role playing the materials in this manual can help those working with young gifted/talented handicapped children to become more effective in talent programming.

RAPYHT: The Outreach Stage

RAPYHT is entering the first year of a three-year cycle referred to by BEH as Outreach. Its charge is to help others replicate the model. The current plan is to work with five states each year; thus, over the three-year period at least 15 states will utilize the RAPYHT model.

It was felt that the most effective way to disseminate information generated by RAPYHT and to insure effective replication is for outreach specialists to work closely with state consultants in both the gifted and early childhood handicapped. State personnel, however, take the lead in promoting the RAPYHT model in programs in their states while RAPYHT outreach staff work with state personnel to plan and provide training in RAPYHT procedures to personnel in the selected local replication/demonstration sites and in other special education programs throughout the state.

The states selected for RAPYHT outreach activities are chosen on the basis of the following criteria:

1. Commitment of the state to the gifted and handicapped as reflected by the existence of staff consultants in both gifted and early childhood special education and concomitant legislation.

2. A written agreement from state consultants to work with RAPYHT staff by:

    a. Attending a workshop at the University of Illinois to learn in depth the process of identification and programming for young gifted/talented children developed by RAPYHT.

    b. Identifying at least one site in their state at which to replicate the RAPYHT approach.

    c. Working cooperatively with RAPYHT Outreach specialists to help the site replicate and demonstrate the approach.

As a result of working with RAPYHT Outreach staff, the state consultants will be prepared to:

1. Train local program staff to identify and assess strengths and talents often overlooked in the young handicapped child.

2. IDENTIFICATION

2. Consult with local program staff in the development of individualized education programs designed to nurture and enhance the talents of young handicapped children.

3. Help teachers of young handicapped children to acquire the knowledge, skills, and attitudes required to effectively implement talent-oriented programming.

4. Support teachers of identified talented/handicapped children by providing access to new information and materials relevant to the implementation of talent-oriented programming.

Thus, the state personnel are first trained by RAPYHT Outreach specialists at the University of Illinois for a period of three days in the early fall. They then work with RAPYHT staff in training personnel at a selected replication/demonstration site in their respective states. The training of local replication/demonstration sites takes place in a series of workshops conducted by the state consultants with the assistance of a RAPYHT Outreach specialist. As a result of this cooperative relationship, state consultants gain a greater understanding of RAPYHT procedures and become more proficient in training personnel to use these procedures.

Currently RAPYHT replication specialists are working with state consultants at local demonstration sites in Minnesota, Michigan, Connecticut, Wisconsin and Illinois. The Outreach project will continue working with these personnel during 1979-1980 and will add 5 more states. Commitments have been received from Iowa, Florida, Louisana, Indiana and Georgia. Nine other states (Alabama, California, Idaho, Kansas, New York, North Carolina, Ohio, Pennsylvania and Texas) have expressed an interest in receiving future assistance, for a total of 19 states with consultants in the preschool handicapped and the gifted having indicated an interest in replicating RAPYHT procedures.

In addition to work with the state consultants and selected early childhood special education programs which agree to replicate and demonstrate the RAPYHT model, RAPYHT staff will also work with early childhood program staff who will be the demonstration audience of the selected replication/demonstration sites, with private and public schools, with state agencies such as the Department of Mental Health, Head Start, and with university faculties, students and other groups interested in appropriate programs for young gifted/talented handicapped children. These contracts will not be as intensive or extensive as those provided the demonstration sites.

Based on the experiences gained during the development/demonstration period at the home site and with distal sites over the past three years, RAPYHT staff has developed a set of procedures that have been applied in several settings.

1. Procedures for continued staff development. Inservice training for staff focuses on development of skills, knowledge, and attitudes necessary to identify talented handicapped children and to provide programs to develop their talents. Strategies for training include workshops and consultation visits by RAPYHT Outreach specialists to sites which adopt the RAPYHT model.

2. Procedures for screening and assessing handicapped children to identify talents.
3. Procedures for applying selection criteria to determine child eligibility for talent programming.
4. Procedures for establishing individualized goals and objectives to develop the child's abilities in each area of talent.
5. Procedures for planning and presenting individualized instructional activities designed to challenge and stimulate the talented, handicapped child.
6. Procedures for objectively documenting child progress in all instructional areas.
7. Procedures for involving parents in the education of their gifted/talented handicapped child at a level commensurate with their needs, interests, values, skills and knowledge.

SUMMARY

One segment of the handicapped population that is currently under-served is the gifted/talented handicapped. These children are defined as those whose full development is impaired through physical, sensory, social-emotional and/or learning deficits and who also show evidence of outstanding abilities in one or more areas of talent: intellectual, academic, creative, leadership, visual and performing arts, and psychomotor. At present, such children are served in preschool special education programs, but their talents are seldom recognized or developed. Until recently, specialists in the gifted have shown only limited concern for identifying and programming for the gifted/talented handicapped children, especially at the preschool level. Similarly, personnel trained to serve the handicapped have demonstrated little interest and few skills in identifying the gifted among the handicapped populations and programming for them. Thus RAPYHT is in a unique position to promote interest in better serving the young gifted/talented handicapped population through training key persons in select states which have demonstrated a commitment to educating both the young handicapped and the gifted. These key persons will in turn, with the help of RAPYHT replication specialists, train personnel in local programs to replicate RAPYHT procedures.

The old saying that "giftedness will out" is not true among non-handicapped gifted/talented children, and it is even less true among the gifted/talented handicapped whose handicaps may obscure their talents or inhibit their development. Of course outstanding figures over the years have made important contributions to society despite their handicaps—Edison, Beethoven, Helen Keller, and Van Gogh to name only a few. Nevertheless, one must question how many others with comparable potential have gone unidentified and unnutured. RAPYHT has the potential of helping special educators to serve potentially and functionally gifted/talented children much better than they have in the past. Parents can also become more accepting of the handicaps of their child if they are helped to identify his/her strengths and to assist in developing individualized education programs in areas of strength as well as weakness. As mentioned previously, the teacher's perception of the child is reflected in the child's perception of himself, and it is equally true that parent's perception of the child affects how the handicapped child feels about himself.

2. IDENTIFICATION

RAPYHT during its three-year development/demonstration phase defined procedures for screening, diagnosing and programming for gifted/talented handicapped children and for involving family members and evaluating child progress and family involvement. Through the technical assistance of RAPYHT Outreach replication specialists working with the state consultants, benefits are expected in the following areas:

1. Increased awareness among state consultants in the gifted and in early childhood of the need to identify and better serve gifted/talented handicapped children.
2. Greater awareness among preschool special education personnel that a segment of their population may be gifted/talented and thus in need of more appropriate programming.
3. An awareness of viable strategies for identifying and providing appropriate individualized educational programs for young gifted/talented handicapped children.
4. The development of interdependency between state and local personnel working in the specialized area of the handicapped and of the gifted to develop better programs for young gifted/talented handicapped children.
5. Increased awareness among university faculty of the need to include training for working with the gifted/talented handicapped in teacher training programs.
6. Better communication among states as to what each is doing to better serve the gifted/talented handicapped through the project newsletter.
7. Increased sensitivity to the need to identify gifted/talented handicapped children who are older and to program for them, as a result of the diffusion of information generated by the project relating to better serving the preschool gifted/talented handicapped.
8. Enhancement of the quality of programming for all children in sites adopting the RAPYHT model as a result of attention given to programming in the child's areas of strength as well as in areas of weakness.
9. Increased sensitivity of parents of the handicapped included in the replication/demonstration projects to the gifts/talents of their handicapped child and greater skill in helping their child to progress in areas of strength as well as weakness.
10. Refinement and documentation of strategies for working with state personnel to transport the model from the original demonstration site to practitioners in the field.

REFERENCES

Davidson, H. H. and Lang, G. Children's perceptions of their teachers' feelings toward them related to self-perception, school achievement and behavior. *Journal of Experimental Education*, December 1960, *29* (2), 107-118.

Karnes, M. B. and Bertschi, J. D. Identifying and educating gifted/talented nonhandicapped and handicapped preschoolers. *Teaching Exceptional Children*, Summer 1978, 114-119.

Karnes, M. B. and Strong, P. S. *Nurturing academic talent in early childhood - Science.* Urbana, Ill.: Publications Office, Institute for Child Behavior and Development, University of Illinois 1978a.

FACTORS COMPOUNDING THE HANDICAPPING OF SOME GIFTED CHILDREN

Charles Meisgeier
Constance Meisgeier
Dorothy Werblo[*]

Three o'clock in the morning and the jarring sound of the phone demands response. A frantic mother is calling from the hospital emergency room while doctors work feverishly to save her son's life. A suicide attempt in early adolescence -- and the prime reason given is "I'd rather die than go back to school."

The boy's name was John. The following picture of John emerged from a careful review of the test records already available at John's school. At age 10, John was given a reading test on which he scored at the 99th percentile. At the same time, he was given the Wisc and his total recorded score was translated to an IQ of 80. John had a perceptual handicap that interferred with his ability to do the assignments in school.

On the Metropolitan Readiness, Test, Form B, John had a percentile rank of 61. A year later, on the Otis Lennon Test of Mental Ability, his record shows he tested at stanine 7. John was assigned to a class of children with learning disabilities and worked with peers who had IQ scores between 70 and 80. Despite the reading skills that placed him in the 99th percentile, John's reading lessons consisted of circling one of many pictures when the teacher said the name of the picture. He endured this for two years before the climactic suicide attempt.

Is John gifted? Surely his ability to read at such a high level indicates some kind of unique endowment. Is John handicapped? Without question, John's inability to perform at even the average level on many school-related tasks indicates serious deficit.

---

[*]Dr. Charles Meisgeier is Professor of Education and Chairperson of the Special Education Program at the University of Houston. Constance Meisgeier is a writer, editor and consultant. Dr. Dorothy Werblo is the Project Coordinator of the Gifted/Handicapped Project at the University of Houston.

"Factors Compounding the Handicapping of Some Gifted Children," Charles Meisgeier, Constance Meisgeier, Dorothy Werblo, *Gifted Child Quarterly*, Vol. XXII, No. 3, Fall 1978. Copyright 1978 by The National Association for Gifted Children, all rights reserved.

children it should prove helpful to define the gifted child and the handicapped child separately.

A gifted child demonstrates the ability to perform with excellence, tasks requiring general intellectual ability, specific academic aptitude, creative or productive thinking, leadership ability, or employing unique ability in visual or performing arts and/or psychomotor ability.

A handicapped child is impaired in his function by one or more of the following conditions: mental retardation, hearing loss, deafness, speech impairment, visual impairment, serious emotional disturbance, orthopedic impairment and/or other health problems or specific learning disabilities that require special educational services.

If handicap is defined as a manifestation of a condition that impedes functioning and gifted as highly intelligent and/or creative or talented, then a gifted/handicapped child is highly intelligent, creative or talented with one or more normal functions impeded.

A gifted/handicapped child demonstrates at least one attribute of educational, emotional or physical/sensory impairment. A gifted/handicapped child may deviate from 'norma' substantially both above and beneath when measured by objective testing procedures.

It is generally recognized that the educational system as a whole has been slow to respond to the special needs of handicapped children. Less well recognized is the probability that giftedness puts its own kind of stress on the system. The behavior of gifted children deviates from the norm. The child who deviates will almost surely feel the weight of the system being brought to bear to make him conform. For some, the process may have the effect of punishing the expression of his giftedness. If, as stated above, the gifted child is more than normally able to perceive and understand the implications of each stimuli, then it follows that creative behaviors may be more easily extinguished in him subtle punishments and pressure than in other children.

The Problem
When the problems of giftedness and the problems of handicap coexist--or stated another way--when the unacceptability of the 'abnormal' behaviors that spring from giftedness exist concomitantly with the unacceptability of the performances resulting from the handicap--a child may tend to withdraw from meaningful interaction with the learning environment. The even partial isolation then produced may interfere with social growth and yet another need for remediation programs becomes evident.

The expectation that gifted/handicapped children will be seriously impaired in their school performance is more than conjecture. Studies done in Texas thru the University of Houston have shown that, far more often than anyone would like to believe, gifted children with some kind of learning problem or other handicap have disengaged in school to such a degree that they are discovered in special education classes limping along with very little or no evidence of the giftedness being manifested. Other states are finding the same inappropriate placement of gifted children in classes for children with

2. IDENTIFICATION

educational deficits. In "Guidelines for the Operation of Special Education Programs for the Mentally Gifted," issued by the Pennsylvania State Department of Education Maker cites, "...too often the handicap is emphasized rather than the strength. In its worst extreme, instances have been found where gifted, but emotionally disturbed adolescents are being taught with procedures better suited for work with retarded youngsters." (p. 38) The same document further observes, "...perhaps the important statement to be made is that youngsters who are treated as if disabled will tend toward becoming so, while the youngster who is challenged and encouraged may take pride in his uniqueness and may well produce original ideas and accomplishments." (p. 39) Of course not every gifted child has disengaged or allowed his/her giftedness to be suppressed. Susan is a colorful example.

Teacher Response to Giftedness

Susan certainly was a case of mismanaged giftedness who was able to maintain a measure of assertiveness even in the first grade. Susan started reading at three years of age. When she went to first grade, she patiently endured a reading class that laboriously worked its way through *ABC and Me* and then a book called *Little Pig*. After weeks, the teacher asked the children to write a story about *Little Pig*. Susan wrote:

> "Little Pig. Little Pig.
> I'll tell you what you
> can do with Little Pig.
>   You can take this book and ---------."

Susan's teacher investigated and discovered that Susan was reading the encyclopedia for recreation. She appropriately modified Susan's program. Not every teacher is as understanding as Susan's teacher. Some punish. The following are several examples of harsh treatment that illustrate the tendency of schools to punish giftedness.

One first grade teacher freely and often announced that she would "whip this little upstart into shape," and "show her who is boss," until she is willing to "toe the line." In this harsh environment a precocious little girl was trying to cope with marked perceptual problems. Before long, she was eating her fingernails and her hair and suffering from nightmares. Another little boy was grabbed by his teacher and marched to the principal's office for placement in another class when the teacher discovered, on the first day of school, that he could read his own name. She told the boy, "I won't have you, little trouble maker, in my class."

Stereotyping

Society's stereotype of the gifted child has undergone a wide sweep. In the last century, a genius was thought to be a "...puny, bespectacled little boy in a corner by himself, pouring over scientific journals or working calculus problems while the other children were simply being children; he grew up to be nearly insane, weird, and ostracized by society" (Maker, p. 7). After Lewis Terman's longitudinal studies of over 1000 gifted individuals reversed that notion (Maker), students in teacher training programs were probably taught that gifted children were larger, heavier, physically more attractive and emotionally more stable than their less gifted schoolmates. While the socio-economic factors that related to health, growth, appearance and social advantages probably tend to corroborate the second view (Maker) as more realistic, the truth is probably somewhere in the middle. The gifted can be large or small, more or less attractive, and handicapping conditions such as learning disabilities, emotional disorder and physical impairment probably occur about as frequently among the gifted as they do in the population as a whole.

C. June Maker states early in her book Providing Programs for the Gifted Handicapped that "...one of the most difficult tasks in considering the topic of the gifted with learning problems is to communicate effectively the notion that gifted people have problems learning." (p. 7) She further points out that the gifted are individuals, some of whom are attractive and some not, some popular and some not, some successful and some not. Just as some of the general population are blond and some brunette, some gifted children are blond and some brunette. Just as some children in the general population may have perceptual problems or poor coordination, some children who are gifted or talented may also be poorly coordinated or experience perceptual problems.

The tendency to look at a handicapped individual and predict his performance on the basis of the label he carries rather than on an individualized assessments of his strengths and weaknesses is evident in the school experiences of the gifted youngsters described above. Just as handicapped children should not be stereotyped by a label neither should gifted children be stereotyped whether a handicap is present or not.

Summary

Some gifted children have learning, behavior or physical-sensory problems. Programs for the gifted/handicapped are virtually nonexistent. Educational personnel often place them in programs for the handicapped which many times are designed to remediate the weak areas and offer little or no stimulus in the area of giftedness. More careful evaluation of handicapped students suspected of being gifted is needed and individualized programs are needed to foster full development of their potential. Each child's school program must be individualized in such a way that it is responsive to the total child and not merely to the most glaring label attached to the child. Each child is unique. Each child's school experience should be just as unique to his individual needs.

REFERENCES

Maker, C. June *Providing Programs for the Gifted Handicapped*, Reston Virginia: Council for Exceptional Children, 1977.

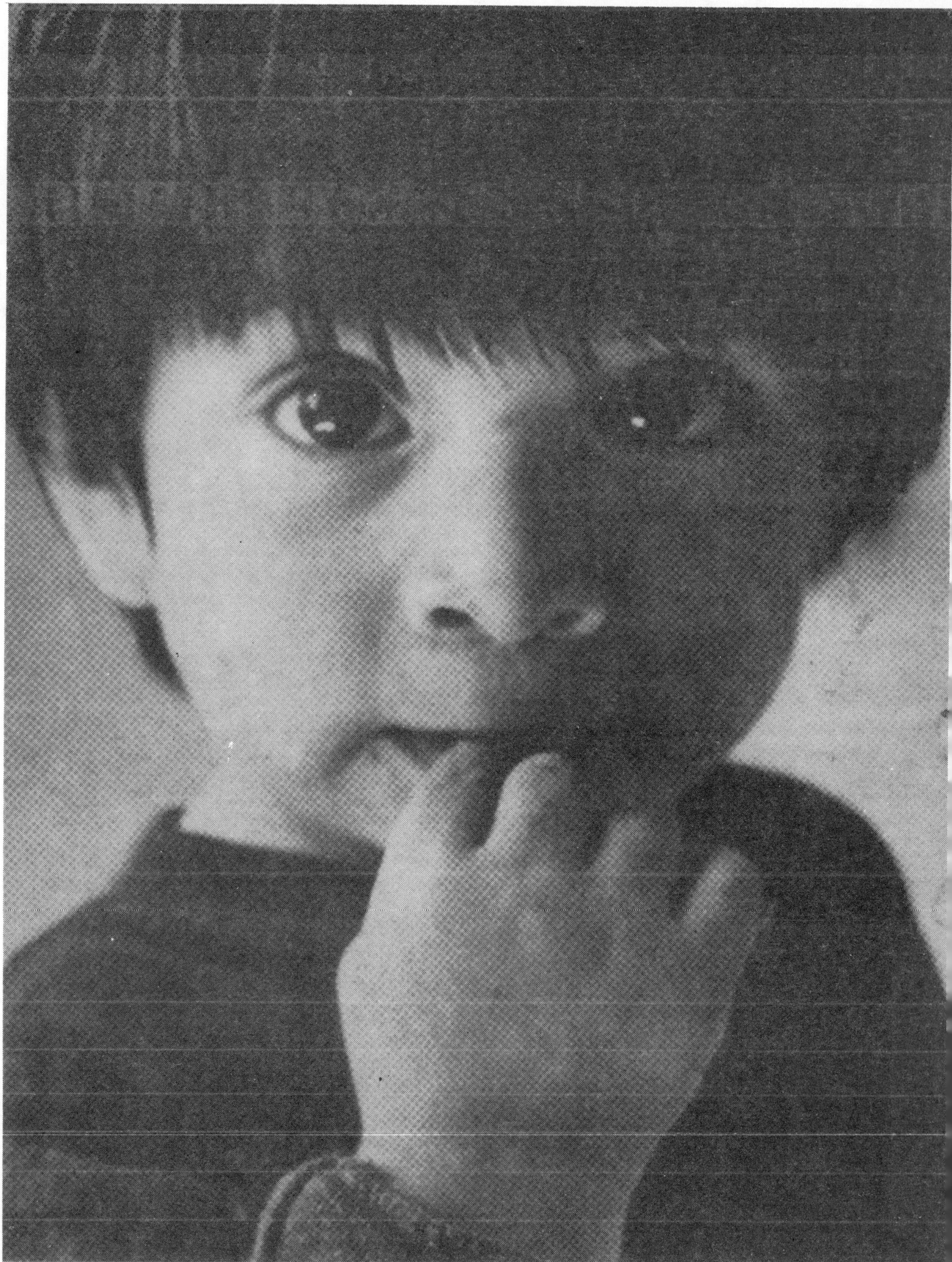

The Culturally disadvantaged gifted youth

AN ADDRESS BY THE HONORABLE SHIRLEY CHISHOLM BEFORE THE NATIONAL FORUM ON MINORITY DISADVANTAGED GIFTED AND TALENTED (MAY 15, 1978)

MRS. SHIRLEY CHISHOLM:

It is both an honor and a pleasure for me to be with you this morning to begin this important conference on a topic which for me has the deepest personal meaning.

This conference represents a significant breakthrough in the attitudes of our federal educational policymakers who traditionally, have paid little attention to the disadvantaged gifted and talented. It is my hope that this conference represents the winds of change, and that federal policy, and our educational institutions recognize the vast untapped resources in culturally different children.

Last November, when I introduced legislation to expand and improve programs in the Elementary and Secondary Education Act, I included provisions to establish a separate authorization for the gifted and talented program. A major feature of my bill required the targeting of at least 25% of funds on the disadvantaged gifted. It was only then that I fully realized how misunderstood the disadvantaged gifted are in our society.

Many of my white colleagues in the Congress seemed disturbed at the realization that there actually could be disadvantaged children who were gifted. Many congresspersons having just accepted the need for compensatory educational programs, exhibit their racist tendencies in their belief that all of "our" children are in need of academic remediation.

To be truthful, even a couple of my black colleagues in Congress felt compelled to pull me aside to ask what my problem was pushing these so called "gifted" programs which do nothing but promote I.Q. testing and money for affluent white children.

As someone who has had a long history as an educator and a maverick, I believe both are wrong. Furthermore these attitudes are representative, and explain why our American system of education has so ignored this group of children who have such special educational needs.

Too often, educators have failed to recognize the large number of gifted children in poor communities, due to their reliance on culturally-biased standardized testing to identify gifted children.

As a result there is little recognition of the gifts and talents in those children who are culturally different. In addition, educational institutions in general, and so many of our teachers in particular, are not only unable to iden-

2. IDENTIFICATION

tify the giftedness of minority students, but tragically are also unable to respond in a manner which encourages these students to reach their potential.

In fact our schools not only fail to nurture the talents of our disadvantaged, often the system reacts with hostility to skill it cannot measure — potential it cannot understand.

Those few states which have taken a lead in meeting the needs of the gifted are beginning to see the magnitude of educational mis-labeling. According to the Pennsylvania State Consultant on the Gifted, up to 50% of the students referred to emotionally disturbed classes who were subsequently tested, were found to be gifted. It is frightening to think of the many talented minority youth who have landed on the educational trash heap, simply because the system is not prepared to deal with them. Our schools too often clutch tightly to traditions which were designed for the children we read about in "Dick & Jane" books.

The time has come to let go of traditions when it is painfully clear that they are no longer the answers to the problems we face in the classrooms of today.

An article on the black gifted in Harvard's Educational Review identifies this problem simply:

> "--Until public schools are held responsible for responding to children rather than the other way around, no test of public instruction will have occurred."

I feel very strongly about the need to expand initiatives in inner city and poor rural areas on behalf of the gifted.

For a moment, I would like to discuss the direction school-based programs for the gifted should take:

We must realize that the traditional criteria for giftedness are irrelevant to minority and disadvantaged children. Measurements based upon majority culture present obstacles to identifying the talents of our black and brown-young people.

I am pleased by the breadth of criteria which HEW's Office of Gifted and Talented has embraced in the identification of giftedness, which includes:

1. the academically gifted
2. specific academic aptitude
3. creative, productive thinking giftedness
4. giftedness in visual and performing arts
5. leadership giftedness
6. psychomotor giftedness

As we develop means of better identifying the latter non-traditional qualities, I believe that larger numbers of disadvantaged and culturally different children will be identified for special programs and opportunities.

I hope that we will begin to develop models for the identification of disadvantaged and minority gifted, realizing the cultural differences between Black, Hispanic, Asian, and native-American children, we will probably need to evolve a number of models.

As I have indicated, there is a desperate need to reorient the attitudes and approaches of teachers if they are to stimulate, and not stifle the potential of their disadvantaged pupils.

Expansion of the federal role in this area is critical if we are to bring about changes in the classroom.

PARENT INVOLVEMENT

I am probably the Congress' most forthright advocate of meaningful parent involvement, as I firmly believe that no educational program can be successful in helping the disadvantaged child without building a partnership between parents and teachers to insure that the home environment supports the efforts made in the classroom.

So often teachers and school administrators will respond by citing poor participation of these parents at P.T.A. meetings or parent-teacher conferences as examples of a lack of parent interest or commitment to their child's academic success. Unfortunately, they conveniently forget that it is these same parents whose own experiences with school were so hostile and alienating that they either dropped out, were forced out, or they simply stopped caring. It is not enough to mail out mimeographed flyers, and expect that it will eliminate their impression of schools as a source of frustration and shame. Any program to improve the quality of education must be built solidly on a commitment to find new ways to involve parents in the schools, and more importantly to develop respect, cooperation and understanding between parents and teachers for the benefit of all our children.

I believe that the potential for parent involvement with gifted and talented by far exceeds that which we can accomplish with the traditional compensatory efforts. Parents can be involved in selecting students, advising on program design, working in the classroom, and of course developing approaches in the home to stimulate and support the gifted child.

Here too, we must realize that the parent him or herself, may face difficulties in raising a gifted child, and the support and encouragement offered through these school-based efforts are important to the parenting process.

9. Disadvantaged

This concept was presented in a paper on the disadvantaged gifted at the Third National Conference on the Disadvantaged Gifted, and I quote:

> It requires an extraordinarily powerful device to break up the highly entrenched cycles of poverty which exist in the society. One of the key factors certainly appears to be centered around the involvement of the powerless. Consequently, the goal of any significant cycle-breaker *must* be to include the powerless in the decision-making processes. Certainly this is basic to functional participation in a democratic society since those affected by decisions must participate in their development. Without such participation, effective change is usually impossible.

Through my exposure to gifted programs for minority youngsters, I have seen black students, heretofore silent and apathetic in formal classroom situations come to life as vibrant, articulate, dynamos in the more personalized enrichment settings. There have been a number of exciting "youth-teaching youth" efforts where one disadvantaged child has successfully imparted knowledge to a somewhat younger child when all of a teacher's effort had failed. Gifted programs which relate to the special qualities and needs of a minority child can promote cooperation and understanding with gifted peers from the mainstream culture.

Of course, there are a number of additional approaches to meeting the needs of the disadvantaged gifted, and the expertise to expand them is certainly here in this room today. In order to fulfill this potential, we need to bring about a change in society's attitude and understanding of giftedness. More importantly, we have got to impact upon federal policy to bring about the needed resources to establish a national commitment.

My good friend and colleague from H.E.W., Dr. Marry Berry, is certainly doing her part to re-orient and refocus the attention of the bureaucracy on the disadvantaged gifted. Her impact on educational policy has been extremely important, and it is important that we support the initiatives she has undertaken.

At the same time, my legislative concept to mandate a set-aside for the disadvantaged gifted has been adopted in similar forms by the House Education and Labor Committee, and the Senate Human Resources Committee. I am confident that the final Elementary and Secondary Education Act which is passed by the Congress will contain provisions to insure focus on the disadvantaged gifted.

Our troubles are in the piddling amount which Congress has appropriated for the gifted. Presently, only $2.56 million is appropriated for gifted programs. New legislation for the disadvantaged will have little meaning if it is not backed up with appro-

2. IDENTIFICATION

priations to fund programs.

This year, almost 500 proposals were submitted to the Office of Gifted and Talented; yet only 50 will be funded due to a lack of money. Let me say that Dr. Dorothy Sisk has been able to do a remarkably good job in light of the financial obstacles her program has faced.

Just last month I testified before the House Labor-HEW Appropriations Subcommittee, and I spoke strongly to the need to increase funds for gifted and talented to a level next year of at least $8-$10 Million. Yet I was shocked to learn that last week this Subcommittee reported a bill to the Full Appropriations Committee recommending the same $2.56 million which starved the program last year.

At this very moment, I am working on an amendment which would hopefully be offered in the Full Appropriations Committee during its consideration of the Labor-HEW Appropriations Bill around June 1st. If it is not offered in Committee, I will definitely work to offer an amendment on the House Floor to increase the funding levels. I will definitely need your support and interest though, if I am to work with a few of my other colleagues to bring about this funding increase. For too long, educators have treated politics as though it were dirty laundry — to be pushed in the corner and forgotten. I think that we, as individuals committed to improving educational opportunity for disadvantaged and minority children, cannot afford the luxury of ignoring the political processes which impact upon all facets of our lives.

I hope that you will work with me to develop the needed resources for the disadvantaged gifted, our most neglected group in American education. Together I believe we can bring about the type of change that will make their tomorrow more hopeful.

DR. MOSHE SMILANSKY:

AN ADDRESS BY DR. MOSHE SMILANSKY AT NORFOLK STATE COLLEGE ON ISRAEL'S DISADVANTAGED GIFTED YOUTH (FEBRUARY 27, 1978)

To begin, I want to thank you for inviting me and, for the opportunity to discuss Culturally Disadvantaged Gifted Adolescents with you today. Unfortunately, I too, feel disadvantaged working with your group. I am, of course, disadvantaged by my restricted language facility. In addition, I do not know the members of this group and therefore find it difficult to speak directly to specific needs. I will, however, try to answer some of the basic questions that are most often asked of me.

The first question is always, "Why adolescence?" Why do we suggest beginning with adolescence rather than the pre-school, or elementary grades, or any other stage in the life span?" The next question is, "Why are the more gifted adolescents given priority?" Then, "What are the possible organizational approaches used which may be relevant to our discussion?" and finally, "What is the focus of such a program?"

The question, "Why adolescence" seems to me rather irrelevant because we all recognize that each person at each stage of life can use support of his intellectual, social, and emotional growth or development. Let us therefore consider priorities. It is essential that in education as in any other area of endeavor we identify "priorities".

I see the main reason for the priority in adolescent education to be the fact that adolescence is a three generation impact proposition. The adolescent lives with his family of origin. He has impact both on his parents and on his siblings. Therefore, any problem areas that deal with younger siblings, I assume, would not be successful regarding attitudes and behavior, if the adolescent himself is not humane in the sense or if he is frustrated or if he does not believe in the values, attitudes, and behaviors that are fostered in early childhood or elementary education programs. He, as a model and as a reference to the young, would actually be producing the counterbalancing negative impact to that program for the early childhood or elementary education programs aimed at his siblings. But what is more important, while he is in the family of origin, he is continually in confrontation with his family and he represents to his family the prospects of today and tomorrow. Next, the adolescent is going to build, of course, the next generation family. By his choice of partner, by his marriage, by his choice of residence, and by his family planning, he decides on the meaning of the second generation family.

Thirdly, by his decision to become a parent or by the reality of becoming a parent, even if he did not decide about it, he already has impact on the third generation and on those who will have impact on this society until, perhaps, the 21st century.

In other words, even those who advocate priority to early childhood education should see the adolescent as a family builder, as a citizen, and as a parent. He is the one who will have the strongest impact on tomorrow's family and on tomorrow's early childhood education. This is one reason I call it the three generation impact proposition.

Adolescence is a stage that I would call very crucial in the lifespan development. There are some who use the word "critical". I don't use this word because I don't believe that we really have evidence that there is a period in life that is critical in the sense of *irreversibility* of the impact of that period. In a series of lectures before the heads of education departments from throughout the world, who were interested in deciding between priorities for pre-school or adolescence, I tried to convince them that even though early childhood may be considered by some a "critical" period, we have enough evidence of reversibility options to indicate why we should not be using that concept.

But, if we just say a "crucial" stage in human development, there is no question that adolescence is a crucial stage. It is crucial because of a number of factors and I will illustrate just those that seem to be very important for our program.

First of all, except for early childhood, there is no period in human development in which three or four years produce the transformation of a person and his capacities to such an extent as adolescence. That transformation from a child to a man or woman, the biological transformation, the transformation in cognitive abilities (whether one accepts exactly the propositions by Inhelder and by Piaget or one would use other ways of describing that capacity), is the poten-

9. Disadvantaged

tial for transforming from a stage of concrete experiences to the ability for abstraction, hypothetical proposition, etc. It is a crucial stage in terms of the development of moral reasoning and political commitment. Anyone who wants to do something in terms of values, in terms of commitment to the political process, knows that adolescence is a crucial stage. It is a crucial stage in one's own self development. It is the stage in which one differentiates from the family of origin and establishes self identity. As I have already mentioned, it is a stage in which the adolescent is building his family. He is establishing a lifespan proposition. Even with the growing rate of divorce and the other options that are available in modern societies, there is no question that decisions made and happenings that we perceive are under the impact of events in the adolescent stage. One can define and elaborate, if he has time, on each of ten or twelve points regarding the importance — the crucial importance — of adolescence. Time does not permit this and I shall go on to the second question.

"Why the more gifted among the adolescents?" My reply is that they are the ones who experience success within their group, within their community, and within their schools. They have the self esteem and the motivation to persevere toward goals that they choose or we suggest to them. They are able to believe that they can make it. Because of that, they are partners in the reorientation process called a positive disintegration proposition. In other words, they are stronger in their capacity to develop all those qualities that I mentioned earlier because in addition to those, they have the potential for cognitive development, moral development, and self knowledge. This enables them to exhibit and demonstrate to themselves and others that it

2. IDENTIFICATION

is possible to make it in this society.

Secondly, the more gifted among the disadvantaged, and I shall define this later, are nearer in terms of potential capacity, potential capabilities to the norm of the group in a society made on merit judgments. In other words, if they are supported they can get equality that is available in the society.

Thirdly, they are potentially those who can be leaders, models, or a reference group for others in their group. They can prove by their performance that it is possible to achieve success and because of that they are able to upgrade the entire group feeling of power to continue to confront reality, etc. They are the ones who can upgrade the total group from which they come in programs where they are not completely separated but differentiated only part of the time.

Now, the gifted group is the most disadvantaged group relative to its potential. In other words, growing in a socially disadvantaged area as well as growing in a school where the average ability and level of performance is relatively low, they are placed in a situation where the teacher always uses the average norm as the frame of reference for what can be done. Also, because there are students who don't even perform to a minimal threshhold, most of the efforts of the regular teachers are directed to bringing up the basic skills and to coping with the constant struggle to make education a priority. The gifted pay the price more than anyone else in a relatively homogeneous ethnic or social elementary school.

The program offered as an alternative works three ways to accomplish its goals. It uses the children's potential for their own enrichment and their own service in the front-line of social mobility and social integration. The children are the ones who have the most impact. If they receive the proper enrichment, they are the ones who are able to make any homogeneous classroom a heterogeneous classroom. Instead of having one teacher assigned to enrich 30 to 40 youngsters in a classroom, the youngsters in the upper quarter or the upper third of that classroom, because of their own enrichment activities, can act as assistants. Through their experiences, they prove to the other group, the dominant group in many societies, that ethnic prejudice or social-class prejudice *can* be overcome.

Let us look at the options for organizing a program both in terms of administrative options and in terms of content. I personally subscribe to three models for dealing with the issue. They are not instead of the other in terms of my orientation but they are supportive. They are directed to different groups of the population.

The first approach I call the enrichment of the upper quarter of any disadvantaged area school. Personally, I tried it both in Tel Aviv and Jerusalem with 16 schools in two centers and it later was spread in 29 other cities in Israel. The proposition there is that those who are in the upper quarter of the elementary school according to teacher judgment and those who are in the upper quarter according to test criteria, should be accepted as belonging to the upper quarter.

Why this criterion? Each will identify certain groups of the population. Each will not be identifying specific individuals. In reality, from our experience, the use of both measures enlarges the group from 25% to somewhere between 30 to 35%. In reality, we are speaking about including a third of the upper group in each elementary school while we still speak as if it is the upper quarter. We call this a program for the gifted assuming that these children are the more gifted in their group. In other words, it is not the regular assignment of giftedness as the upper 2%, or the upper any other percentage that somebody uses, but, it is the assumption that they are potentially the more gifted in their own group. For purposes of their motivation and the motivation of their parents, we are able to say on the basis of follow-up studies that although the average I.Q. of the upper quarter or the upper 30%, as I defined them, is somewhere around 102 on the Wechsler — an average group in terms of national norms — they are the upper group or the more gifted *within their own group.*

Because we take such a relatively large group, we are sure, as far as humans can be sure, that we are not discriminating, nor lowering the potential of identifying anyone who potentially may be lower than the more gifted among the disadvantaged.

In this type of program, the children meet twice a week in the afternoon and during the entire summer for 3 consecutive years. The program includes sixth, seventh, and eighth grades.

In the United States, you have another option that is not available to us. We teach 6 days per week, from 8 AM until 1 PM.

However, you teach only 5 days per week and actually can use one of the weekend days for the enrichment of that upper quarter group in addition to the summer. Our experience has shown that by working together with the regular school, the identified students and their parents, we are able to maintain the motivation necessary. During the 3 years of the continuous program, from the beginning of the 6th until the end of 8th grade, about 90% of the children remain voluntarily in the program.

The youngsters meet in a center—usually a high school, because a high school has very important connotations. It has the status and it has the facilities that an elementary school does not have. This says, "Look here. We are preparing you to perform according to expectations of a quality high school."

The children come to the program and then return to their own school. In this way, we achieve many important options simultaneously. First, because they go as a group, not as individuals, they are the "upper quarter". There is an "esprit de corps". There is a group feeling that as a group "we" can create a different culture emphasizing intellectual development and giving priority to learning as a counter-culture to the dominant one in the disadvantaged area where other values predominate.

As a group the children return to their classroom and, as I said before in talking about the teacher, enrich that classroom. Because they go weekly to the enrichment center, they bring back new ideas and force the teacher both to use them and to confront their contributions. From what they receive at the enrichment center, they prove constantly their readiness for confrontation with their peer culture in the school and in the neighborhoods. Individuals usually have to adjust to such a reference group within a dominant culture, in a neighborhood, or in a school. As a group, however, they are strong enough to create that counterculture experience.

Another model that is very meaningful for us and works unusually well, is what we call the boarding school for our gifted disadvantaged. The supposition is that some children need additional assistance to develop their potential because they are growing up in areas where quality education is unavailable to them. We take them out to boarding schools or boarding centers. In operation since 1960 with 60 youngsters, today it includes 4,000 students. It is an option for those who need this kind of experience.

The third model is a day program which identifies those who need the boarding program, but who are unable to leave home for some reason.

The results show that a boarding school program costs twice as much as regular high school. The results also indicate, however, double the level of those who graduate who are college bound and double the proportion of those who then graduate from the universities. In other words, it costs twice as much, but, produces twice as many graduates both at the level of college entrance and completion of the university program.

It is our assumption that a program should focus on a number of important components. One is called self development in coping capacities. This develops the capacity of the individual to understand himself, to understand the environment with which he must cope, and to prepare him to take part in that environment. This program must be handled in a very systematic way and not just by chance.

During the last few years, we developed modular units of curriculum that deal with that general concept. It begins with what you may call sexual identity, or "Who am I as a man or woman?" Sex education is one component of sexual identity. The idea is to understand sex roles, sex role typing, sex education, career education, and a component dealing with relations between the adolescent and his family. The latter because adolescence is a period of differentiation from the family. There must be a systematic confrontation asking, "Who is my father? Why is he the way he is? Who am I? I may love my father and not want to be like him. When I choose a girlfriend, do I want her to be like my mother or do I want her to be just the opposite because of experiences I had with my mother?" This systematic confrontation between adolescent and parent is necessary both to release the parents and the adolescents from confrontation about daily events of the right to autonomy, the right to decide to date, go out on weekends, etc.

A second important component to mention is the curriculum we develop. This is what we call the unit of leadership. It deals with the community. It attempts to help the adolescent understand his community environment and leadership. Its goal is to prepare him for his future role.

Another aspect that seems to be important is the component of peer counseling. The student learns to give orders and to receive them. This responsibility is placed parallel to receiving privileges. One way to confront the question of responsibility is by asking, "What type of responsibilities can the youngsters have?"

The assumption of responsibility to upgrade the total level of learning and living in the classroom and the school and the responsibility for specific roles in counseling younger students or adults, as well as other responsibilities that can be defined in the context of what is relevant in a specific community, are of prime importance.

In summary, then, let me state that the high ability, culturally disadvantaged adolescent given appropriate education in an appropriate setting helps himself, his present and future family, and his society.

Photo: Office of Human Resources, Department of Health, Education and Welfare

PROBLEMS IN EVALUATING SPECIAL PROGRAMS

There definitely are problems of evaluating programs for a gifted segment of a total school population, such as those which arise from the limitations of existing tests and those which relate to gaps in operationally feasible means of approaching some very general objectives. Even so, some agencies are finding practical solutions to these and other problems, and they are producing useful written evaluative studies of district-wide special programs. Instruments for such studies are becoming available.

Two of John Ferrell's evaluation instruments are included in this section. The first, "The Ferrell Gifted Program Evaluation Instrument for Teachers" is a form for teachers for the purpose of gathering information, based on qualitative changes in student thinking, as well as quantitative content changes. The second, "Evaluation of Instructional Programs for Gifted and Talented Children" is based on two identified local (Illinois) education needs: 1) "A concern for the total progam for gifted education offered within the local school district." and 2) "The extent to which the local program is meeting the assessed needs of the individual gifted student within the program."

By including a summary of a three year study of a program for talented elementary students, and a general article on the problems facing the evaluating team, this section will better prepare the reader to establish similar procedures, or perhaps more successful measuring devices.

Issues and Procedures in Evaluating Programs

JOSEPH S. RENZULLI AND LINDA H. SMITH

The purpose of this chapter is threefold. First, a brief overview of some of the major concepts that define the field of program evaluation is presented. The focus of this section is upon general issues and problems related to each concept and the ways in which these issues and problems have special relevance to the task of evaluating programs for the gifted. Second, some of the relatively unique characteristics of programs for the gifted are discussed. These characteristics require that special considerations be taken into account in the process of developing evaluative studies that are designed to assess particular objectives and populations. The third purpose is to present an overview of a model that hopefully will provide some practical guidance in designing evaluative studies.

Basic Concepts in Program Evaluation

As the literature on evaluation grows in size and complexity, a whole new language of evaluation is emerging that describes the concepts which have helped to create this area of specialization. The concepts discussed below reflect some of the basic ideas that have been set forth in the general evaluation models of Stake, Stufflebeam, and Provus.[1] The first two concepts, formative and summative evaluations, may be thought of as evaluation designs. They represent the predetermined plans that guide the ways in which an evaluation will be carried out and the role that evaluation will fulfill in the overall operation of a project or program. It should be emphasized that an evaluation need not be either formative or summative, but rather can be a combination of both designs.

The other three concepts—product, process, and presage evaluations—should be thought of as types of evaluative data, that is, the kind of information that an evaluator focuses upon in organizing and conducting an evaluative study. Decisions regarding which types of data an evaluator will seek are, of course, also based on the role that evaluation is expected to play; and thus, there is a relation-

---

1. Robert E. Stake, "Measuring What Learners Learn," in *School Evaluation: The Politics and Process,* ed. Ernest R. House (Berkeley, Calif.: McCutchan Publishing Corp., 1973), chapter 16; Daniel L. Stufflebeam, *Educational Evaluation and Decision Making* (Itasca, Ill.: F. E. Peacock Publishers, 1971); Malcolm M. Provus, *Discrepancy Evaluation* (Berkeley, Calif.: McCutchan Publishing Corp., 1972).

From *The Gifted and the Talented: Their Education and Development,* ©1979, by the National Society for the Study of Education, reprinted with permission.

ship between formative and summative evaluations on one hand, and product, process, and presage evaluations on the other.

FORMATIVE EVALUATION

Scriven, the originator of the concept, defines formative evaluation as "simply outcome evaluation at an intermediate stage in the development of [whatever it is that you are evaluating]."[2] The role of formative evaluation "is to discover deficiencies and successes in the intermediate versions" of educational programs and activities.[3] The emphasis is on when the data are gathered (intermediate stages as opposed to end-of-program data) rather than on the types of data that are being used. The major purpose of formative evaluation is to provide continuous in-process feedback so that appropriate modifications and revisions can be made in a program as the program develops and matures. One of the primary advantages of formative evaluation is that the data are gathered in close proximity to specific components of a program, and thus it has greater potential for pinpointing the successes and failures of particular activities in a program.

All types of data (product, process, presage) can be used in formative evaluation but it is important to keep the following guidelines in mind. First, a systematic feedback mechanism must be developed so that information reaches decision makers in time to institute changes that are deemed necessary. Second, decision makers at each level of decision-making responsibility must make a sincere commitment to change. Third, and perhaps most importantly, information should be collected on identifiable program activities about which something can be done. Formative evaluation data are useless unless they indicate where to make changes and unless the changes are within the realm of possibility.

An evaluator expected to engage in formative curriculum evaluation can benefit from some of the strategies that have grown out of experimental curriculum projects. These projects have generally relied on carefully developed mastery tests bearing direct relationship to specific areas of the curriculum. The strategies recommended are based on a detailed analysis of content areas and process objectives which are classified according to the taxonomies of educational objectives.[4] Instructions are given for drawing up tables of specifications and constructing formative evaluation tests.

Curriculum evaluation based on mastery testing represents only one dimension of total program evaluation. Persons who are engaged in formative evaluation will no doubt want to provide continuous feedback in other areas where corrective action can be

---

2. Michael Scriven, "The Methodology of Evaluation," in *Perspectives of Curriculum Evaluation*, ed. Ralph W. Tyler, Robert M. Gagné, and Michael Scriven, American Educational Research Association Monograph Series on Evaluation, no. 1 (Chicago: Rand McNally, 1967), p. 51.

3. Ibid.

4. Benjamin S. Bloom et al., *Taxonomy of Educational Objectives, Handbook I: Cognitive Domain* (New York: Longman, 1956); David R. Krathwohl et al., *Taxonomy of Educational Objectives, Handbook II: Affective Domain* (New York: David McKay, 1964).

3. EVALUATING

taken, such as reactions of parents toward the program, the effectiveness of in-service training, and so forth.

SUMMATIVE EVALUATION

Summative evaluation differs from formative evaluation mainly in the role that it fulfills. Whereas formative evaluation is directed toward program revision and improvement through continuous feedback, summative evaluation is more concerned with overall program effectiveness. Thus, summative information is more likely to be used in making decisions about the adoption or continuation of a program. While the results of this type of evaluation are no doubt of interest to persons who may develop and operate programs, they may be of greater interest to boards of education or funding agencies.

Although summative data might be gathered through the course of a program, the summative evaluator usually avoids giving any feedback until the end of the program in order to see how the program works in its natural (unaltered) form. In this respect, summative evaluation resembles the classic approach to experimental research design, that is, holding the independent variable (program) constant in order to discover what changes it produces. The main difference between summative evaluation and experimental research design is that the researcher is usually comparing alternative treatments under highly controlled conditions. These conditions almost always include the random assignment of students to experimental treatment groups and to control groups. Although most evaluators would like to respect as many of the mandates of good research as possible, it is difficult to do so in field evaluations. Programs for the gifted are often characterized by a great deal of variety and individualization, and it would be difficult to do high quality research without very substantial resources. The summative evaluator can, however, use the same instruments as the formative evaluator in documenting the overall effects of a program. But in this case there is a greater need to show growth over relatively long periods of time, and for this reason it may be necessary to gather data at the beginning and end of a program.

In actual practice, the evaluator will most often use a combination of approaches and some of his instruments can serve the dual purpose of providing in process feedback for practitioners and documenting student growth for decision-making bodies. The best guide for determining what types of data will be most useful for practitioners and decision makers is to survey each group at the outset of an evaluation study. The techniques for doing this are discussed in a later section under "Front-End Analysis."

PRODUCT OR "PAY-OFF" EVALUATION

Since educational programs are intended to produce certain changes in the attributes of students, product evaluation can be thought of as the assessment of observable and measurable student outcomes that result from a particular educational endeavor. Assuming that there is some consensus about the desirability of intended outcomes, these outcomes then become the pure "pay-off" of an educational program. The important evaluative data are documented indications of change in student performance, change that would not have taken place had the student not been enrolled in a particular course or taken part in a certain educational activity.

Merely obtaining objective measures or descriptions of student growth does not enable the evaluator to make qualitative judgments about what has been learned (for example, how good is an increase of ten points in the mean score for a particular group?). The problem of establishing abstract criteria for judging educational products is compounded as attention is focused on higher-level processes such as creativity and problem-solving abilities. In the final analysis, some form of human judgment must be brought to bear on objective findings; and thus, one of the major responsibilities of the product evaluator is to determine what types of information are most necessary for facilitating the judgment process.

The most obvious and popular type of product evaluation data has been scores on standardized and teacher-made tests. Scriven has pointed out that "the performance of students on the final tests, as upon the tests at intermediate stages, must be analyzed in order to determine the exact location of shortcomings of comprehension, shortages of essential facts, lack of practice in basic skills, and so forth."[5] In other words, test scores, in and of themselves, tell us nothing about cause and effect relationships and the only way to pinpoint such relationships is through a thorough analysis of test items as they relate to course content.

The development of criterion-referenced measurement shows promise of making more effective use of tests in program evaluation.[6] Whereas traditional norm-referenced tests yield only scores that show an individual's relative standing in comparison to a norm group, criterion-referenced tests are designed to show a student's accomplishments in particular areas in relation to a level of performance that the student will be expected to achieve. As such, criterion-referenced tests can help to determine exactly where remedial instruction may be necessary and/or whether or not a student is ready to go on to the next step in a learning hierarchy.

Until the present, criterion-referenced testing has been closely tied to the behavioral objectives movement and because of this there has been a tendency to concentrate mainly on basic skills and limited types of learning activities. Unless these tests truly assess the types of learning that are appropriate for gifted and talented students, their use may have the same limiting effects on programs as the rigid application of norm-referenced tests.

Product information can be gathered from a number of sources other than tests. Ratings of student products (or of performance) by experts is one way in which the quality of creative work can be assessed. For example, in a program for gifted and talented students in Warwick, Rhode Island, a group of professional artists and writers were asked to rate students' work that was completed at

---

5. Scriven, "The Methodology of Evaluation," p. 61.

6. Jason Millman, "Criterion-referenced Measurement," in *Evaluation in Education: Current Applications*, ed. W. James Popham (Berkeley, Calif.: McCutchan Publishing Corp., 1974), chapter 6.

3. EVALUATING

various stages throughout the program. If specific student attitudes are listed as objectives of a program, the measurement of such attitudes can also be considered product data. Instruments for the measurement of all types of attitudes have been collected in a variety of sourcebooks.

Another type of product data falls under the classification of "frequency counts." This type of data is typically gathered through the use of logs, checklists, or an analysis of school records. Frequency counts qualify as product data if they reflect the accomplishment of an important program objective. Thus, for example, if one of the stated objectives of a particular program is "To increase by 50 percent the number of science books that students select for independent reading," this objective can be evaluated by some relatively simple record keeping. This is a very different kind of product from the qualitative assessment of student performance.

PROCESS EVALUATION

In view of the many problems that product evaluation presents in assessing for the gifted and talented, there is a clear need to seek additional kinds of data that show promise of determining the effectiveness of particular program activities. Process evaluation is concerned with assessing those aspects of student and teacher behavior considered to be worthwhile in their own right. These behaviors or processes are the teaching strategies and learning activities that are believed to be necessary in order to bring about desired educational products. In other words, process evaluation is concerned with "what goes on" in a learning situation rather than "what comes out of it."

Although there is some disagreement among educators about what constitutes a process, most evaluators agree that assessing the actual dynamics of a learning activity can provide very valuable insights about the strengths and weaknesses of certain educational practices. The assessment of educational processes is almost always used in formative evaluation studies. Process data are usually gathered to give immediate feedback to teachers so that they can be used in summative evaluation reports, but a great deal of caution must be exercised when such data are used for summative purposes. Teachers may be genuinely interested in "taking a look at themselves" so that they can improve their teaching techniques, but may feel threatened if they think that process data will be used by others to make judgments about their teaching ability.

The use of process data for purposes of program evaluation can best be discussed by focusing on two specific approaches to systematic observation techniques and to the analysis of classroom climate. One of the most highly developed and widely used systems for gathering observational data is the Flanders Interaction Analysis System.[7] This system focuses on the distinction between direct and indirect teacher influence in the classroom, the underlying assump-

---

7. Edmund J. Amidon and Ned A. Flanders, *The Role of the Teacher in the Classroom: A Manual for Understanding and Improving Teacher Classroom Behavior* (Minneapolis, Minn.: Association for Productive Teaching, 1971).

tion being that the first step in modifying one's teaching behaviors is to understand more fully how the teacher is influencing the learning situation. Implicit in the target behaviors of this system (that is, direct and indirect influence) is Flanders's belief that teachers should develop the capability to make their own behaviors appropriate to the requirements of particular learning situations.

Higher achievement, less dependence, and greater self-direction have usually been found in the classrooms of teachers who were classified as highly indirect. Thus, the Flanders system represents a technique that has relevance to the task of evaluating the processes that are frequently encouraged in gifted education. The system is especially useful in gathering data at lower grade levels because students are not required to complete questionnaires or rating scales.

A second approach to the evaluation of process offers some possibilities for overcoming some of the problems of observers in the classroom. Rather than having one or two observers in the classroom for a very limited period of time, the questionnaire or rating-scale approach is based on observations made by numerous observers who are in the classroom all the time. These observers are, of course, the students themselves.

The *Class Activities Questionnaire* (CAQ) was developed by Steele as part of the instrumentation that was used to evaluate the Illinois Gifted Program. Both cognitive and affective dimensions of the instructional climate are measured through a thirty-item instrument that is completed by both students and teachers. Steele describes the dimensions of the instrument as follows:

1 and 2. Lower Thought Processes and Higher Thought Processes assess the dimensions of cognitive emphasis. This part of the CAQ is based on Bloom's taxonomy. Each higher level of thinking is believed to involve the use of all the lower levels. The difference between lower and higher levels is one of complexity. There can be a range of difficulty of activities at each level of thinking.
3. The Classroom Focus dimension assesses whether focus is on the teacher as information-giver with students having a passive role, or on the students being given an active role with the teacher being the facilitator.
4. The Classroom Climate dimension deals with the affective domain. It assesses factors such as how relaxed and open the class is.
5. The Student Opinions dimension represents mini-interviews with each student on the best things and changes to make in the class.[8]

Student responses are considered to be the "actual" emphasis that is placed on each of the factors and these are summarized. Teachers fill out two copies of the questionnaire. On one copy they record the *intended* or *ideal* amount of emphasis that they would like to place on each factor. The second copy records their *predicted* emphasis. In analyzing their results teachers can determine how successful they were in achieving their ideal behavior and how accurately they estimated the way students viewed the class. Discrepancies can be used as the basis for improving instruction through self-analysis and/or inservice training activities.

---

8. Joe M. Steele, *Dimensions of the Class Activities Questionnaire* (Urbana, Ill.: Center for Instructional Research and Curriculum Evaluation, University of Illinois, 1969), p. 3.

3. EVALUATING

The fact that the CAQ is based, in part, on Bloom's *Taxonomy of Educational Objectives* makes it particularly relevant to process evaluation in gifted education. As was indicated above, a system such as the taxonomy helps focus attention on those higher cognitive and affective processes which should be given major emphasis in programs for the gifted and talented.

PRESAGE OR INTRINSIC EVALUATION

Some evaluators would argue that due to deficiencies in instruments that measure products (payoff), especially higher-level cognitive and affective products, it is necessary to look for other sources of evaluative data. Presage or intrinsic evaluation focuses on factors which are assumed to have a significant impact on outcomes or products. Thus, intrinsic factors may be thought of as the purposefully planned activities that are designed to bring about changes in student performance. According to Scriven, persons who advocate this approach in curriculum evaluation are likely to be concerned with certain "qualities of a curriculum such as elegance, modernity, structure, integrity, readiness considerations, and so forth, which can best be judged by looking at the materials directly."[9] Renzulli and Ward have used the presage approach more broadly in the development of the *Diagnostic and Evaluation Scale for Differential Education for the Gifted* (DESDEG) by pointing out several dimensions of a program that can be studied through the assessment of information that has an assumed relationship to the quality of a program.[10]

The major problem with presage or intrinsic evaluation is the logical jump that must be made from intrinsic factors to program outcomes. Indeed, very few contemporary evaluation theorists advocate a wholly presage approach, and yet, this concept is of value in considering the assessment of programs for the gifted and talented because the outcome objectives of such programs are oftentimes not easily measured by existing instruments.

The presage approach also offers a useful model of evaluating nonproduct dimensions of a program. For example, in the DESDEG model, Renzulli and Ward have developed several forms that help to provide an analytic look at identification systems. The comprehensiveness of screening and placement procedures, the variety of criteria used in identification, and the proportion of students selected at each grade level are revealed through the use of these forms. The forms force a breakdown of the information and thus enable the evaluator to see the identification system more clearly and to ask more meaningful questions. A clearer picture of all aspects of the identification process should help the evaluator come to more accurate judgments.

The presage or intrinsic approach is probably more in keeping with Stake's belief that careful and accurate description is a neces-

---

9. Scriven, "The Methodology of Evaluation," p. 54.

10. Joseph S. Renzulli and Virgil S. Ward, *Diagnostic and Evaluation Scale for Differential Education for the Gifted* (Storrs, Conn.: Bureau of Educational Research, University of Connecticut, 1969).

sary prerequisite to the judgmental process.[11] Information (data) does not in and of itself render opinions; and in the final analysis, it is people who must make judgments. The presage approach can facilitate the judgmental process by helping to present information in its clearest and most useful format.

Special Problems in Evaluating Programs for the Gifted and Talented

THE PROBLEM OF "HIGHER-LEVEL" OBJECTIVES

Programs for the gifted are often characterized by a commitment to the development of higher powers of mind and advanced levels of awareness, interest, and other affective behaviors. This presents a somewhat unique problem for the evaluator because these objectives cannot be measured as easily and precisely as those objectives that deal mainly with the acquisition of basic skills. As one moves up the scale of learning behaviors, from the simple acquisition of knowledge to the development of higher mental processes, it becomes increasingly difficult to find measuring instruments that meet the scientific and practical requirements necessary for good evaluation studies.

A second dimension of this problem is that gifted programs are frequently characterized by highly individualized objectives for each student. Whereas a reading skills program for average or slow learners may have enough uniformity in its objectives to warrant large-scale standardized testing, a program for gifted students may have many *different* objectives for each student. Standardized tests can, of course, be used effectively in evaluating programs for the gifted if they (a) are valid (appropriate) measures of particular objectives, and (b) if they are used in situations where reasonable levels of reliability can be obtained. But when a teacher devises individualized objectives for each child, the appropriateness of tests based on systemwide or nationwide objectives must be seriously questioned.

In recent years there has been a great deal of concern in education about the specification of objectives in terms of observable and measurable student behaviors. Many evaluators have looked upon the "behavioral objectives model" as a panacea for conducting evaluation studies. The nature of gifted programs, however, and their concern for developing higher thought processes may make this model too cumbersome to be applied practically to programs for the gifted and talented. In fact, when the behavioral objectives approach is used in its most rigid form, it may even force program developers to focus their attention on the trivial rather than important behaviors of superior learners.

The rigid behavioral objectives model is inappropriate for programs for the gifted because it forces one to be primarily concerned with those behaviors that are readily measured. Although many experts in testing believe that complex objectives can be evaluated, Stake has suggested that the total cost of measuring such objectives

---

11. Robert E. Stake, "The Countenance of Educational Evaluation," *Teachers College Record* 68 (1967): 523-40.

3. EVALUATING

may be one hundred times that of administering a forty-five minute standardized paper-and-pencil test; and the amount of time, personnel, and facilities necessary for such evaluation may be astronomical. Stake also points out that the errors of testing increase markedly when we move from highly specific areas of performance to items which attempt to measure higher mental processes and unreached human potential.[12]

MEASUREMENT AND STATISTICAL PROBLEMS

Measurement and formal testing often play a major role in evaluation studies, but certain cautions are necessary when considering the use of standardized tests in evaluating programs for the gifted. By definition, the gifted student initially scores at the upper end of the normal curve, where it is much more difficult to show an increase in percentile score points. The same is true for age and grade scores. Generally, there is a slowing down of gains at the upper levels of most performance tests that were normed on the general population. For this reason, when the evaluator uses standardized tests, he should avoid making comparisons between gifted students and other populations. This can be done by developing separate sets of norms for each distinct population whose growth is being evaluated, provided of course, that the test has a broad enough range to allow students to show maximum growth. If a test does not have enough "top" or "ceiling" in it, highly able students may score at the upper limits, but their true growth cannot be determined because of the low ceiling of the test. Since many standardized tests are designed to provide achievement information for the vast middle ranges of ability, their content and interpretive data may not be valid for children who deviate markedly upward from the mean.

The use of conventional tests with gifted and talented students also presents some problems in the statistical treatment of evaluative data. One such problem relates to the fact that test reliability is a function of group diversity—the more heterogeneous the group, the higher the reliability. When dealing with a relatively homogeneous group of students, caution must be exercised in examining the reported reliabilities of standardized tests. Unfortunately, most test publishers do not report reliabilities for subpopulations within their standardization sample and therefore it is necessary to conduct a local reliability study whenever conventional tests are used with special populations.

Another statistical problem encountered when working with the test scores of superior students is the well-known effect of regression toward the mean. Simply stated, this means that predicted scores tend to "move in" toward the mean of the distribution. Thus, if a pretest and posttest design is used to evaluate the effects of a program for the gifted, and if the students' scores on the pretest are initially high, it is quite likely their posttest scores will actually decrease somewhat due to the regression effect. It is for

---

12. Stake, "Measuring What Learners Learn," pp. 196-99.

this reason the evaluator must exercise great caution when considering the pre/post design and other statistical designs that do not take into account the lack of normality in the distribution of gifted students' test scores.

PRACTICAL PROBLEMS

The evaluation of programs for the gifted, like evaluation in all other areas, requires time, money, and trained personnel. When evaluation is "tacked on" to a program as an afterthought, and when the human and financial resources necessary for carrying out a comprehensive evaluation are not available, the evaluator may very well end up being asked to do the impossible. Even when time and resources are available, the evaluator is frequently called upon to develop a plan of evaluation for programs with poorly defined objectives and a very limited conception about what will constitute a successful program.

What can be done about practical problems in evaluation such as time, money, and personnel? There is agreement on the importance of involving the evaluator from the very beginning of any educational endeavor. Through such involvement, the evaluator can continually bring to the attention of program developers the steps that must be taken and the resources that must be allocated if evaluation is to serve useful purposes. Early and continuous involvement on the part of the evaluator will help to overcome many of the difficulties that arise when evaluation is tacked-on as an afterthought.

Another practical problem relates to the attitude that many educators hold toward evaluation. Teachers and other professional personnel often view evaluation as a means of controlling or checking up on a program and the persons responsible for operating a program. In short, evaluation can be very threatening and might result in some rather harsh actions, especially if the evaluation is mandated by a decision-making body or by an outside funding agency.

The evaluator must walk a very thin line in the process of gaining the acceptance and cooperation of persons over whom he may eventually have to pass judgment. In spite of all of the rhetoric about friendly and cooperative relations between evaluator and staff, the fact remains that the evaluator may sometimes have to recommend actions or changes unpleasant to the persons who sponsor and operate a program. This problem can be minimized by spelling out the responsibilities of the evaluator and the staff at the very beginning of an evaluation study.

The Key Features Evaluation System

The Key Features System is a general evaluation design that has proven to be effective in documenting the value of programs for the gifted and talented. It is an approach that translates many of the theoretical concepts in program evaluation into a practical, usable plan and is flexible enough to account for the relatively unique characteristics of programs for the gifted and talented. As indicated in figure 1, this system consists of four sequential steps

3. EVALUATING

or phases. The purpose of these steps and the specific activities or procedures involved in each are described in the narrative that follows.

STEP I: FRONT-END ANALYSIS

The purpose of Front-End Analysis is to help the evaluator identify "key features" in a project or program. Key features may be thought of as major factors or variables that contribute to the effectiveness of a program. Before instruments can be selected and data gathered it is important to determine which factors influence the operation of the program and contribute most to an understanding of it. It is also important to learn what types of information are of major concern to various "Prime Interest Groups." Prime interest groups consist of people who have a direct or indirect interest in the program being evaluated. These groups will almost always include students, parents, teachers, administrators, and school board members. But, depending on the nature of the program, prime interest groups may also include persons who are involved in the program indirectly.

As noted in figure 1, the evaluator can identify key features by

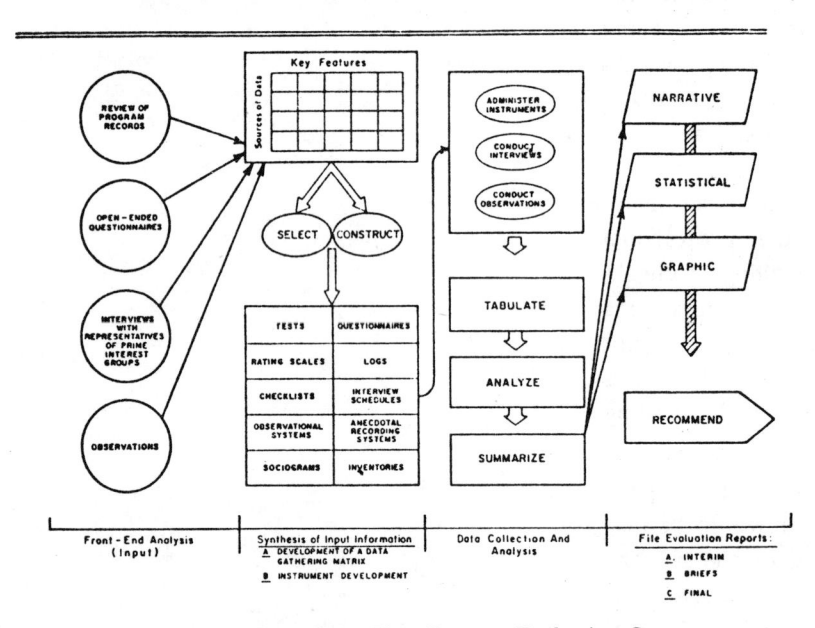

FIG. 1. Overview of the Key Features Evaluation System
Source: Joseph S. Renzulli, *A Guidebook for Evaluating Programs for the Gifted and Talented* (Ventura, Calif.: Office of the Ventura County Superintendent of Schools, 1975), p. 51.

compiling "input" information from four main sources, the first of which is a comprehensive review of all written material relating to the program. These documents should provide the evaluator with an overview of program objectives and a description of the general mode of operation of the program.

As a second source of information, the evaluator can design and administer open-ended questionnaires. These questionnaires should be completed by a representative sample of each prime interest group and should enable the respondents to describe their main concerns about the program. Respondents may simply be asked, for example, to list the major questions that they would like to have answered by the evaluation report.

Knowledge gained from reviewing documents and the questionnaires will enable the evaluator to ask meaningful questions during the third step of Front-End Analysis: interviews with representatives of each prime interest group. Interviews should begin with the director and persons who were involved in the planning phase of the program. These persons will more than likely provide an understanding of the way in which the program was ideally conceived, whereas interviews with teachers and students will probably deal more closely with the way in which the program is actually operating. In all Front-End Analysis interviews, the evaluator should essentially be asking: "How can I help you?" "What information will help to make the program better for you?" "What are the things that are bothering you?"

In the final stage of Front-End Analysis, the evaluator observes the program in operation so as to help clarify and verify some of the concerns identified through previous input procedures. This type of "reality orientation" gives a much better perspective of "the way it is" rather than the ways in which it has been described and discussed.

STEP 2: SYNTHESIS OF INPUT INFORMATION AND INSTRUMENT DEVELOPMENT

At the conclusion of Front-End Analysis the evaluator should be able to list the *major* concerns of each prime interest group. These concerns should be classified and organized according to similarities among the groups and the list which evolves should make up the key features upon which the evaluation will focus. Once identified, these key features should be listed along one dimension of a chart such as the one presented in figure 2. The evaluator must now ask himself two questions: (a) What types of instruments and/or techniques will provide information relevant to each key feature? and (b) From whom can this information be obtained?

The answers to these questions provide the information necessary for completing the other dimension of the chart (Sources of Data) and filling in the actual content, which consists of the instruments that will be used to gather data related to each key feature.

Selecting and constructing appropriate data gathering instruments is perhaps the most difficult aspect of evaluating programs for the gifted and talented. As mentioned in the previous section, standardized tests of cognitive and affective abilities may fail to yield valid information about student growth and it may therefore be necessary to seek out special instruments or to construct instruments that will provide more accurate information about program effectiveness. The list of assessment devices that can be used to supplement or replace standardized evaluation tools is quite lengthy and includes such items as rating scales, checklists, interview schedules, logs, sociograms, and observation techniques. It is important to point out that selection and/or development of these evaluation measures requires a strong background in tests and mea-

3. EVALUATING

Key Features

	Student Growth	Levels of Thinking and Classroom Conditions	Attitudes Toward Program	Identification Procedures	Etc.
Students	Pre- and Post-Tests of Creativity, Critical Thinking, etc.	*Class Activities Questionnaire* Interviews	Questionnaires Interviews (Random Sample)		
Program Teachers	Evaluation of Student Growth Forms (A Structured Anecdotal Report)*	*Class Activities Questionnaire* Logs	Interviews	Time and Effort Reports Follow-up Questionnaire	
Parents			Questionnaires Interviews (Random Sample)	Follow-up Questionnaire	
Student Selection Committee (Including Records)				Time and Effort Reports Rating Scale (on Usefulness of Information) Interviews Analysis of Records	
Non-Program Teachers	Rating Scale		Questionnaires Interviews (Random Sample)	Time and Effort Reports Follow-up Questionnaire	
Consultants	Student Product Rating Form				
Building Principals and Coordinators		Questionnaires	Interviews "Problems" Log	Time and Effort Reports "Problems" Log	
Secretaries				Time and Effort Reports	

Sources of Data

FIG. 2. Matrix of Key Features and Sources of Data
Source: Renzulli, *A Guidebook for Evaluating Programs for the Gifted and Talented*, p. 57.

surements. The field evaluator without such training should obtain the assistance of a consultant with experience in this area of specialization.

STEP 3: DATA COLLECTION AND ANALYSIS

After the evaluator has identified key features, sources of data, and instruments necessary for obtaining the data, he then begins the third step of the Key Features Evaluation System—data collection and analysis. Data collection requires careful and comprehensive planning so that important information will not be lost due to conflicts with school vacations, special events, or final examinations. Timing is also important in terms of how often information is gathered and how much time is required to obtain the information.

Once data related to each key feature are obtained, they must be broken down into component parts. There are two basic methods of data analysis open to the evaluator: logical analysis and statistical analysis. In logical analysis, information is categorized according to some common characteristic and an attempt is made to discover patterns, trends, or discrepancies that exist within each clearly discernible category. The statistical approach, which incorporates both descriptive and inferential techniques, provides the evaluator with the means by which to summarize large sets of numerical information and to make probability statements regarding the significance of observed differences among groups. Generally speaking, the nature of the data collected will determine which type of analysis is most appropriate for answering specific evaluation questions.

STEP 4: PREPARING EVALUATION REPORTS

Once data are collected and analyzed, the evaluator is ready to prepare a final report. The report should begin with an introductory chapter that contains a description of the program and an overview of the evaluation design. Each chapter that follows should be organized around one key feature. The methods for data collection and techniques for data analysis should be described, followed by the results as they relate to each activity being evaluated. Statistical information should always be described in narrative form and each chapter should end with a brief summary that highlights the major conclusions derived from the results. The final chapter of the report should contain a general summary of the entire evaluation, highlights of the strengths of the program and areas that are in need of improvement, and recommendations that seem warranted by the findings.

Concluding Remarks

All too often, evaluations have been launched as last-ditch efforts to save programs that are in danger of being eliminated or sharply reduced in the amount of support they receive from sponsoring agencies. Although a hastily conducted evaluation may be better than no evaluation at all, the best weapon in the battle for program support and survival is a carefully planned and comprehensive evaluation that will accurately document all aspects of the services being provided for gifted and talented youngsters. Evaluation should be an essential and ongoing part of total programming and each step of the planning and development phases of a program for the gifted should give careful attention to the ways in which evaluative information can be gathered, organized, and presented to decision-making individuals or groups.

FOCUS...
WISDOM AND CLEVERNESS

by EDWARD DE BONO

Wisdom is the wide-angle lens and cleverness the sharp focus. Wisdom is the navigator and cleverness the rally driver. Wisdom does not exclude cleverness but too often cleverness seems to exclude wisdom. If you focus clearly on something there seems more point in exploring that something in detail than casting a scanning eye over the surroundings. To know that you are right makes it superfluous to look around at the context in which you are exercising that righteousness. To defend a point of view with well articulated logic seems preferable to exploring the situation and considering alternative views without yet knowing which one you will choose in the end.

Quite recently I was giving a seminar in Toronto and afterwards one of those attending came up and told me that his great tragedy in life was that he had been good at mathematics. Because he was good at mathematics he was encouraged into that direction and his university career and subsequent life were largely determined by that starting point. Only recently had he become aware of other areas which he found he preferred. But it seemed to him too late to change. So excellence can become a trap because by leading fiercely in one direction it makes it difficult to explore others.

When I was at Harvard I tried a simple block arranging experiment on some of my academic colleagues. They took the first step which was right and then the second and the third — and then they found themselves blocked. They knew they had been 'right' in their initial steps so they insisted on going forward. Some of them gave up and others took as long as eleven minutes over the task. Yet the same task given to some children was solved much more quickly. The children took the same steps at first but then, finding themselves blocked, they assumed (quite incorrectly) that they had taken the wrong step and so they went back to the beginning and

"Wisdom and Cleverness" by Edward de Bono, from the *Journal of the Gifted Child*, Vol. 1, No. 1, Autumn 1979. ©1979 National Association for Gifted Children.

tried a different approach.

It may be the things we learn successfully that make future learning difficult if that learning is not a direct continuation of the initial learning.

Is this 'excellence trap' a reason for proceeding slowly or clouding our vision lest we be ensnared? Can we hold back on cleverness in the hope that wisdom will get a chance to develop? Probably not. The best we can do is to choose for thinking exercise situations that require wisdom and breadth rather than cleverness. We might have to move away from puzzles, mathematics and games which tend to be closed ended to situations that require a broader situation where there is no one right answer but where a practical answer of a sort is demanded. Puzzles are too tight and passive contemplation is too uncommitted. Somewhere in between we should be able to exercise thinking in a constructive manner.

To the clever mind being negative may be more attractive than being constructive — and for several good reasons. The achievement is immediate. There is a sense of superiority. The attacker is less liable to further attack than the originator of the idea. I sometimes feel that we ought to make people earn the right to be negative by requiring them to be positive first.

Is wisdom more than well-filed experience and if it is not is there any way of buying that experience without having to pay in time? I believe that wisdom is less of a gift and more of an attitude. The attitude then creates the experience that strengthens the wisdom. Perhaps wisdom is a thinking strategy and if so we may be able to teach it much more easily than we could ever teach intelligence. At least that is the basic presumption of the Cognitive Research Trust approach to the teaching of thinking as a curriculum subject in schools.

Evaluation of the Alexandria, Virginia Program for Talented Elementary Students, 1974-1977

Frank Morra, Jr. Ph.D., *Frank Morra & Associates, Inc.*
Richard Hills, Assistant Superintendent for Instruction, *Alexandria Public Schools*
Sponsor: Linda Geldman Morra, DHEW/BEH

*Presented at the
1978 Convention of the American Educational Research Association:
Toronto, March 30. 1978*

This paper summarizes a three-year longitudinal study of a differentiated education program for elementary students who have demonstrated exceptionalities in academic and arts areas. Three program options were examined:

- *Interest Activity:* students participated in activities in the area of their gift as supervised by a trained teacher. This took place outside the regular classroom and did not substitute for regular instruction.

- *Curriculum Area Learning Center:* pupils participated in an advanced class in the subject-area of their gift; this class substituted for regular instruction in the subject.

- *Enrichment:* a special teacher assisted the regular teacher in providing additional materials to enrich the child's classroom work. The "enrichment" teacher met frequently with the child to provide additional instruction and to monitor progress.

The evaluation study involved the pre- and post-administration of these instruments during each of the three years of the study:

- *SRA Achievement Tests**
- *Torrance Tests of Creative Thinking*
- *Piers-Harris Children's Self-Concept Test*
- *FIRO-BC*

---

*A special testing procedure was developed in conjunction with Dr. Lee Van Arsdale of Science Research Associates for the prevention of ceiling effects.

- A specially constructed self-report instrument which measured attitude toward school and learning.

In addition, during the spring of each year both parents and classroom teachers were surveyed about the development of the pupils in the five areas of testing.

Two comparison groups were selected and tested with the same instruments:

- A group of pupils not in the program with IQ and achievement scores similar to those of pupils in the program.

- A group of pupils selected at random from the general school population in grades four-through six.

The full results from interim reports for each of the three years are available through the ERIC Clearing-House for Handicapped and Gifted Children, Reston, Virginia. Data tapes of all information are available at the cost of reproduction from Frank Morra and Associates, 3510 McKinley Street, N. W., Washington, D. C. 20015.

Selection into the Program

Pupils in grades four through six are nominated to the program by parents, teachers and other interested persons in the community. Pupils in *academic* areas are selected upon the basis of their school records (gross screening) and a program of individual testing by the school psychologist. Pupils enter the *arts* areas after review of either performance or portfolio by a jury composed of teachers in each subject field.

The effects of this selection process were studied by comparing pupils in the program with a random sample of pupils from the general school population. A comparison of the distribution of pupils in each group was made with respect to ethnic background, sex, and socioeconomic status which indicated that the selection was *fair* (i. e., the distribution of pupils in the program was very similar to those in the general population, according to a chi-square test). Further, the program casts a "wide net" in forming the pool of candidates: an estimated twenty-five percent (25%) of all pupils were considered for the program. Finally, a comparison of test scores among these groups found that academic achievement was not the sole basis for selection—and that creativity played an important role in the process.

Thus, the data support the essential "fairness" and sensitivity of the program criteria.

Effect on Academic Achievement

The data show that pupils met the performance standards which had been set in conjunction with the state education agency for all three years of program operation and that the gains in achievement by pupils in the program generally

3. EVALUATING

Effect on Social Relations

During all three years, concern was expressed by a number of regular teachers and a few parents about the social consequences of providing differentiated education for the gifted: the problems of "elitism" on the part of pupils in the program and of reactivity on the part of those not in the program.

The program has been attentive to these problems through a careful monitoring of the social relations of pupils in the evaluation data.

The results are quite unequivocal: *the program has little or no effect on the social relations of pupils:*

- Pupils are, for the most part, very close to the statistical norms set for the measures of social relations—with the sole exception that they *begin and end* the program with an unusually high degree of independence.

- With the exception of the independence factor, the social relations scores of pupils in the Gifted and Talented Program are virtually indistinguishable from those of pupils who were sampled randomly from the general school population.

The evidence indicates that the program has little or no effect on social relations. In particular, the evidence indicates that the program has not contributed to any social pathologies, such as "elitism."

Effect on Self-Concept

The program has monitored carefully the self-concept of pupils to detect adverse changes, such as "stigmatism" or "over confidence." All sources of information indicate that the pupils began the program with generally normal scores, and that the program has had no significant effect on self-concept.

A "summer" effect was observed in self-concept scores: although there was little change observed *during* the school year, there was a trend toward mild increases, on the order of three points on an eighty-point scale, during the summers.

In comparison with the general population, pupils in the Gifted and Talented Program were found to have slightly higher scores on the self-concept measure. However, both groups were within the statistically normal range.

In addition, the ratings of parents and teachers agreed with the results observed in the student testing program.

Effect on Attitude Toward School and Learning

The program intends to produce a positive attitude toward school and learning, consequently eliminating problems stemming from lack of challenge in the regular classroom.

The student test data showed consistent *decline* in attitude during the school year. However, the longitudinal analysis showed a strong "bounce back" effect during the summers. The net change over the three years is in the direction of a more positive attitude toward school and learning.

surpassed those of pupils in both the general population *and* those who initially had high achievement scores but were not selected into the program. The performance of pupils in the program has improved beyond the expectations of normal maturation and development during each of the three years of the program.

The highest gains in achievement were made by multitalented pupils—those with gifts in both academic and arts areas. No meaningful differences in achievement were found with respect to socioeconomic status.

Of the three program options, the Curriculum Learning Center appears to produce the largest gains in achievement, particularly in the area of mathematics. However, all program options met or exceeded the performacne standard for achievement.

The data indicated also that there is considerable change in test scores during the *summers* (i. e., between the last measurement in one year and the first measurement in the succeeding year). This effect was not explained in terms of the existing data base and may represent the effects of maturity, consolidation of knowledge or additional learning experiences gained outside the schools.

Effect on Creativity

The data show that pupils in the program are clearly "more creative" than the general population on all four dimensions (i. e., fluency, flexibility, originality, elaboration) measured by the tests. Pupils in the program have had meaningful growth in "creativity" during their association with the program, which meets or exceeds the performance standards set in the area.

The gains in creativity vary according to the program option:

- The *Interest Activity* group scores highest on the *flexibility* subscale which is linked to the *diversity* of production of ideas.

- The *Curriculum Learning Center* group excels on the *originality* and *elaboration* subscales which are linked, respectively, to the production of novel and of well-defined ideas.

- The *Enrichment* group has its best performance on the *fluency* subscale which is linked to the *rate* of production of ideas.

These trends have persisted throughout the study; a full analysis of this phenomenon is beyond the scope of the existing data.

Multitalented pupils have higher scores on the four creativity subscales than those with gifts in one area only. However, there do not appear to be major differences in the creativity scores of academic and arts pupils. This indicates that the growth observed in the scores represents enhanced creativity rather than the manifestation of artistic skills and technqiues.

Further, the changes in creativity do *not* show any appreciable "summer" effect—indicating that growth on the measure is primarily determined by activities which occur during the school year.

3. EVALUATING

Further, in the comparison studies, pupils in the Gifted and Talented Program had more positive attitudes schooling than the general population. These findings have led to the conclusion that the declines observed during the school year may represent the temporary effects of fatigue or a general end-of-year let-down.

When the longitudinal analysis, comparison studies, parent and teacher surveys are combined, they lead to the conclusion that the program indeed has a beneficial effect in enhancing students' attitudes toward school and learning.

Other Issues

The teacher survey data indicate that the program has not had an appreciable effect in the enhancement of regular classroom activities. Teachers gave less than average ratings to the exchange of information among the program and the regular classes, and gave only average ratings to the enhancement of classroom activities.

During Year One, parents criticized the amount of information received about the program. Program management began information dissemination activities. The nature of parent comments have changed during Years Two and Three: parents have moved from a concern about the nature of the program's activities to an interest in the regular reporting of pupils' progress.

Some parents offered comments to the effect that regular classroom teachers were not supportive of the program. However, the survey of teachers established that teachers have a positive attitude toward the differentiated education of the gifted. Thus, teacher resentment of the program seems to be unlikely—although teachers do give the program the lowest ratings of all groups surveyed during the study.

Overall Summary

The bast bulk of the evidence indicates that during the program's three years of funding under Title IV-C ESEA, it has been successful in meeting its stated goals. The program has stimulated the growth of pupils in academic achievement and creativity while preserving their social relations. In addition, the program has a mildly beneficial effect on self-concept and attitude toward school and learning.

FOCUS...

"Science Flies on Wings of Measurement"

Gallagher Speaks on Measuring Devices for Future Programs for Gifted

Without adequate measuring instruments, the broad definition of giftedness—intellectual, specific academic, creativity, leadership, visual and performing arts, psychomotor—is only a noble gesture, says James Gallagher, Director of Frank Porter Graham Child Development Center, University of North Carolina.

"We need more sophisticated theory and better instruments before such a definition is operational," he told the Educational Testing Service Conference on Measurement and Educational Policy, late last year. "Science flies on the wings of its measuring instruments."

"We now appear to be caught in a seam of history," he continues. "We have emerged from six decades of a serious attempt to measure individual characteristics in order to understand and predict that individual's future behavior and performance. This has worked reasonably well in the area of achievement and cognitive development. It has worked less well in areas such as creativity or leadership."

Another special problem Gallagher points out is the assessment of abilities of gifted and talented minorities who are raised in different cultures from those used in standard IQ tests. He lists three general approaches to this problem: (1) statistical adjustment, such as J. Mercer's System of Multicultural Puralistic Assessments; (2) assessment of characteristics particularly stressed in the cultural subgroups, such as tests developed by Ernest Bernal, Mary Meeker, and Paul Torrance; and (3) a combination of tests, rating scales, and peer and adult nominations, such as Alexinia Baldwin's identification matrix.

On the subject of measuring creativity, Gallagher mentions past interest and theoretical work on this subject. "This movement created a blizzard of measuring instruments of dubious validity and reliability." he says. "Such simple instruments, of course, did not measure *creativity*, which is a complex process that cannot be viewed apart from the subject and the environment. such tests did seem to measure some characteristics of intellectual fluency and flexibility, which may be more cognitive style than a separate intellectual operation. The tests miss the essence of the complex process of creativity, as noted in the study of the creative person by Frank Barron."

Gallagher speaks of the "brief but exciting marriage between scholars and educators" in the early 1960s in mathematics, physical and social sciences. "These programs emphasized the basic structure of the discipline," he explains, "the importance of having the student behave as the physicist or historian, or whatever, and the introduction of complex ideas as early as possible in the school program. These are all goals that fit the needs of gifted children very well."

A few excerpts from J. Bronowski's *Ascent of Man*, a television series produced by the BBC, serve as Gallagher's example of major ideas that the gifted and talented child can grasp from preadolescence onward:

War, organized war, is not a human instinct. It is a highly planned and cooperative theft. And that form of theft began ten thousand years ago when the harvesters of wheat accumulated a surplus and the nomads rose out of the desert to rob them of what they themselves could not provide.

The different cultures have used fire for the same purposes: to keep warm, to drive off predators, and clear woodland, and to make simple transformations of everyday life, to cook, to dry and harden wood, to heat and split stones. But, of course, the great transformation that helped us make our civilization goes deeper; it is the use of fire to disclose a wholly new class of materials, the metals.

From the *Bulletin of the National/State Leadership Training Institute for the Gifted and Talented*, February/March 1979, Barbara Johnson, Editor.

THE FERRELL GIFTED PROGRAM EVALUATION INSTRUMENT FOR TEACHERS AND EVALUATION OF INSTRUCTIONAL PROGRAMS FOR GIFTED AND TALENTED CHILDREN

John Ferrell, Director of the Area Service Center for Educators of Gifted Children, John A. Logan College, Carterville, Illinois, has provided two evaluative devices which reflect a growing concern for realistic evaluations of programs for the gifted and talented. In the first, The Ferrell Gifted Program Evaluation Instrument for Teachers, the author has developed a form for teachers for the purpose of gathering information based on the assumption that a gifted program involves qualitative changes in student thinking, as well as quantitative content changes. The major divisions of the instrument are:

1. Identification Procedures

2. Needs Assessment Procedures

3. Instructional Procedures

4. Administrative Aspects

5. Personal Teacher Judgments

The second, Evaluation of Instructional Programs for Gifted and Talented Children, was produced from a week long meeting of all Area Service Center (ASC) staff members. The evaluation data were gathered from many sources, including ASC staff members and developments by specific Illinois schools. The evaluation is based upon two identified local education association needs:

1. "A concern for the total program for gifted education offered within the local district." The models in this section, referred to as Formative Evaluation, assess the ongoing progress through personal reactions and insights of field evaluators, teachers, students, and parents.

2. "The extent to which the local program is meeting the assessed needs of the individual gifted student within the program." The models included in this section, referred to as Summative Evaluation, assess end products by focusing on initial identification procedures, program objectives, and teacher opinions.

Reprinted form *Sample Instruments for the Evaluation of Programs for the Gifted and Talented,* Compiled and Edited by Members of the TAG Evaluation Committee, Joseph S. Renzulli, Chairman, by The Association for the Gifted, A Division of The Council for Exceptional Children. Copyright 1979 by The Council for Exceptional Children, 1920 Association Drive, Reston, Virginia 22091.

THE FERRELL GIFTED PROGRAM EVALUATION INSTRUMENT FOR TEACHERS

_____   _____   _____
  Date   Grade Level   Teacher's Name

This instrument was designed to help you document your instructional attempts for gifted children. It is important that you give specific responses when possible.

I. <u>Identification Procedures</u>

   A. Instruments or procedures used (If check lists are used, file a copy with this evaluation.)
      1.

      2.

      3.

      4.

   B. Categories of gifted children involved in your program.

   C. Number of children identified. _____

      Number of children in total population. _____

   D. What changes or improvements in the identification process do you intend to make.

   E. When was the identification completed?

II. <u>Needs Assessment Procedures</u>

   A. The starting point
      1. Students were selected for an existing program. _____
      2. Students were selected and then a program was designed. _____

   B. Describe how you determined the needs of your gifted students.
      1. Interview _____
      2. Check list — teacher _____, student _____, parent _____
      3. Other

3. EVALUATING

    4. Comments on the needs process

  C. How much time did you take for the needs assessment?

  D. What changes or improvements in the needs assessment process do you plan to make?

III. <u>Instructional Procedures</u>

  A. Gifted learning objectives

    1. What objectives did you establish for your gifted program that differ from your general education objectives?

    2. Who was involved in the production of these objectives?

      a. teachers only
      b. teachers and students
      c. student only
      d. other

    3. What changes or improvement do you plan to make in your objectives?

    4. If you established a set of written objectives for your program attach them to the evaluation.

  B. Student-teacher role in the classroom

    1. How does the classroom role of your gifted students differ from the classroom role of your general education students?

    2. How does your role as a teacher differ when working with the gifted students when compared to the way you teach general education students?

  C. Description of your instructional procedure

    1. Describe your instructional procedures for your gifted program.

    2. Describe as best you can the relevant differences between your instructional procedures for the gifted students and for your general education students.

  D. Evaluation of gifted students

    1. Describe how you evaluate your gifted students.

2. Describe the differences if any of your evaluation procedure for gifted students and for general education students.

3. What kinds of grades do you use (A, E - pass, fail etc.)

   a. for gifted students _____

   b. for general education students _____

E. What changes or improvements in the instruction procedures do you plan to make?

F. If appropriate, include examples of the products of your gifted students.

IV. Administrative aspects of your gifted program

   A. Number of days per week your gifted students meet. _____

   B. In what ways are your gifted students grouped?

   C. What changes have been made in meeting times, locations, materials, or equipment for your gifted programs when compared to the general education program?

V. Your judgements on your gifted program

   A. How successful were your students in working toward the objectives?

   B. What unanticipated objectives did your students reach?

   C. In what ways was the gifted program

      1. suitable for your gifted students.

      2. not suitable for your gifted students.

   D. Other judgements you have about this year's gifted program.

3. EVALUATING

EVALUATION OF INSTRUCTIONAL PROGRAMS FOR GIFTED AND TALENTED CHILDREN

Evaluation is a measurement of effectiveness – It's an assessment of our performance.
– Anonymous

Since LEA districts with funded gifted programs are not provided with evaluation specialists and are not as heavily funded for gifted education as for other programs, it would be unrealistic to expect bulky, comprehensive evaluative efforts.

Somewhere between the two attitudinal extremes of "we must have complete, comprehensive evaluation"; and "if we can't do a big job of evaluation, we won't do it at all" can be the honest, straightforward effort to find what is and is not effective in local programs.

Glowing gains are welcome, but steady, purposeful evaluative improvement of programming is essential.

Though exemplary programs are an ultimate goal, a dedicated desire for forward progressive momentum towards the ultimate goal is of prime importance!

Evaluation – General Overview

There is a need for the LEA to address itself to two separate, distinct evaluations:

1. The total program for gifted education offered within the local district.

2. The extent to which the local program is meeting the assessed needs of the individual gifted student within that program.

The evaluation should assume two forms:

1. Formative evaluation designed to highlight the worth of the ongoing progress of the program during the school year.

2. Summative evaluation designed to highlight the state of the end product of the year's programming.

The above evaluations, if shared, would be of benefit to three agencies involved in Illinois' gifted programming: the LEA, the ASC, and the State gifted office.

The local education district would use its evaluation as a check in assessing:

1. Whether the funded proposal objectives were being met or had been accomplished.

2. Whether the existing program(s) reflected the needs of specific gifted students within the LEA.

3. Whether the current program provided a firm base for the following year's program proposal.

4. Whether an expanded version of the present program, an alternative to the present program, or a new direction in programming for the following year needed clarification and articulation.

5. Whether unintended outcomes were present, readily discernable, and able to be capitalized upon in further enhancing the local program.

To the Area Service Centers a systematic evaluation by LEA's would be of assistance in:

1. Checking the efficacy and efficiency of the rules and regulations for establishing viable programs, and other such publications intended to shape LEA gifted programming.

2. Providing a means of obtaining a realistic perspective of the broad scope and sequence of the State of Illinois provision for gifted students.

A relatively efficient delivery system for assistance by ASC's to LEA's in the writing and use of effective, succinct, formative and summative evaluation would include:

1. An early fall inservice for reimbursement directors outlining steps in the production of a model in existence for each of the two above types of evaluative procedures.

2. A method by which the reimbursement directors could cause the LEA personnel involved to be cognizant of and efficient with use of such evaluations, and

3. Guidance by ASC's as requested by LEA's.

Some areas of concern inherent in the above would include:

1. The time and personnel resources of LEA's to conduct evaluation. For example, LEA personnel involved in gifted programming are generally well involved in general education, filling each day with active planning. Any evaluation would of necessity need to be concise and readily transferable to a final usable form.

2. A commitment by the LEA staff to the use of evaluation not as "something to be done," but as a vehicle for shaping and improving gifted programming. In other words, LEA personnel must be objectively not subjectively involved with the findings contained within the evaluation, and be able, as a team, to build constructively on the program's strengths as revealed by the evaluation and reform or revamp parts of the program that contain elements of futility or failure even though the evaluation indicates the setting aside of "pet projects," "favorite techniques," etc. if those projects/techniques prove unproductive.

3. Fitting a LEA evaluative timetable into the state timetable and dates for proposals.

4. A recognition by the LEA that facets of gifted programming such as identification, needs assessment, programs, and evaluation procedures each feed into and support one another.

3. EVALUATING

The program and the student within the program will not feel success unless the above elements are treated not as separate entities but one continuously evolving, circular movement. Each year's cycle fulfilling its purpose prepares for the following year - with NO END POINT. Each so-called end point turns into a beginning position for a new thrust.

5. A realization by the LEA's that elaborate, involved impressive evaluation is not necessary. Simple, straight-forward, easily-interpretable data are much to be preferred. Less time and energy expended on involved, contrived, evaluation means greater facility and delight in implementing and sustaining enthused personnel and students in gifted programs.

Formative Evaluation

In the formative evaluation of the total LEA program, the essential ingredient is a precise representation of the areas of strengths and concerns as reflected in an assessment of "what is going on" in the day-to-day program procedure.

Essentially then, formative evaluation is on-going, and used for express purposes at stated intervals giving the program direction and assessment during the year.

Examples of formative evaluation models follow.

In Model A, an evaluation is conducted by a LEA reimbursement director or other designated person.

Models B, C, D, E, and F are for teachers, students, and parents involved with the program. Value can be seen both from a present vantage point, as well as providing future projection.

It can be stated at this point that the models presented are interchangeable and applicable to uses as formative or summative evaluation for both general program and individual student assessment of strengths and concerns. The models have been placed in what were perceived as each model's optimum use.

Summative Evaluation

In the summative evaluation of the total LEA program, the essential ingredient is a precise representation of the areas of strengths and concerns as reflected in an overview of the year's total program. The evaluation of the program and the teacher's performance within the program is included in the area of self-assessment.

Summative evaluation is inextricably bound into the objectives and intent of the proposal. Summative evaluation, in essence, assures that the needs assessment conducted, identification procedures utilized, specific program techniques selected, and implementation of the above have been, in fact, accomplished as stated in the proposal objectives.

This cannot be stressed too firmly! Good objectives, good follow-through, generally produce good programs for gifted students.

Examples of summative evaluation models are also attached.

Evaluation Inservice for LEA's Use

It is felt that an early fall evaluation workshop would be of paramount benefit to reimbursement directors of local LEA's. The experience has been that too often school personnel, even though they know evaluation is due at the end of the year, tend to let evaluation slip off until the last few days. An early fall workshop would allow LEA's to think of and plan for evaluation at the beginning of the year's program. Some concrete formative and summative models could then be initiated into and provided for early enough to reflect beneficial program assessment. The inservice personnel conceivably would include ASC staff, SEA staff members, and the reimbursement director or a representative from each LEA in a particular ASC's sphere of influence.

The purpose of the inservice would be:

1. To define and emphasize the power which formative and summative evaluation can have in delineating a program's objectives and the successful meeting of those objectives.

2. To discuss design formative and summative evaluation models.

3. To explore various evaluation models.

4. To present suggested formats for the reimbursement director to relay the information to his/her LEA gifted program personnel.

Concluding Statement

The preceding pages are clearly idealized conceptions, but from idealized conceptions come upward striving realities! If each succeeding year brings more LEA districts into a commitment to the extreme importance of and value in purposeful formative and summative evaluation, the Illinois Plan for Gifted Education will be well served.

I. MODEL A

Evaluation Team: Chicago   Staff Form - REV. 7/73

_____(Team Reporter)

_____   Date of Visitation _____

_____

GIFTED PROGRAM - FIELD EVALUATION

Program Title _____ Program Number _____

Program Site _____ Dist. _____ Area _____

Contact _____ Phone _____

3. EVALUATING

Teacher _____

Starting Date of Program _____ No. of Students by Grade _____

	PROGRAM DESCRIPTION	OK	PROBLEM	DID NOT OBSERVE
1.	Are the depth and focus of activities in the program generally such that they meet the special needs of gifted children?			
2.	Are children placed out of certain aspects of the regular program as a consequence of gifted program participation?			
3.	Are the program's activities compatible with the program's objectives?			
	PROGRAM IDENTIFICATION			
4.	Do the identification procedures correspond to those stated in the current proposal?			
5.	Is student identification based primarily on objective data?			
6.	Does the number of students in the program approximate the number of students stated in the current proposal?			
7.	Are the students involved in the program at least 150 minutes per week?			
8.	Does the program allow for an amount of student participation in setting objectives, planning activities, and evaluation progress?			
9.	Is the interaction between teacher and students generally appropriate to the program objectives?			
10.	Does student involvement in the program activities seem generally to be high?			
11.	Are special counseling and/or guidance provisions made available to all students in the gifted program?			
	PROGRAM EVALUATION			
12.	Is a systematic plan of evaluation being used to assess the program?			
13.	Does the evaluation include measuring program objectives with respect to pupil growth?			

14. Does the evaluation provide necessary information to assess the effectiveness of the program?			

PROGRAM ADMINISTRATION

15. Were the teachers in the program involved in developing the current proposal?			
16. Do the teachers in the program have copies of the current proposal?			
17. Are materials and services being purchased necessary to the activities which comprise the program?			
18. Do the teachers in the program have access to all materials purchased specifically for the program?			
19. Are program funds being utilized mainly for program development rather than program maintenance?			
20. Is budget record kept of current balance?			
21. Are teachers aware of balance of funds allocated and deadlines for submission of requisitions?			
22. Do school clerks have special ordering instructions for materials and services for gifted programs?			

PROGRAM SERVICES

23. Are materials and services ordered for the program received within a reasonable length of time?			
24. Are you receiving the services and consultative help necessary to assist you in implementing your program?			

25. Indicate in which of the following areas you would like to receive additional assistance from the gifted program staff, such as:

      _____ Identification of gifted children

      _____ Developing program objectives in behavioral terms

      _____ Program evaluation

      _____ Teaching strategies

Other: _____

Summary: _____

3. EVALUATING

MODEL B

This model represents the formative evaluation involving personnel from one school building. Two easily filled-out forms from that program are included.

C. Henry Bloom Elementary School
Rockford, Illinois

Evaluation Procedures for Program

    I. Teaching Teacher Evaluates
        A. Lesson (Form 1-A)
           Was behavioral goal met?

        B. Children
           1. Performance (daily) (Form 1-B)
           2. Makes comment on child's self-evaluation.

        C. Short narrative note to parents at end of teaching period.

    II. Coordinators Evaluation Responsibility
        A. Look over records of children and lesson plans monthly.

        B. Teaching teachers and coordinators in each area (Math and Language Arts) meet once monthly to assess over-all continuity and progress of Directed Study Program within their area.

    III. Director

        Following each monthly meeting (See II-B above) coordinators meet with director to assess over-all continuity and progress of entire Directed Study Program.

    IV. Faculty

        Meet once monthly at noon to exchange ideas and discuss pupil's reactions (teaching teachers plus interested faculty members).

FORM 1-A

EVALUATION OF LESSON   To be filled in by teacher.

LESSON TITLE	BEHAVIORAL OBJECTIVE	SUCCESSFULLY MET OBJECTIVE	PROBLEM AREAS

FORM 1-B

CHILDREN'S PERFORMANCE (AGE____)
  To be filled in by a
  teacher and the student.

_____
STUDENT'S NAME
_____
SUBJECT

Student Evaluation

1 – I understood it and did it well.

2 – I understood it and did it poorly.

3 – I didn't understand it.

Teacher Evaluation

1 – He understood it and did it well.

2 – He understood it and did it poorly.

3 – He didn't understand it.

LESSON	STUDENT EVALUATION	TEACHER EVALUATION	COMMENTS

MODEL C

This model presents two types of evaluation that if used would indicate trends of strength or concern that the individual student expresses. Taken over a period of several months formative evaluation as to the worth of emphasis or area of study could be ascertained.

PERSONAL REACTIONS AND INSIGHTS

Block No. _____   Exercise Name and No. _____

1. What were your feelings while doing this exercise?
   (e.g., uneasy, awkward, confused, pleasurable, etc.)

2. What new thoughts or insights about your problem-solving style were you made aware of as a result of this exercise?
   (Such as your: initial approach, follow-through, general work style, relations with others, etc.)

3. How does this experience relate to the work problems you brought to this program?

Source Unknown

3. EVALUATING

MODEL D

INDEPENDENT STUDY EVALUATION

How useful was this unit to you?

Do you feel you accomplished (reached) your goals?

Did the teacher give you enough help, materials, guidance?

Evaluate your use of time.

Would you choose independent study again? Why or why not?

Write a paragraph on what you learned in this unit.

Source Unknown

MODEL E

STUDENT QUESTIONNAIRE

To children participating in the gifted program:

Child's Name _____

School _____

Gifted Program Enrolled In _____

1. What is the name of the special program you are in? _____

12. Ferrell

2. How were you chosen for this program? (See the next page)
   _____

3. How often does this class meet?
   _____ Everyday
   _____ Several times a week
   _____ Once in a while

4. What do you do in this class that is different from your other classes? _____
   _____

5. Tell what you especially like about this class? _____
   _____

6. What would you change about this class if you could? _____
   _____

7. What things do you do in this class that you would like to do in your other classes during the day? _____
   _____

8. What things do you do in your other classes that you wish you could do in this class? _____
   _____

9. Would you like this class to be continued next year?
   Yes _____   No _____
   Why? _____
   Why not? _____
   _____

10. How do you think you were chosen for this program?

    _____ Teacher invited me.

    _____ I said I was interested in it.

    _____ I can work well independently.

    _____ I can read well.

    _____ I'm one of the smartest people in my class.

    _____ My name was drawn out of a hat.

    _____ My parents wanted me to participate.

    _____ I was in it last year.

    _____ My whole class participates.

    _____ I don't know.

133

3. EVALUATING

MODEL F

PARENT QUESTIONNAIRE

Parent's Name _____

Name of Child _____

Grade of Child _____ School _____

1. How did you learn your child was in a gifted program?
   _____ Principal
   _____ Teacher
   _____ Child
   _____ Letter sent home
   _____ This questionnaire
   _____ Notified of gifted parents' meeting
   _____ Not informed

2. Did you know previous to selection for this program that your child was gifted?
   _____ Yes
   _____ No

3. Does your child talk to you about the program in which he is participating?
   _____ Yes
   _____ No

4. How do you perceive your child is responding to this program?
   _____ Is enthusiastic
   _____ Accepts without enthusiasm
   _____ Comments favorably
   _____ Comments unfavorably

5. Do you favor the continuation of this program?
   _____ Yes
   _____ No
   _____ Don't care
   _____ No response

6. Do you favor the establishment of additional gifted opportunities for your child?
   _____ Yes
   _____ No
   _____ Don't care
   _____ No response

YOUR COMMENTS: _____
_____

II. MODEL A

SUMMATIVE EVALUATION - DESCRIPTIVE MODEL

Program in Operation Since: 19__ - __

Contact Person:

Grade Level:

Number of Students:

Number of Teachers:

Program Description:

Identification Criteria:

Program Objectives:

Plan for Evaluation:

Materials Acquired During 19 __ - __:

Comments:

MODEL B

SUMMATIVE EVALUATION FORM

EVALUATION OF YOUR GIFTED PROGRAM - 19__ - 19__

OBJECTIVES OF PROGRAM	MEASURING INSTRUMENTS	EVALUATION RESULTS
(List the main objectives as stated in your proposal.)	(Indicate the measuring instrument(s) or procedure(s) by which you evaluated each of the corresponding objectives. If teacher made tests were used, please attach sample copies.)	(Summarize the date indicating the degree to which each of the corresponding objectives was accomplished.)

3. EVALUATING

MODEL C

TEACHER QUESTIONNAIRE

PLEASE HAVE ONLY THOSE TEACHERS INVOLVED IN A GIFTED PROGRAM FILL OUT THIS QUESTIONNAIRE.

SCHOOL _____

1. With what program are you involved? _____

2. Does the program operate
   _____ regularly in a classroom situation.
   _____ independent basis
   _____ irregularly
   _____ other, specify _____

3. List names and times of workshops you have attended that pertain to this program.
   _____
   _____
   _____

4. How were children selected for the program?
   _____ Teacher nomination
   _____ Academic achievement
   _____ IQ scores
   _____ Other

5. How do you think children should be selected?
   _____ Teacher nomination
   _____ Academic achievement
   _____ IQ scores
   _____ Other

6. List materials used in the program. _____
   _____
   _____

7. How were these materials acquired?
   _____ Regular budget
   _____ Gifted program
   _____ PTA
   _____ Other
   _____ Don't know

8. List materials or other aids you need to better this program.
   _____

9. Please identify what you perceive to be the strongest aspect of this program. _____

10. What do you perceive to be its chief weakness? _____
    _____

11. Do you think this program should be extended to other classrooms in your building?
    _____ Yes
    _____ No

12. List changes you would make in this program if you could. _____
    _____

13. Do you feel this program should be continued next year?
    _____ Yes
    _____ No

    If no, please state your reasons. _____
    _____
    _____

Photo: Office of Human Resources, Department of Health, Education and Welfare

BUILDING PROFESSIONAL AND PUBLIC SUPPORT FOR THE GIFTED

The dimensions of the tasks which are part of building professional and public support for the gifted are awesome in scope. Educational professionals number some two and a quarter million, and the American public number more than 200 million. Yet the beginning which has been made in this decade to increase professional awareness and to awaken public consciousness is impressive, especially in view of the modest resources devoted to these tasks.

In the next decade, perhaps many who are aware, and who clearly see society's stake in the full development of talents and problem-solving abilities, will grasp the tools that are available in public reactions, in access to the media, and in relation to corporations, labor unions and the private sector. If these and other tools are used effectively and imaginatively, we may see in the next decade an accelerated rate of progress in building support for growth in services to America's gifted-talented-creative children and youth.

The final section gives direction for the future of gifted programs, and possible areas to go to for support. It is not just parents that are instrumental in helping the school system create a viable program, but the "establishment" and media can and will give assistance. It is a group project to improve the current status of the gifted in today's educational systems.

The Emerging National and State Concern

David M. Jackson

I wish to acknowledge the assistance of Dr. Bruce O. Boston in the preparation of this paper.

A slow but steady development has characterized the federal concern for the gifted and talented since the late 1960s. This effort has coalesced with the diffused efforts of several pioneering states to produce what can now be viewed as an initial effort of truly national dimensions. While the most recent attention on the part of federal and state governments is best viewed as continuous with earlier attempts, current federal activity springs most directly from the Education Amendments of 1969, and specifically from an amendment offered by Congressman John Erlenborn of Illinois.

Erlenborn had been impressed with the efforts made on behalf of the gifted and talented by the Illinois Department of Public Instruction, particularly by its efforts to provide a comprehensive identification program, by the variety of programs offered, and by the quality of in-service education for teachers available through the state's network of resource centers. Moreover, he had been convinced of the critical needs of gifted and talented children for differentiated educational experiences. His amendment voiced a congressional intent that gifted and talented children should benefit from federal legislation, particularly from Titles III and V of the Elementary and Secondary Education Act, as well as from the teacher education provisions of the Higher Education Act of 1965.

Most significantly, however, the amendment directed the U.S. Commissioner of Education to launch a study that was to have four basic objectives: (a) to discover the extent to which special education provisions were necessary to meet the needs of gifted and talented children, (b) to discover whether any existing federal programs were currently meeting some of those needs, (c) to evaluate how programs of federal educational assistance could become more effective in meeting these needs, and (d) to recommend what new programs were needed to meet them.

The congressional mandate was fulfilled on October 6, 1971, when Commissioner Sidney P. Marland submitted to the Congress a document that can be viewed as the embryo of recent developments in gifted child education.[1] Its recommendations and consequences have been more far-reaching than one might ordinarily expect from yet another report from the U.S. Office of Education. The Marland report offered recommendations for eleven actions to be taken under then existing legislative authority (P.L. 91-230, Sec. 806). The recommendations called for (a) a planning report on implementing a federal role in educating the gifted and talented; (b) the establishment of a staff within USOE for gifted education; (c) a national survey of programs to find costs, evaluation procedures, and model programs and to develop a clearinghouse on gifted/talented education; (d) the utilization of Title V of the Elementary and Secondary Education Act to strengthen capabilities for gifted/talented education; (e) two national summer leadership training institutes to upgrade supervisory personnel in state education agencies; (f) program and research support for institutions interested in gifted children in minority groups; (g) program ac-

---

1. Sidney P. Marland, Jr., *Education of the Gifted and Talented*, vol. 1, Report to the Congress of the United States by the U.S. Commissioner of Education (Washington, D.C.: U.S. Government Printing Office, 1972).

From *The Gifted and the Talented: Their Education and Development*, ©1979 by the National Society for the Study of Education, reprinted with permission.

13. Concern

tivities specific to career education for the gifted and talented; (h) special attention in one experimental school to project the relation between gifted and talented education and comprehensive school reform; (i) cooperation with Title III programs; (j) one staff member for each of the ten regional Offices of Education to be assigned to gifted and talented education; and (k) the study of Office of Education programs relating to higher education to optimize their potential for the gifted and talented.

The record of the Office of Education in fully or partially implementing most of these recommendations is impressive, especially in view of the normal organizational and policy fluctuations within the agency that caused some programs to disappear, the reassignment of personnel, and the reevaluation of policy goals.

Beyond its recommendations, Commissioner Marland's report provided some notable "firsts" for a serious federal involvement in the education of the gifted and talented. Specifically, the following steps were taken for the first time:

1. Gifted and talented children were attended to as a specific population with special educational needs. Thus a crippling assumption, that these children could somehow "make it on their own," was officially undercut. Previous efforts benefitting gifted and talented children had entered the school house via the back door, through programs under the National Defense Education Act, the National Science Foundation, and others. Now gifted and talented children were seen as worthy of assistance in their own right—a significant step forward.

2. A definition of "gifted and talented" was attempted for purposes of identifying this population. Significantly, the definition was a broad one and not circumscribed by a view of giftedness that focused on cognitive superstars. The new definition sought to encompass not only generalized intellectual ability, but also specific academic aptitude, original and creative abilities, leadership abilities, talent in the visual and performing arts, and psychomotor abilities.

3. Staff attention within USOE was to be directed toward improving the educational lot of gifted and talented children.

4. Elements of a national strategy for the education of the gifted and talented began to take shape.

The Role of the Office of Education: From Advocacy to Categorical Funding

The rudiments of what eventually became the Office of Gifted and Talented (OGT) in the U.S. Office of Education were already present in the staff that gathered the material, conducted the regional hearings, and prepared the final draft of the Marland report. The recommendation that such an office be established was very quickly implemented.

The Office of the Gifted and Talented faced the immediate problem of how to foster a truly national effort without program funds. By dint of circumstance, the new office was in a position where it could not attempt to develop, or even coordinate, a national program nor promulgate a national policy for educating the gifted. In the absence of programmatic clout, a pluralistic tack was

4. SUPPORT

taken in which OGT tried to stimulate activity at several levels simultaneously. The strategy was one of identifying when and where interesting and productive things were happening, to call attention to them, to persuade, to advocate, and to bear witness. This stance of persuasive advocacy was manifested in different but related strands of activity.

First, in order best to fulfill the advocacy role for the gifted and talented, OGT had to know what was in fact happening. This investigative task had already been accomplished in some measure by the needs assessment survey completed for the Marland report. The survey results were not encouraging, but they did provide OGT with an agenda for advocacy. Among the findings were the following:

1. Differential educational provisions for the gifted and talented had an extremely low priority in the competition for the federal, state, and local educational dollar. Programmatic concern was found to be "miniscule."

2. Minority and culturally different gifted and talented children were scarcely being reached.

3. While twenty-one states made some legislative or regulatory provisions for these children, more often than not such provisions represented mere intent. Only ten states had full-time personnel in their state education agencies concerned with gifted child education. There was a gap between what should be and what actually was.

4. Gifted and talented children, contrary to myth, were *not* succeeding on their own. In fact, the reverse was true. Research had convincingly demonstrated that they required specialized educational programs to live up to their potential.

5. Identification of the gifted and talented suffered woefully from lack of adequate testing procedures, inadequate funds, and in some cases from apathy and downright hostility to their educational needs on the part of teachers and administrators.

6. When differentiated programs for the gifted and talented were implemented, the effects were measurable.

7. Perhaps most disturbing of all, from the point of view of OGT, was the finding that while people tended to look to the federal government for help for the gifted and talented, the federal role in the delivery of services to these children was for all practical purposes nonexistent.

Clearly the job to be done was enormous and the resources for doing it meagre. But the Marland report did provide the context for significant opportunity. It scarcely mattered where one began since so little was being done. The needs assessment survey provided a justification for a pluralistic approach to problems; the lack of federal funds precluded throwing money at the situation and pointed to a strategy of sustained advocacy.

Second, while casting about for a way to make a demonstrable impact on the gifted scene nationally, OGT resorted to the time-honored American approach of federalism. A leadership training effort at the state level was mounted in order to (a) shore up already existing support among those in the field who had long been committed to gifted child education, (b) reach key educators, opinion shapers, and legislators, and to begin to develop the potential parent constituency, and (c) provide concrete skills in planning and program building at the state level. Because no specifically earmarked funds were available for leadership training in the gifted and talented area, OGT turned to the funding possibilities contained in the Education Professions Development Act. This initiative is discussed below.

Third, in pursuit of more effective advocacy for the gifted, and in order to focus national attention on the problems brought to light by the needs assessment, a number of other initiatives were taken. Official federal and state inattention could be remediated in part by calling on private foundations, business, industry, and community groups to invest in programming and support for the gifted and talented.[2] An extensive national travel and speaking schedule, numerous network and local TV and radio appearances, and a lengthening series of articles in popular and professional journals, newspapers, and magazines were undertaken. Greater visibility for the gifted and talented was gained through programs like Exploration Scholarships, a national symposium for gifted high school students, jointly sponsored with the American Association for Gifted Children. OGT also took over administrative responsibility for the Presidential Scholars Program initiated by President Lyndon B. Johnson in 1964. Local and state education agencies were alerted to the funding possibilities for programs for gifted students that could be developed by applying the techniques of creative grantsmanship to various Titles (for example, Titles I, II, V, IX) of the Elementary and Secondary Education Act and its amendments. Vocational and career education funds were also tapped for the gifted and talented. Other sources within the federal education establishment were also sought out, such as the National Endowment for the Arts and the Humanities, the National Science Foundation, and others. Little by little the needs of gifted children and existing resources were brought together. Applications were made for funds, programs were initiated, interest was stimulated, and results were generated.

In 1975 a breakthrough occurred. Under the provisions of the Special Projects Act of P.L. 93-380, Section 404, categorical funds were for the first time made available for the education of the gifted and talented. The hopes of OGT and the gifted education community had come to fruition. Appropriations for gifted child education were set at $2.56 million, to be apportioned as shown in table 1.

Three points may be made about these funds and the uses to which they were put. First, the categorical funding was a cause for both rejoicing and dismay: rejoicing because the gifted and talented children had emerged from the welter of 50 million American school children as worthy of attention in their own right, and

2. Jane Case Williams, *The Gifted and Talented: A Role for the Private Sector* (Washington, D.C.: U.S. Office of Education, 1972).

4. SUPPORT

TABLE 1

APPROPRIATIONS FOR GIFTED CHILD EDUCATION FOR 1976 IN THE SPECIAL PROJECTS ACT OF P.L. 93-380, SECTION 404

PURPOSE	NUMBER OF GRANTS	APPROPRIATION (IN DOLLARS)
Information services	1	$ 125,000
Grants to state education agencies	26	1,500,000
Local projects grants	18	260,000
Graduate training for leadership personnel	1	190,000
Inservice training and technical assistance	1	165,000
Internships to train leaders	1	70,000
Research, research training, surveys, dissemination of findings	0	0
Model projects for special categories: early childhood, community-based mentor programs, visual and performing arts, exceptionally disadvantaged, creativity, sparsely populated areas	6*	260,000

* One grant made in each of the special categories.

dismay because the amount appropriated was so disproportionate to the need.[3] Nonetheless, it was a beginning.

Second, the uses to which the funds were put indicate two wagers that are mutually reinforcing. One took seriously the success of the strategy adopted by the National/State Leadership Training Institute on the Gifted and Talented as well as a significant finding of the Marland report that a commitment to gifted and talented education on the part of professionals at the state level was the most determinative factor in the development of strong programming. This had certainly been the experience of those states that were already leaders in the field long before federal interest was manifested. Therefore, fully half of the available funds were channeled into state education agencies for professional staff development.

The other wager was a commitment to the "ripple effect" that could be generated from local levels outward and upward. Thus, a total of $520,000 was awarded to proposals for local projects and model programs that had a built-in replicability factor. The overall effect of concentrating funds in state capitals and in selected geographical and project areas would be to create wave and splash at the same time—a combination of sustained activity and raised visibility for experimental approaches in targeted program areas.

Finally, a look at the history of the OGT reveals that categorical funding for gifted and talented education at the federal level is as much a consequence of emerging concern at state and local levels as it has been a stimulus to that concern. In other words, the traditional federal function of pump priming has now met the

---

3. Congress had originally authorized $12.25 million for the gifted and talented, but had later accepted the administration's figure of $2.56 million. The larger figure had been arrived at through prolonged consultation with leaders in the field and had been considered a bare minimum for effective action nationwide.

13. Concern

water table of local concerns and activities that have been very quietly percolating beneath the surface for many years. To alter the metaphor, this federal/local encounter over the needs of our nation's gifted and talented students is fast approaching a critical mass, indicating that the encounter now has the definite potential for breaking out of the cyclicism which has plagued that concern over the last two generations and for becoming a continuing priority over the long term.

The major lacuna of the federal effort has been the lack of funding for research. Federal support in this area has been negligible, and such activity as has occurred has resulted from the individual interests of leading educators in the field who have managed to capture foundation, departmental, or private funds to sponsor research in which they have personally been interested. This state of affairs is likely to continue for the foreseeable future, casting a baleful influence over the entire effort.

A further cause for concern is the fact that categorical funding for gifted and talented education has emerged in the context of "Special Projects," on a par with and tied to metric education, educational programs related to women's rights, and the like. The congressional intent regarding all these programs is that they be phased out once the need for them is mitigated. Federal appropriations were continued for the gifted and talented until 1978 as a kind of "extra." While it is possible to believe that once American school children have been taught to "think metric" they will continue to do so without a further infusion of federal funding, and that textbook and curriculum publishers will sustain initial efforts in this area, it is unlikely that the parents of the United States will cease producing gifted and talented children for whom special educational provisions must be made. A post-1978 strategy was needed to assure continued attention to the needs of these children.

Gathering and Disseminating Information: The ERIC Clearinghouse

While not self-consciously a part of an overall federal strategy, the ERIC Clearinghouse on Handicapped and Gifted Children nevertheless functions as an active component of the federal effort. One of a number of such clearinghouses funded by the ERIC (Education Resources and Information Center) subdivision of the National Institute of Education, it has been operated by the Council for Exceptional Children since its official inception in 1972.[4] With respect to the education of gifted children, the Clearinghouse performs five main functions:

1. Gathers, evaluates, abstracts, and disseminates information on all aspects of gifted child education on an ongoing basis. Dissemination generally occurs by way of regularly published bibliographies of abstracted documents that are grouped generically (for example, "Identification of the Gifted and Talented," "Creativity," "Programming for the Gifted and Talented," "Mathematics and Science for the Gifted and Talented," and so forth);

2. Sponsors and publishes "information analysis products" in the form of published monographs, studies, manuals, and reports;

4. SUPPORT

3. Conducts a computer search service on specialized topics;
4. Sponsors workshops for potential users of the ERIC system;
5. Responds to client requests for information on all aspects of gifted child education.

The most important function performed by the Clearinghouse is its role as a repository and dissemination center for a national data base on the entire gamut of information available on the education of gifted and talented children. The growth of this data base in the last several years has been little short of phenomenal. Thousands of abstracts of documents on gifted child education are accessible in the DIALOG computer system. Since 1972, the Clearinghouse has published bibliographies and information analysis products related to the education of the gifted and talented. While the greatest volume of the activity in information gathering and dissemination relates to various handicapping conditions, it is significant to note that a full 15 percent of its client services relates to information requests on gifted child education, as much as for any other single need in special education.

Bridge to the States: The National/State Leadership Training Institute

In August of 1972, some five months after the appearance of the Marland report, the National/State Leadership Training Institute on the Gifted and Talented (LTI) was formed. It was funded primarily through a grant released under the authority of the Education Professions Development Act and administered under the fiscal aegis of the Ventura County (California) Superintendent of Schools. Perhaps more than any other actor in the field, the LTI has directed its efforts to changes at the state level, translating a federally articulated vision into planning and program activity by state and local education agencies.

The basic rationale for the LTI has always been that in order for gifted and talented students to achieve the instructional benefits that would best develop their abilities and talents, and in order for gifted child education to achieve the level of presence and recognition called for at the federal level, decision makers had to be involved at both state and local levels at the crucial points where educational policy is made.

Accordingly, the early goals of the LTI have remained in effect over the long term. These goals may be expressed as follows: (a) to formulate and initiate activities to be carried out by uniquely constituted state-level planning teams; (b) to establish a working communications network among USOE/OGT, regional offices of education, the states, and local education agencies; (c) to specify measurable objectives that can be met in identifiable time periods for implementing the national commitment to the education of the gifted and talented called for in the Marland report; (d) to develop training modules for regional offices, states, local education

---

4. The Council for Exceptional Children began data gathering and information dissemination activities some three years prior to 1972 and functioned as an ERIC Clearinghouse without being officially designated or funded as such.

agencies, schools, and parent groups, which would suggest action steps to be taken in the development of a gifted and talented program at state and local levels; (e) to provide technical assistance in adapting these training modules to the unique circumstances of the above-named groups; (f) to develop and disseminate effective publications and media resources on the problems and promise of the gifted and talented; (g) to create a clearinghouse for the gifted and talented that would identify, analyze, and disseminate information on ongoing programs for this population.

This diversity of goals was focused fundamentally on bringing about the policy changes necessary for successful programming for the gifted and talented at state and local levels. These changes have run the gamut from legislation and funding to in-service and curriculum development.

The overall LTI goal of policy change has taken shape around three strategies: (a) developing awareness of the educational needs of gifted and talented children; (b) training educational leaders in appropriate pedagogical strategies for thtse children; and, most importantly, (c) planning for the educational needs of gifted and talented children at state and local levels.

In pursuit of these goals the LTI held three national and nine regional conferences between 1973 and 1976. Five-member teams were recruited and invited for training in educational planning. Teams were comprised of one representative each from the decision-making level and one from the operating level of the state agency; one representative from local education agencies; and two or more representatives chosen from among teachers of the gifted and talented, parents, the academic community, a local school board, and the private sector. One noneducator was to be represented on each team.

In the three-year period during which the LTI conducted its national institutes, a total of forty-eight state teams received training and developed state plans. Teams from the New York City and from the Los Angeles schools were also trained. Literally hundreds of educators, administrators, parents, and other policy makers participated in the institutes.

The training sessions took as their major objective the writing of a long-range plan for the development of strategy and programming for gifted and talented children in each participating state. State-level goals, objectives, and strategies were delineated. Responsibilities were assigned, time frames established, and points of impact and leverage identified. Upon returning to their states, the teams sought to implement their state plans in a variety of ways. Team members pushed for enabling legislation and for categorical funds, and lobbied in state and local education agencies for both policy and personnel support for gifted and talented education. Sometimes the private sector was approached. Media attention was sought. Participants and teams also worked to organize programs and advocacy support.

A second objective of the LTI was the development of what amounted to a national network of persons and agencies committed to gifted and talented education. Several strategies were undertaken

4. SUPPORT

in the service of network development, including the following: (a) follow-up visits by national LTI staff members; (b) the forging of linkages at and across local, state, and federal levels; (c) the publication of a monthly newsletter providing information regarding national developments, changes in state policies, innovative practices and programs instituted in local school districts, the activities of parent groups, news of local, state, and regional conferences on the gifted and talented, and the like; (d) on-site technical assistance; (e) recruitment and deployment of consultant assistance across local, state, and regional lines; (f) the organization of topical regional conferences on appropriate strategies for teaching the gifted, on the problems of disadvantaged gifted children, and on culturally different gifted children; and (g) the "recycling" of both knowledge and personnel from previous regional and national institutes and conferences into the ongoing activities of the LTI in other locations.

A third long-range objective of the LTI has been the establishment of a continuing publication program designed to meet the policy-making and instructional needs of those involved in or advocating gifted child education. As a consequence of a sustained effort, more than ten major publications have been developed covering such diverse topics as "Developing a Written Plan for the Education of the Gifted and Talented," "The Identification of the Gifted and Talented," "Providing Programs for the Gifted and Talented," "Parentspeak," and "Evaluating Programs for the Gifted and Talented."

According to one study, the policy impact of the LTI on the states has been significant.[5] Of the top twenty-five states with which the LTI has had the greatest amount of interaction since 1972, sixteen (64 percent) ranked among the states having the highest percentage of policy changes most often mentioned in connection with LTI activity. These policies include: (a) the utilization of LTI methods, including a broadening of the terms used, for identifying gifted and talented children; (b) higher priority rankings for services to gifted and talented children within the state; (c) the increased representation of minority and female students within the ranks of those identified as gifted and talented; and (d) the establishment and broadening of channels of communication between and among states as they relate to the needs of the gifted and talented.

Other changes noted include an increased level of national public awareness, an increase in the numbers of students and programs for the gifted and talented, and an upsurge in in-service programs devoted to gifted child education. To take but one finding of the evaluation report, 52 percent of those policy makers, administrators, and staff persons in state and local education agencies who were polled indicated that since 1972 gifted and talented programming has received a higher priority in policy and planning as a result of LTI efforts.

---

5. Elsbery Systems Analysis, *Evaluation Summary: National/State Leadership Institute for the Gifted and Talented, 1972-1976* (New York: Elsbery Systems Analysis, 1975).

13. Concern

Activities at the State Level

Until the 1960s, activity at the state level was more or less limited to the developments occurring in California, Connecticut, Florida, Georgia, Illinois, and North Carolina. In these states either a legislative definition of "gifted" was enacted or categorical funds were authorized for the education of the gifted, or both. State-sponsored in-service programs both stimulated, and were stimulated by, local interest.

Today, there are at least thirty-eight states that make provision for the gifted and talented in their legislation, in the regulations of the state education agency, or both. In some cases the legislation expresses intent only, without specific financial provisions. In a growing number of states (sixteen at last count), funding is available to *every* local education agency in the state to provide program support. Only since 1971 have eight of these states instituted their policies of funding local programs. Only about one-fifth of the states had full-time coordinators for gifted education in 1971 but by 1977 this proportion had risen to about one-half of the states.

Since the states and local education agencies bear 92 percent of all educational costs, it is to the state and local levels that we must look for continued development of programming, despite the significant advances that have been made at the federal level since 1972. Clear evidence of this point is seen in the fact that in any given year such states as California, Florida, Illinois, and Pennsylvania devote more funds to gifted and talented education than does the federal government. Approximately one-third of the states fund programs statewide, another third are beginning to show interest in and support for planning, in-service training, and special projects, and the remaining third lack any significant involvement on behalf of their gifted and talented, with the possible exception of some outstanding local programs. In view of these facts, it is fortunate that the categorical funds contained in P.L. 93-380 (Section 404) will probably touch every state in some way, whether directly or indirectly.

An overview of the activities for gifted and talented students at the state level over the past several years reveals five major developments:

1. There has been an increase in both the number and the quality of personnel at the state level devoting professional attention to the educational needs of the gifted and talented. Beyond the administrative attention of full- and part-time personnel, the emerging quality factor entering upon the state scene has probably been the most significant advance for both the short- and long-term future. Increasingly, the professionals emerging at state and local levels have specialized academic training in gifted education (often with masters degrees or doctorates in the field). They also count among their number many who have labored long in the vineyards, and who now feel that their time has come. Thus, at both the state and local level, there are more and more teachers and administrators who are not only highly qualified and willing to take advantage of recent developments across the country, but who are also equipped

4. SUPPORT

to bring pressure to bear on local school boards and state education agencies to assure gifted and talented children their rightful place in the educational sun.

2. There have been significant policy changes at the state level associated with legislative advances and developments within state departments of education. These advances have been of two basic kinds. First, state legislatures, as they respond to both congressional and state initiatives, are slowly undertaking to provide legislative definitions of all manner of exceptional children—the mentally retarded, the handicapped, the learning disabled, and the gifted and talented. Thus, gifted and talented children are reaping the benefit of legislative attention directed at other forms of exceptionality. Their visibility as a "special" population is being more sharply focused. If the historical pattern continues to hold, and program funding follows recognition and legislative or regulatory definition, the outlook is for more rather than less state involvement in the education of the gifted and talented.

Second, state education agencies have taken a different tack with regard to gifted and talented children over the last half decade. Prior to the most recent surge of activity, gifted child education was viewed in most state agencies as an "educational fringe." Such activity and attention as did occur usually came about because of the personal interests and predelictions of a particular state-level bureaucrat. State education agencies are currently faced, however, with two developments that are sure to bring about policy change: a federal initiative and an organized parent and teacher pressure for special programming for these children. In some states this pressure has been exerted through the courts (for example, in Pennsylvania) in due process proceedings. In others, organized local pressure has reached the point where it warrants attention by state administrators with respect to policy.

3. The third significant development in the states has been the shift away from the dominance of cognitively oriented programs toward a massive diversification in programming. The root of this development has been an increasing sophistication on the part of educators, which has led them away from the narrow perspective that the gifted child is basically a cognitive "superstar" with a very high IQ. The six dimensions of giftedness/talent delineated in the Marland report have contributed significantly to broadcasting this academic consensus to an ever-widening audience of parents, teachers, and local program administrators. As a consequence programmatic attention has been construed along a wide variety of lines. Diversification has also been encouraged in state and local education agencies through grants offered by the Office of Gifted and Talented for model projects in 1976. As noted above, proposals were requested in the areas of the visual and performing arts, creativity, early childhood programs for the gifted, the exceptionally disadvantaged gifted, innovative rural programs, and community-based mentor programs. At state and local levels, increasing attention has also been given to career education for the gifted and talented, as well as to vocational education, and to the gifted handicapped.

4. Following this diversification, the states have also been making significant inroads into the development of different pedagogical styles for gifted and talented children. The educational basis for such a movement is not difficult to discern, for it is clear that different kinds of giftedness require different instructional modes. A child who flourishes in a resource room environment or in an independent study program may not get the same educational benefit from an accelerated program or from one based on an intensive relationship with a mentor. While the debate between acceleration and enrichment has not ceased among educators of the gifted and talented, the ground for the discussion has recently begun to shift from a discussion of teaching styles to an exploration of various learning styles. This shift has opened up a variety of programming options. It is worth noting in this regard that one listing of program options for the gifted and talented from a Pennsylvania intermediate unit lists over fifty kinds of program options. Thus, not only is programming being diversified to meet the needs of different gifts and talents, but different modes of working with these children are emerging within program types.

5. A fifth and final factor of significance in state-level development of programming for the gifted and talented is the propensity to "piggyback" on community and private sector resources. This strategy has been found to be effective for the gifted and talented. Pupils like it because it brings them into direct contact with more people and resources that can both stimulate and direct their interests. Teachers like it because it provides an alternative to what is offered in the classroom and hence an educational environment that can be brought into a truly dialectical tension with classroom instruction and independent study. Administrators like it because it brings down per pupil expenditures.

Involvement of the community and of the private sector in the education of the gifted and talented has gone far beyond the restricted perspective of attempting to secure private funding for public education. The most significant developments include the enlistment of skilled persons from the private sector (for example, business, the professions, artists, artisans, industry) as both a support system for and a complement to what goes on in the public schools. Typical examples of public school/private sector cooperation in support of gifted education would be the seminars in probability theory for gifted inner-city mathematics students conducted by an insurance company actuary in the northeast, or the internships in city management conducted by a west coast city manager for a small coterie of gifted social science students.

Beyond the involvement of competent community-based persons, gifted and talented programs have also made effective use of a wide variety of community resources such as museums, libraries, theaters, laboratories, hospitals, clinics, recreation programs, and the like.

Since 1972, then, there has been a notable resurgence of interest in and attention to gifted and talented children at both federal and state levels. Federal leadership has been significant symbolically, even if not financially determinative. State-level advances have

It's A New Day For Gifted Children

by Dorothy Sisk

EDUCATION FOR the gifted is emerging as a national priority. In every classroom, from three to five students could be considered as gifted and talented, and with the increased interest in excellence at the national level, educators are beginning to realize that the notion of equality upon which the United States is founded does not preclude the development of special talents and abilities.

True equality demands that we maintain equal awareness, respect and freedom for every individual to develop his or her uniqueness. This would, of course, mean an equal opportunity to develop unequal abilities to the fullest

Dr. Dorothy Sisk is a Consultant to the Office of Gifted and Talented, Department of Health, Education and Welfare.

extent. This rationale can underlie program offerings for all children, including the handicapped and gifted.

For educators to view all children as having equal capacities, learning styles or interests can only lead to mediocrity in education, whereas the realization that special abilities and talents need and can be developed can only lead to excellence.

An interagency task force on the education of the gifted and talented has been announced by the U.S. Commissioner of Education, Dr. Ernest Boyer. Task force members are drawn from seventeen other U.S. Office of Education agencies, as well as from representatives of professional and advocacy organizations whose purposes and programs affect the nation's 2.56 million gifted and talented children.

The group has been charged with the responsibility of developing a plan for maximizing the educational opportunities for gifted and talented, focusing on the interaction among human, material and fiscal resources. As part of their work, members will explore avenues of interagency cooperation and recommend a national policy for educating the nation's gifted and talented.

Gifted students have a right to educational opportunities in which their unique abilities can be developed. In order to develop the gifted student's potential, educators may need to provide certain types of materials, teaching strategies, and even environments.

Years ago, as a classroom teacher of the gifted, I remember the supervisor of the gifted, Jeanne Delp, explaining that high level intelligence makes certain demands upon the gifted child and behaviors of gifted children result from these demands and that there are curriculum implications inherent in these

4. SUPPORT

demands. Throughout my career as a classroom teacher of the gifted, a counselor of gifted and talented children, a coordinator of a county program for the gifted and talented, a teacher-trainer in gifted/talented education, a consultant to national, state and local agencies, and lastly as the Director of the Office of Gifted and Talented, the wisdom of those premises has stayed with me. The demands are as follows:

DEMANDS OF GIFTEDNESS

1. To crave knowledge—to satisfy the need to feel progress in what they are learning.
2. To feel the need to focus on or devour a subject.
3. To make observations and to see relationships.
4. To place high standards on themselves.
5. To be creative or inventive; to seek an unusual or unique approach to an assignment.
6. To question generalizations.
7. To be serious-minded; to be intolerant (usually) of foolishness or silliness.
8. To concentrate—to become totally absorbed in a task; to have a longer attention span.
9. To explore wide interests at a maturity beyond their chronological age.
10. To be sensitive to honor and truth.
11. **To express ideas and reactions (sometimes viewed as argumentative).**
12. **To resist routine and drill; to require unique ways of pursuing a drill.**
13. To work alone.
14. To be intolerant of stupidity.
15. To seek order, structure and consistency.
16. To do critical, evaluative thinking (may lead to critical attitude toward self and others).
17. To be rarely satisfied with the simple and obvious.
18. To be impatient with sloppy or disorganized thinking.
19. To be sensitive and empathetic.
20. To have their intelligence responded to.
21. To seek out their mental peers.
22. To be friendly and outgoing.
23. To use their power of abstraction; to see and point out cause and effect relationships.
24. To have time for thinking—solitude.
25. To pursue a learning pace of their own (may be fast or slow).
26. To be outstanding in several areas but average in some. (Delp, 1958)

Teachers noting the above list can begin to plan curriculum modification for gifted within the regular classroom, for use in resource rooms, or in special classes for gifted and talented.

The gifted child craves knowledge and has a need to feel progress in what he is learning. Coupled with the need to focus or devour a subject, an excellent technique to use with gifted and talented to meet these needs is to utilize a *Panel of Experts*.

When a topic is to be introduced, such as the *American Desert* at the fifth grade level, the teacher who is providing for the gifted child's need to feel progress (1)* and to devour a subject (2) could assign the entire chapter in the regular classroom text to the class as a whole and choose two or three "experts," one of whom may not be gifted and two of whom are gifted to lessen the likelihood of the gifted children feeling singled out for excess attention. These three students can then be given time to explore books at any level in the library, to view films or filmstrips during "free time," and to become "experts." Their task can be plotted along with Bloom's taxonomy (Bloom, 1956), in this case, first utilizing *Knowledge: recall of previously learned materials*.

Many gifted already know much about a given topic such as the *American Desert* and as they seek materials for the class and a meaningful way to present it as a panel of experts, they move from *Knowledge* to *Analysis: ability to break down material into its component parts so the whole structure is understood*. At this point, they may decide to divide the task into topics that they each can present. Soon the students are into the *Synthesis* level in which they use the *ability to put the parts together to form a new whole*.

Often the teacher can urge the panel of experts to be practical and illustrate to the rest of the class how this new knowledge about the *American Desert* can be demonstrated. With these activities the gifted move into *Application: the ability to use materials in concrete situations*.

Finally, as the panel of experts prepares its report, the children move into *Evaluation: the ability to judge the value of material for a given purpose*. That is, what should they use to best present a topic?

This technique meets several needs: craving for knowledge (1), to focus on or devour a subject (2), and to make observations and see relationships (3). It also causes the gifted to place high standards on themselves (4) as they are introducing a new topic to the class. Their need to be creative or inventive (5) can be encouraged by seeking a unique approach to the assignment.

As the panel of experts presents its findings, other children can question their generalizations (6), identify gaps in the information, and begin to set individual learning goals.

The wise teacher will afford each child the opportunity to plot his or her questions to pursue further learning. It can be as simple as the following breakdown.

Questions I need to pursue . . .
1. What are popular myths about the American Desert?
Sources of information . . .
1. local museums.
2. articles, "Classroom in the Cactus," *American Education*, Vol. 13, 1978.
Application activities . . .
1. Chart with myths and realities indicated.

For secondary and upper level students, the topical guides could be as follows:
Guiding questions or hypotheses . . .
Sources of information . . .
Product . . .

In this way students can seek order, structure and consistency (15) in their learning and in a sense satisfy the desire to work alone (13).

As the teacher views each child's attempt at plotting questions, it is an excellent opportunity to respond to the intelligence (20) of the gifted student.

As I listened one empathetic teacher told an eight-year-old who was trying his hand at plotting questions, "I'm looking forward to your results. Those are excellent questions you have identi-

---
*The bracketed ( ) numbers refer to items in the Delp list.

fied. When do you think you will have it ready to share with me or the class?"

With the last statement, she wisely moved to affording the gifted student the chance to pursue his own learning pace (25).

Morning Talks were introduced to me as a technique by the late Dorothy Norris, who was so instrumental in the continual success of the Cleveland Major Work Classes for gifted students in Cleveland, OH.

In *Morning Talks*, the gifted student is given an opportunity to share information which he or she has chosen to present to the class from compiled notes. I modified *Morning Talks* to just plain *Talks* and successfully used the technique with gifted students at any time during the day.

Each child was given an opportunity to choose (e.g., in reading) an author to devour (2). One gifted third grader chose James Fenimore Cooper and proceeded to regale his classmates at every opportunity (22) with the latest adventures of Cooper. This particular gifted child was placed in an administrative arrangement called "cluster-grouping" in which 10 gifted students are grouped with 10 average students and 10 above average. He not only gave vent to his need to express ideas and reactions (11), but encouraged his classmates to follow suit. This latter phenomenon is one of the spillover values of cluster-grouping—the positive effect the gifted and talented students have on average and above average students.

Several of the demands of giftedness often make gifted children's behavior less than a joy in the regular classroom—to question generalizations (6), particularly if they are the teacher's or other students' generalizations; this needs to be done *carefully*. To be intolerant of stupidity (14), whether it takes the form of senseless cruelty or just foolish intuitive leaps from A to Z must also be dealt with.

A great technique called *Side Stepping Negative Energy* can be used quite effectively with gifted and talented students. This, along with many other fine techniques, can be found in *The Centering Book*, by Gay Hendricks and Russel Wills (1975).

In this technique, they urge the child to do the following when people say bad things to them:

- Imagine the bad thing is like a breeze that you can feel go by you.
- Imagine the bad thing is like an arrow that sails by you as you step aside.
- Ask, "Are you sure you're mad at the right person?"
- Say, "It hurts when I get yelled at."
- Imagine you are a duck and the bad things slip like water off a duck's back.

Another one I often use is:

- "Oh, my, you must feel better *now*."

It is difficult to cope with the slings and arrows of criticism, and the gifted child's own critical nature, but these techniques can certainly help gifted children adapt to their peers and the learning situation.

"Let's round robin and see if we need a test," shouted fifth grade Polly. She was demonstrating a need to resist routine and drill (12), requiring instead unique ways of pursuing drill. Quickly a chorus of "Yes, yes!" greeted the teacher of a gifted class in Orlando, FL, and she began with the first child in the first seat. Each child enthusiastically responded to oral math problems on square root and not a single error was made. "See," said Polly. "We don't need a review. Let's do logarithms."

Round Robin can be used as a review with each child given an opportunity to state one important fact on a topic to demonstrate skills such as math, spelling, or to carry out other routine drills. Gifted children enjoy the competition of *Round Robin* and widely appreciate skipping page after page of more of the same.

Erich Fromm says, "Education for creativity is nothing short of education for living." What do you think he means by this pithy saying? How can you apply it to gifted education?

For gifted students, placing pithy sayings on the top of papers, on the board for all to see, will meet their demand to use their power of abstraction (23) to go beyond the simple and obvious (17).

Bob Eberle and Rosie Hall (1975) list the following proverbs that adapt beautifully to lessons in interpersonal relations:

"Gentle words open iron gates." (Bulgaria)

"Even the ladle and the cooking pot collide." (Malaysian)

"Rich together, poor if separated." (Laotian)

14. New Day

"Pound the water and it is still water." (Saudi Arabian)

"Whoever lies down with a dog will get up with fleas." (Hebrew)

Eberle and Hall suggest using a structured series of questions to provide opportunities to think and discuss human behavior. After posting the proverbs, the teacher would ask the following questions (Eberle and Hall, 1975):

- What do you think this proverb means?
- Will you given an example of the meaning?
- What kind of feeling does this proverb generate in you?
- Why do you feel this way about it?
- Can you think of any reasons why this proverb might be associated with the country where it originated?
- How can we apply this proverb to our everyday relations with others?
- If you were to rewrite the proverb, how would you say it to convey the same idea?

Again one can quickly see that in using *Pithy Sayings*, the teacher can have gifted and talented children utilize knowledge, comprehension, application, analysis, synthesis and evaluative activities. Also it includes an opportunity for the gifted student to work alone (13) and to be creative or inventive (5).

One of my favorite activities to use with gifted students and adults is boundary breaking (Sisk, 1976). It meets the need of the gifted and talented to be serious minded (7), to express reactions (11), and to be sensitive and emphathetic (19). To conduct a boundary breaking session, a teacher chooses a series of open questions and gives each child an opportunity to respond off the top of his or her head. All responses are to be accepted without evaluation.

It is best to seat the children in a circle of about fifteen students, if at all possible. However, I have successfully used this technique with a much larger group, even as many as fifty.

Boundary breakers can be used to introduce units of work, lessons or as pleasant moments to relax and get to know one another better. If a child cannot respond or chooses not to respond, he or she can say "Pass." However, the child who passes should be given another opportunity to respond. In this case, "Pass, Pass" can indicate "I still

4. SUPPORT

choose not to respond." The children respond in clockwise or counterclockwise fashion. Sessions usually last 10-15 minutes.

For example, boundary breaking questions which begin a unit on jewels might include:
- If you could design your own ring, what kind of stone would you use?
- If you thought of yourself as a jewel, what kind would you be?
- When you think of regal jewels, what kind do you think of?
- There is a magic jewel box in the room. What jewel would you take out of it?

Or more indirect boundary breakers, such as . . .
- If you could be a note in any song, what song would you choose?
- If you could visit any country, what country would you choose?
- Think of yourself as a color. What color are you?
- When you are happy, what do you do?
- If you could be any character in a book, who would you be?

The insightful teacher who listens carefully to her students' responses can get to know their interests, values and ideas much more keenly in these open-ended activities than in more structured lessons and build upon them to personalize the learning experiences.

The teacher who utilizes the behaviors (1-26) of the gifted and talented to plan a curriculum will find that he or she will become creative and flexible and will have produced an enriched, challenging and individualized curriculum suited to every student's needs.

PARENT TALK

Willard Abraham

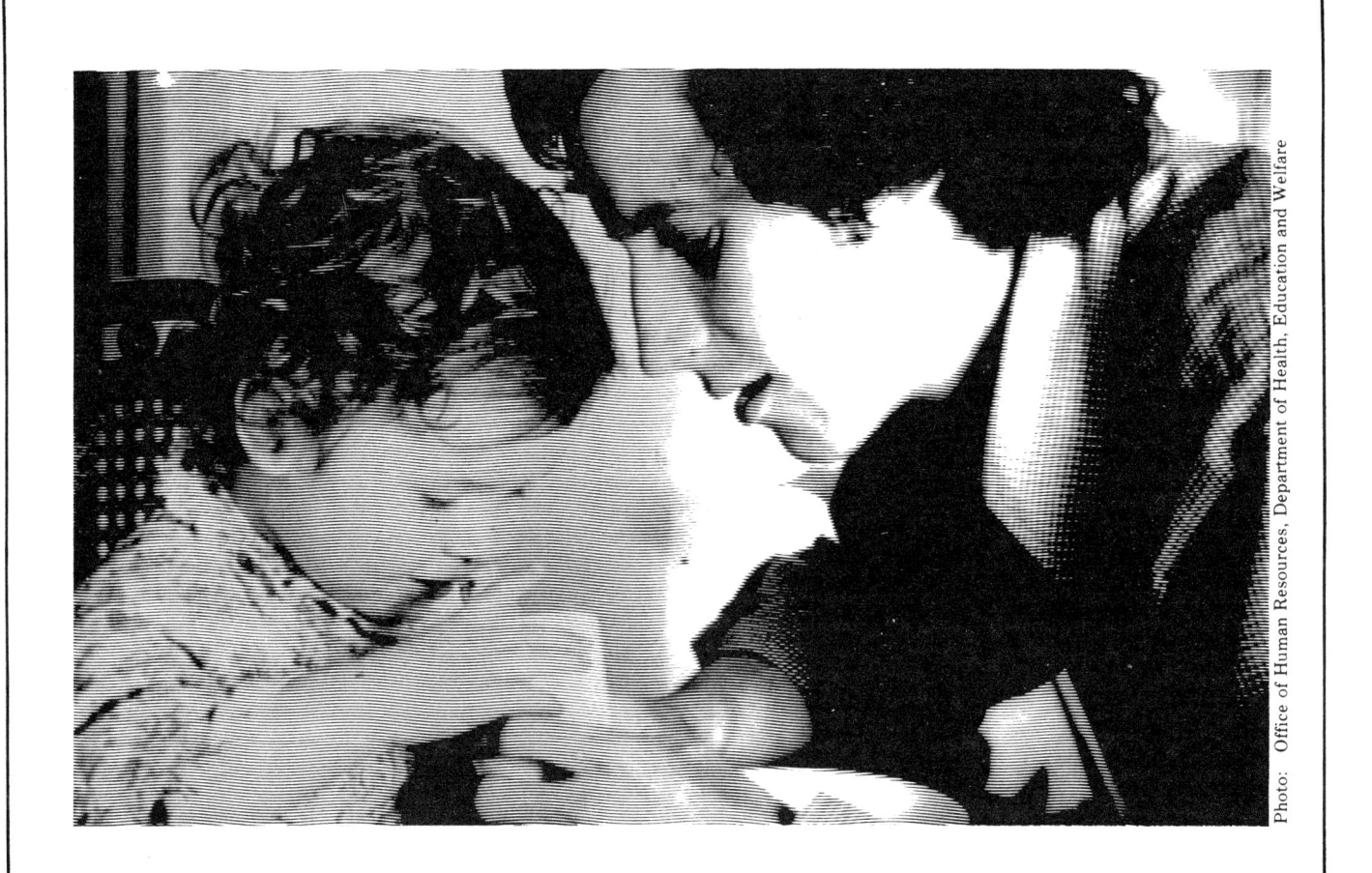

Many parents are sure that their young children are bright — but it is so easy to be wrong.

Because they say clever things, put words together in unusual ways, and ask questions that may be hard for you to answer, you might think they are gifted. After all, if a child asks, "What makes the sky blue?" or "What makes thunder?", doesn't that mean he's very smart?

4. SUPPORT

The problem parents face is that they often don't see their youngster in comparison with others. He or she may seem so quick — but others might be faster.

So here's a check list which can help you tell whether your preschool child is gifted. It is not necessary to score high on all 20 points, but if your youngster is strong on at least half of them, you can be quite sure he or she is bright.

---

1. Started to walk and talk before most other children you know about.
2. Is at least a little taller, heavier and stronger than others his or her age.
3. Shows an interest in time — clocks, calendars, yesterday and tomorrow, and days of the week.
4. Learned to read even though not yet five years old. Likes to read.
5. Arranges toys and other possessions, putting the same kinds of things together.
6. Knows which numbers are larger than others.
7. Can count, and point to each item as he or she correctly says the number.
8. Creates make-believe playmates as he or she "plays house" or different games.
9. Is interested in what is on television and in newspapers, in addition to cartoons and comics.
10. Learns easily, so that you have to tell him or her something only once.
11. Shows impatience with jobs around the house that seem to have no meaning — like putting toys away when he or she is just going to have to take them out again.
12. Asks "Why?" often, and really wants to know the answer. Is curious about a lot of things, from a tiny insect and how it's "made," to a car and how it works.
13. Doesn't like to wait for other children to catch up.
14. Sticks with a task longer than others do. Won't give up easily.
15. Does things differently in ways that make good sense, whether it's piling up blocks, setting the table, or drying dishes.
16. Likes to be with older children, and can keep up with them.
17. Collects things, likes to organize them, and doesn't want anyone to mess them up — but doesn't always collect neatly.
18. Can carry on a conversation, and enjoys it. Wants your ideas and likes you to listen to his or hers. Uses big words and knows what they mean.

19. Shows an interest in drawing and music, knows colors, and has rhythm.

20. Makes up jokes. has a good sense of humor.

How does your preschool youngster come out on that list? Strong enough so that you feel he or she is gifted? All right — then are you ready for the next step?

Before going on, try to make up your own list of what to do. Here's a space, or write it on another sheet of paper. Cover up the rest of this page until you do.

Did your list include these: (1) Talk to him about what he does, likes, and thinks; (2) listen to him; (3) read to him; (4) take him places; (5) enroll him in the best preschool, nursery school or day care center you can find and afford. And when he goes to school try to find the most creative, brightest teachers for him. (Ed. note: or *her!*)

Your list, and mine, may make you think about something kind of interesting: These are, of course, the same things that parents should do for *all* of their young children.

The Early Years — Don't Waste Them!

"The young child needs friends his age and size with whom he can communicate and cooperate. He needs recognition and social acceptance for his abilities, character and personality. The family alone, as precious and good as it is, cannot meet all of these needs."

Frances Horwich
("Miss Frances", Ding Dong School)

Authorities in this field know that an early childhood program can pay off — if it is (1) prepared especially for young children and (2) operated by competent persons who understand them, know how they develop and work closely with their parents.

Those who believe in the value of preschools feel that a well-planned early experience in such settings can pay rich dividends. Both the child and his or her parents will benefit from it.

Respectable researchers say it all in different ways. It is sometimes difficult to cut through their big words, but their ideas are very clear as they write about young children who receive this early enrichment.

- ". . . one might expect the environment to have its greatest impact during the first years of life."
- ". . . gains in 'intelligence', as well as . . . language growth."
- ". . . durable effects on IQ scores and reading level . . ."
- ". . . more socially accepted . . ."
- ". . . higher . . . on measures of academic achievement, IQ, and social-emotional development . . . general information scores and mathematics achievement . . ."

4. SUPPORT

• "... cope more effectively with the demands of school ..."

One skilled researcher in the field said:

"... No thinking person (should) ignore the importance of the first few years of life ... I (can) continue to cite data ... until you could not possibly refuse to conclude that early childhood enrichment produces impressive gains in the intellectual functioning of young children ... At this stage in the history of early childhood education, most of us inside the field are over the hurdle of 'does early childhood education produce positive effects'."

Yes, they answer emphatically, as one did after reviewing 227 studies in this area.

Even in infancy they found less tension and better "social interaction scores" among those with day care experience, and "no evidence that infant day care and the separation from mother leads to emotional insecurity."

All of these ideas relate to a widely quoted statement about the importance of the early years (Dr. Benjamin S. Bloom, University of Chicago). He wrote:

"... in terms of intelligence ... about 50% of the development takes place between conception and age 4, about 30% between ages 4 and 8, and about 20% between ages 8 and 17 ... *as much of the development takes place in the first 4 years of life as in the next 13 years.*" (My emphasis.)

To be fair, it must be stated that a few serious objections have been raised to early childhood programs. It is wrong to take the child from his or her family, they say. Of course it is. No well-planned preschools "take away" children from their families. Their goal is to *add* to a young child's experiences and home environment during these vital early years.

The objectors sometimes talk about the dangers to attitudes, relationships and children's eyes of "early schooling", but this early enrichment is not formal "schooling." The reading to, playing with, number games, music, art, dance and all the rest are related and sometimes preparation for, but not part of, such "schooling." Young children should not sit at desks, read and study. Most of them are not ready to do so. No competent preschool educator says they should.

Some of those who oppose these programs cite the danger of "depriving children of warmth and security." It is of course possible, but a sound early childhood program provides both in abundance. The skills and personalities of their teachers add to what a child can receive from a warm and secure family and home.

Children can profit from the richness of an expended environment. Researchers, preschool teachers, and thoughtful parents all know this.

The pay-off is in the words and smiles of little boys and girls. Watch them, listen to them, and you will get part of the answer to this question:

"Is an early childhood program worthwhile?"

CONSTRUCTIVE WAYS TO WORK WITH THE ESTABLISHMENT

How "Organized Persuasion" Works for the Gifted in Public Education

by Carol Nathan

A protest, even the most violent protest, becomes legitimated when and only when the affirmations on which it is based are in fact (not just in personal conviction) supported by good reasons, good reasons shared or potentially sharable by the community that is relevant.
Wayne C. Booth, Modern Dogma and the Rhetoric of Assent

When parents with gifted children consider the ways in which they can have an impact on improving educational institutions, they find several approaches that have been used with varying degrees of success over the past few decades. The traditional means developed by parent-teacher associations come first to mind. In the late sixties another mode became fashionable: the hastily organized emotional protest of a crowd of parents united soley by their anger over some local development. An even more recent way of being involved is the parent advisory committee established and controlled by the administration of special programs. Whatever value these methods have in special cases, none has provided the parents of the gifted with a consistently effective means for moving schools and staff toward improved programs for the gifted.

While in some instances parents of the gifted have worked effectively through Parent-Teacher Association committees, their actions are inevitably curtailed by the restrictions of the organization's constitution. No parent-teacher association can favor a particular group of students over the school population as a whole. The adversary stance of emotional protest, because it is based upon the action of a group drawn together by a particular, often momentary crisis, does not provide effective means for establishing a stable and continuing relation with district staff or school board. Finally, the advisory committee, because its parent members are fed only information deemed necessary by the administrators, has also proved ineffective. Only partially informed and made passive by their limited role, parents on these committees find little opportunity to effect improvements in programs.

So it is necessary that parents of gifted students seek alternatives. One such option is what might be called "organized persuasion." This concept does not exclude any of the useful elements of the three other kinds of parent participation when and if they prove useful. Indeed, organized persuasion can be seen as containing these other possibilities because it is based on an inclusive and flexible notion of effective action. It can perhaps be best defined as

"Constructive Ways to Work with the Establishment: How 'Organized Persuasion' Works for the Gifted in Public Education," by Carol Nathan, *Parentspeak*. Reprinted with permission of the author and the National/State Leadership Training Institute on the Gifted and the Talented, Barbara Johnson, Editor, 1976

4. SUPPORT

attempting to establish unassailable reasons for or against a course of conduct.

Organized persuasion becomes possible when a large part of a community working for the gifted reaches a consensus regarding important issues. But consensus is not enough. It gets its force and direction from organization. In this instance, the organization is empowered to represent the interests of the gifted, with a substantial constituency of parents willing to participate actively in pursuing its goals. At the same time it provides an organization with the ability to move beyond the first step, which is too frequently merely a resolution of tensions rather than a prescription for action.

Organization thus becomes consensus institutionalized. It is this organizing of opinion which enables parents to be an enduring force in a community. Further, an organization established upon such a basis derives a justification from the consensus. A coherent body of parents which supports arguments that are persuasive carries more weight than isolated individuals. It presents a business-like face that authorities must take seriously, whether the intention is to move a district to action or to influence legislators to legalize the concept of gifted education within the boundaries of public education. If it sometimes takes effort to identify sympathetic supporters in the public sector, at least when they are located, the organization is there, established and ready to present them with substantial convincing proposals. Proposals, clearly thought-out and offered in convincing form, enable lawmakers to see ways toward possible legislation and provide educators with a view of improving their present offerings to include gifted students.

The Way to Consensus

But how is consensus reached? Anyone at all familiar with parents of gifted children is aware that he is in the presence of a variety of strong independent opinions. Before any constructive action for gifted students can be undertaken, it is necessary for parents to relinquish several all-too-common stances and start to consider the major issue: "how do we get a program going?"

If the answer to that question is to be found in consensus, then parents have to resist the temptation to gather together merely for the purpose of exchanging "horror stories," which are really only camouflage for a reluctance to become actively involved. Parents must also forego the desire to rise up in righteous unexamined indignation to fling strident accusations of incompetence at the system. Attacking an administrator or teacher may somewhat relieve personal frustration, but it usually turns out to be simply another way of avoiding constructive participation in solving problems.

Finally, there are those parents who insist they don't want their children singled out for special attention but complain, both in public and in private, that the schools are wholly failing to educate their children. If what they say is really true, why aren't they applying themselves to remedying such a deplorable situation? Such petulance does often produce results—negative results. It can infect their children with contempt for teachers and for learning generally. Ironically, their attitudes can have precisely the reverse effect of what the parents intend; discontented and contemptuous children are a problem in a classroom. The result is that these children *are* singled out for special attention. The only difference is that the singling out has nothing to do with learning.

"Horror story" telling obviously goes nowhere, since it isn't directed outside the story circle. Vituperation and complaint, if they become aggravating enough, do arouse school boards and administrations to one of two kinds of response, both of which seek to quiet the rage, but rarely address the problems that generate the rage. Placebos are prescribed in the form of "special" field trips or "fun and games" frills. The intention here is to remove the children from the classroom so that the business of learning and teaching can continue. The other response, which is not necessarily exclusive of the first, is a hardening of the status quo opinion that gifted children are frequently figments of neurotic parents' fantasies, or if they are gifted, "they will make it anyhow."

Recrimination and complaint may make individual parents feel good, and "horror stories" may make a group of parents feel good. Neither takes just grievances anywhere important. For that, such attitudes have to be dismissed in favor of thinking through what a good gifted program should be and what can be done to insure that such a program has a chance of thriving in a particular setting.

What must finally take place is a coming together of parents dedicated to developing a serious strategy that speaks reasonably and persuasively to the apathy or hostility of both educators and legislators.

Take a Look at the Options

Options necessarily are various, depending on what the state and/or the individual school district has available for gifted students. In some instances, nothing may be available; then a group must decide where it can best direct its attention. Whether it be the state legislature, the county board of trustees, the local school district, or some independent undertaking such as a lyceum, a campaign strategy must be developed so that the emphasis or organized persuasion directs its arguments to the right audience.

If a group agrees that some kind of statewide legal and financial commitment is needed before anything else, then the group must be prepared to work with state legislators. This strategy requires that a number of local groups work together. Arguments should stress that the needs of gifted students are a legitimate part of the total responsibility of the state to educate all students according to their abilities. The proper education for the gifted is the most economical way a state can assure a pool of citizens competent to become future leaders.

Presenting these arguments means traveling to the state capitol, engaging the interest and support of key legislators, particularly members of education and finance committees. In the beginning, arguments are usually presented in conversation and small group exchange. More formal presentations should wait for an appropriate setting. While it is necessary to contact members of key committees, it is also wise to seek out the state representatives of the local areas of the groups participating. What do they think about education generally and education for the gifted particularly? Most people in government have strong opinions on the subject of education. The object is to influence opinion in the direction one wants it to go, or better yet speak to such opinion in effective arguments.

When the county is the target of organized persuasion, a group representing a number of districts is the most persuasive. The county approach is particularly effective in rural or sparsely-populated areas where centralizing both direction and funding of a gifted program results in better offerings. Gifted students profit from the good will which results from the sharing of the burden of funding and providing materials for gifted courses. The board of trustees, the county superintendent, and any special education departments can be avenues for exploration. If such effort results in a mobile gifted resource center to serve teachers, parents, and students on a rotating basis, possibilities for developing gifted programs are more apt to occur.

4. SUPPORT

Usually, however, a group decides to put its effort on the local level. This is understandable, since it is our own children about whom we are most immediately concerned. Further, success in one district can often stimulate activity in another. Gradually the scope of parent involvement can grow to include county and state.

In a district with no gifted offerings, there is, however, a special problem. What can be found on which to build a gifted program? Without the help of a framework established by either district or state for gifted education, parents of the gifted must turn their efforts to influencing general curriculum decisions. Exploring this possibility in a constructive manner, they can assist in developing a nucleus of offerings open enough to allow the gifted student to stretch without demanding that any teacher establish two mutually exclusive curricula. When such areas of curriculum, preferably in core academic courses, have been identified, parents are likely then to find both teachers and administrators who are amenable to change. If professionals are met with good will and cooperation, they will respond in kind. There are few good educators today who do not welcome any help they can get in improving what schools can do for all students.

If none of these options for working through public institutions seems to be available, a group may decide that it has to begin outside public education. Parents tend to feel—and I think rightly—that this course is an admission of defeat not just for themselves, but for public education itself. And if a group does not establish goals that move it beyond this first hurdle, then the defeat must be laid in large measure, at the feet of parents themselves.

Influencing Public School Responsibility

Organized persuasion—whatever option is selected—is directed toward influencing public schools to assume their responsibility toward gifted students. If this option is elected in preference to any of the others, it can have only one intention: to increase the visibility of the gifted in the eyes of educators and lawmakers. This has been done with some success in a number of cases through a liaison of community people and educators concerned with the fate of gifted students. Saturday classes and summer programs designed for gifted children and offered through a continuing education program at a community college are a frequent practice. In other instances, a lyceum organized by parents is developed, involving interested members of a community—doctors, lawyers, artists, business people, and even concerned educators, to name a few. While neither of the programs is necessarily academic, both offer something beyond average curriculum.

Tuition is a necessary element in either of these programs. In the first, a charge per class is established; in the second, admission to the program is usually on a membership basis, with dues absorbing the expenses. In both cases, costs for books and materials are assumed by the participating students.

How do these programs raise the visibility of gifted children? The enthusiasm of both students and those who on a voluntary basis teach such classes, communicates itself to the whole community. Such opportunities also generate questions about a school system that fails to provide equally challenging activities. Achievements of students are shared with the public through displays, art shows, demonstrations, and performances, for example. The accomplishments of young people always delight, and often amaze, adults and raise more questions about the inadequacy of the educational system.

These parent-generated programs should probably be viewed as short-term activities always directed to the long-range goal: to persuade a district to meet the needs of the gifted students in its jurisdiction. By presenting a variety of teaching styles and curricula, the parent group suggests thoughtful and exciting alternatives to the narrow range of a standard curriculum. As long as public education is a given of our democracy, parents must not settle for a minimal effort on the part of any school system. But care must be taken that these programs are not viewed by the schools as relieving them of their responsibility to the gifted. If this happens, the very intention of such an undertaking is defeated.

I must add that I see parent-generated programs as a last resort. All gifted students deserve an education appropriate to their abilities. The restrictions which private classes must of necessity set up tend to exclude from participation children whose parents cannot afford the tuition. Some of these parents may be spurred to active participation in the organization if its goals are made available to them as parents of students who should qualify. But the climate of exclusiveness often does more harm than good to an organization's long-range endeavor.

If giftedness becomes equated with privileges only available to a particular social or economic status, a whole new set of hostilities have to be dealt with. There is considerable evidence that giftedness is not bound to a social or economic class; all potential must be permitted to realize itself. Theoretically, that is one reason why we have public education. Parents must never forget that they are working for *all* the gifted. Their hopes for their own children's success are ultimately dependent on guaranteeing that all gifted children are offered an equal opportunity to succeed.

A Warning about Expectations

Here though, a word of caution is necessary. Expectations are equally as important as identification of options. Boundless ambition can sink any enterprise. Whether it is one's own or other peoples' minds one wishes to change, it is a slow and difficult process. Often parents of an organization are so convinced of the rightness of their position that they are unprepared to cope with the resistance, the outright hostility to their arguments, which they encounter. Wringing their hands, they cry, "What's the use?" or clenching their fists, they shrug, "What else can you expect from those establishment types?" Both these questions are rhetorical; neither do they require nor receive an answer.

A modest start with modest expectations is almost always the best. That way there is at least some chance of success. Don't undertake to change the entire curriculum or restructure the administration or rewrite the education code. That way lies certain disaster. There really isn't any "establishment" to change; there are only individuals with habits of mind flexible enough to consider alternatives or so rigid that they cannot contemplate change. Of course, there is legislation to be written or programs to be developed but these changes come only through moving individuals to act.

Some of these people will be in positions to assist your effort and will be venturesome enough to experiment. They will want to work for change in the proffered atmosphere of cooperation. If an organization accepts help from such individuals, it can at least waste less time on, if not forget, those others who hesitate out of fear or laziness, to admit that there might be another and better way of doing things. These latter will take their cues from the leaders.

If a few teachers, administrators, or legislators are persuaded that the

4. SUPPORT

argued position makes sense, a beginning has been made. And that should be enough to hope for at first. Getting that far, significant progress has been made. Now there are others out there who will also carry the message. From then on, it is a matter of taking time to consider every step carefully, asking if it will bring the results desired. Know who the audience is in each instance, and what it can accomplish. They should be persuaded to do what is possible for them to do. But the people contacted cannot respond usefully in areas where they have no influence. If the action desired is unrealistic, the result is bound to disappoint.

Organized persuasion is not an instant cure-all; it is a process to influence those who can effect change. And change occurs when such people are convinced that each development grows naturally out of what has preceded it. It takes time to develop, and it takes even more time to grow into that final goal of consensus. An independent and responsible parent organization can be a great asset to teachers, administrators, and legislators in the evolution of this whole process.

It must be remembered that involvement in a parent organization has degrees of commitment; that is, there will be those, usually few in number, who are willing to devote a great deal of time and energy to the work involved in changing the attitudes of educators and legislators. The larger part of the membership will be made up of those who wish to be involved only on special occasions when a show of solidarity is needed, or even more narrowly, when they can be reasonably assured that their efforts will meet with success. They will come to a school board meeting when the subject of gifted education is being considered, or if such a program's existence is being threatened; they may even publicly express their support for the program, but they will consider that having done that, they have done all they need to do.

There is in our society a deeply ingrained timidity before the authority of educators. No one wants to be suspected of meddling or favoring some children over others. These attitudes act as strong deterrents to parents to engage in the kind of prolonged activity that good organization work demands.

But for those undaunted few, who have the toughness to endure and are supported by the results of consensus, the tool of organized persuasion can make meaningful dialogue possible.

Finally, a parent organization must have some notion of the expectations of the people on the other side of the table. Do they view the organization's representatives as reasonable negotiators? If they do not, they cannot take the organization seriously. Arguing persuasively simply means providing those to be influenced with new information, not as a catalog of unrelated facts, but as an organized argument with clear conclusions and concrete proposals subscribed to by a constituency. If they come to expect this, they will listen, even if sometimes it is more out of curiosity for how the presentation is made than for what is actually said. The end result is the same, however; they will have heard from the organization, and if the presentation is also made available in clear and pointed written form; they will have a chance to mull over the position in quieter moments of reflection when there is less obvious pressure on them to act in predictably defensive ways.

No organization should be content to have only one person who does all the work, all the persuading, and all the decision making. When this happens, the organization forfeits the first requirement of organized persuasion—consensus. Particularly in the public arena, putting all affairs in the hands of one active participant, no matter how effective that person may be, will cost a parent group its validity in the minds of those it desires to influence. They will no longer see it as such-and-such an organization but as so-and-so's clique.

When this happens, both the organization and the individual lose their effectiveness. The individual, often unintentionally, usurps powers that belong rightfully to the organization. It is virtually impossible for an individual shouldering total responsibility, not to feel responsible for all decisions. Subtly the role changes from leader to boss, and the first resistance to the boss's decisions leads to internecine conflict. Total power in one place erodes the very flexibility that can make a body based on organized persuasion so beautifully able to deal with changing circumstances.

The governing board of an organization is made up of a number of people, all of whom must be willing to share duties. It also requires some regular turnover in its composition so that new and alternative possibilities can have a hearing. Otherwise, the organization is left with a gap when the time comes that any individual can no longer be involved.

Working on the District Level

But how does parent opinion on the district level get institutionalized? Undeniably deep, if often unspecified, discontent is frequently the primary stimulus for organized parent involvement in education. Certainly this is true in the area of gifted education. Since most involvement grows out of a controversy between parents and schools, the posture of the group toward the schools is naturally that of an adversary. From such a position, strong action can be taken which often results in improving conditions for gifted students. However, after a group's initial success, the adversary posture becomes obsolete and yet is likely to seem, through sheer habit, the only policy to fall back on, unless the organization has considered what it wishes to do next. Organizations which want to remain effective are, in any case, faced with the necessity of adjusting their position to a changed set of circumstances.

Though the conditions for controversy may still remain—for example, the recalcitrance of administrators and the hostility of teachers, to name two conditions—organizations must be prepared to support developing programs and staff. Parent groups have to be able to discriminate between minor issues, usually surfacing at individual school sites, and the major one which is the need to establish stable policies of cooperation with gifted program and staff and support for the overall program. If the issue that initiated the organization in the first place required a strong and agressive position, the stable long-term policy probably, requires thoughtful flexibility. Here, a rigid reliance on the adversary posture can damage not only the organization's effectiveness, but also can ultimately undermine the position gained for gifted students. However, if subsequently an issue does arise that calls for stronger action, an organization which has demonstrated its good will has earned the right to anger and is in a good position to use it.

Changing habits of mind is difficult. But parent groups cannot afford to freeze in some stance that no longer meets the variety of needs demanded by a new program. It is in this context that organized persuasion can provide the flexibility for continuing cooperation. Flexibility, however, does not mean abandonment of standards; it does mean that organizations must avoid crises that militate against program development. And this condition is only possible if there is trust between parents and educators. Part of developing trust involves distinguishing between the legitimate areas of parent involvement and staff responsibility. Parent power has little effect if parents are unwilling to recognize their limits. The legitimacy of a parent organization depends on making proper use of the means provided by the district (or the state) for

4. SUPPORT

gifted education. Understanding the intention of the program, as viewed by the professionals, enhances the ability to bring about change in areas of fundamental disagreement. It is always necessary to keep the door open for dialogue between the organization and the gifted staff.

Both program and fiscal responsibility belong in the domain of the gifted staff and director. Cooperative support will tend to obligate both staff and director to seek the advice and counsel of the parent group regarding program goals and objectives. The director who doesn't include parents in his planning is either arrogant or frightened. Both attitudes are probably a response to the adversary stance and reveal not just the character of the director, but the weakness of the parent organization. It is up to the latter to map out a common ground where both sides can work comfortably without either side losing integrity.

Final decisions are made by the professionals. Parents have to understand this fact and avoid postures that can undermine that authority and lead to hostility or paralysis. This situation serves only to permit higher echelons of administration to stand in neutral territory rejoicing that they have contained another disturbance—and still do nothing for gifted students. While parents can do much to insure a successful program, no program is even possible without the professional's skills. This does not mean that parents need to become rubber stamps. They can assist staff in tasks that are necessary to a successful program without losing their right to question decisions when that need arises.

A balance then has to be maintained that weighs fairly between parent conviction and the knowledge of educators; this balance is achieved by working closely together on all matters, with a steady eye toward the students and their growth. The alert detachment of the professional must outweigh parental emotion when the latter, as it often does, reflects the need of the parent more than that of the student. But parent conviction must not be automatically treated as ignorant intrusion by staff. In short, both parties must learn to respect each other's capacity to contribute. But respect ought not to imply uncritical mutual admiration. It should mean sympathetic honesty. Thus while staff has the right to criticize parents for sometimes indulging their egos, parents have an equal right to criticize staff for occasionally thinking more about public relations than about public education. When these mutual rights are granted by both parties, parents can influence major decisions, staff can respond to constructive criticism, and children profit from the results.

Future of the Organization

After the first hurdle is crossed: where, then, organization? Is an organization's usefulness ended when its efforts result in an identifiable, funded gifted program? By no means. Whether mandated by district policy or established by state law, a gifted program can still suffer from neglect. An independent parent organization can serve as a deterrent to the loss of gifted priorities at higher levels of administration. Strong community support of the program is a great asset to both teachers and director in their struggle to maintain a quality program. With increasing pressures being brought to bear on school systems by a variety of community factions, gifted education requires also continuous support.

Even in California, which has long had a statewide gifted education option funded by "categorical aid" monies, the need for various parent involvement has been demonstrated innumerable times. While the decision to have a gifted program is discretionary at the district level, control of the funding for such programs is with the State Department of Education. Proposed programs must meet specific guidelines before the extra funding can be obtained.

Experience supports the conviction that there is genuine concern and careful assessment done at the state level. What happens in the district after approval is generally where questions of proper administration and program arise. The gap between proposal and implementation is often more like a chasm. One of the most disturbing aspects in gifted education is the large number of "paper" programs that have developed throughout the states. These have no reality beyond lip service and permit institutions to receive monies meant, but not used, for the gifted.

In California, the State Department's Gifted and Talented Education Management Team has developed a full set of guidelines to correct this situation. These guidelines are available in every district having a gifted program, but often parents have found that these useful tools are not properly disseminated throughout a district to enable involved district personnel to be aware of them. Organized parent involvement played an active role both in bringing these discrepancies to the team's attention and in providing suggestions during the development of guidelines. The team has dealt openly and graciously with parent groups since its inception by seeking their advice and cooperation.

This two-way exchange has made it possible for organizations to work more intelligently in their districts. Members have become familiar with the guidelines, the approved program proposal, and its interpretation in specific instances. When evidence of mismanagement is found, the organization is informed sufficiently to be able to discuss the matter with the local school people. Only when questions cannot be resolved in a district does an organization appeal to state authority. To work effectively in this way, organizations need to develop policies on program objectives as set out by the district, either in support of them or to work for their change. The policies should correspond to the program planner's intentions and the state directives to gifted education. The approved program proposal sets the limits on what is to be accomplished. If an organization wants to alter those limits in any way, it must provide constructive suggestions to the program director for his consideration. This is accomplished often by establishing an organization advisory board which meets on a regular basis with the director.

Parent attention generally centers on two essential areas. They are the program of studies and the funding thereof.

Usually considered first, and most important by many, is the program and its relation to the district's curriculum development. The more integral the program is to general curriculum, the greater will be its strength. Program is the very heart of gifted education, and it is through a properly developed and realized program that gifted education earns the support of parents, educators, and legislators. It is the visible manifestation justifying present and future support. Ultimately the form and effectiveness of a gifted program reflects the quality and level of a district's general curriculum offerings, particularly in academic courses.

The requirement, in California, for a "qualitatively different" gifted program assumes a structure that differs in quality or level of complexity. Ideally, this does not mean that fifth graders are doing sixth grade work, or additional fifth grade work, but rather that gifted fifth graders are pursuing the fifth grade curriculum extended and deepened. Because of the limitation on gifted funds, a gifted program minimum of 200 minutes a week has been set. This minimum of qualitatively different education is not going to produce

4. SUPPORT

miracles for any child. Only when the 200 minutes becomes an integral part of a high-level district-wide curriculum is it possible to provide gifted children with the opportunity to learn to their fullest potential.

Of course, it is impossible to address the whole educational design of a district, but it is possible to identify the most glaring problems of gifted education in the context of a district's curriculum and work to solve them. Thus, general curriculum is a legitimate and necessary area for parent involvement.

The other area is the use of gifted funds. These may be used only for staff and materials which would not otherwise be provided for gifted students, and should be so coded in the district's total budget. Parent organizations need to work for a separate, gifted budget within the overall budget. The aim of this effort is to make it possible to watch at key points how gifted funds are spent. Put in their own category, gifted monies are less prone to get lost than if they are included in general funds.

If the law governing the use of gifted funds is not observed, a district may be penalized or lose these monies entirely, and, of course, probably lose its program, too. Accountability is a major concern. A strong organizational policy on this matter can be of great value to a program director in securing jurisdiction of the uses of gifted monies.

When organized persuasion has been used to establish an awareness of gifted education and has helped develop or strengthen a genuine program, the task is far from done. Situations continually change and can imperil all the hard-won accomplishments of the past. Since any achievement is not an immutable perfection, there always is the possibility for future improvements. An organization must stay alive to these possibilities. On the larger scene, laws need making or improving as more gifted students are located and programs continue to expand. As long as there are gifted children, there will be the need for parents organized to protect and improve gifted education. And as long as those in authority are susceptible to effectively offered reason, persuasion will be the best method to reach these ends.

How Media Can Assist In Raising Public Consciousness About The Education Of The Gifted

Raymond P. Ewing, APR, Media Relations Director, Allstate Insurance Company

To begin, I would like to sketch the force we are proposing to rouse in support of the education of the gifted and talented.

James Bryce, the historian, identified it this way: "Towering over Presidents and state Governors, over Congress and state legislatures, over conventions and the vast machinery of party, *public opinion* stands out, in the United States, as the great source of power, the master of servants who tremble before it."

James Russell Lowell put it this way: "The pressure of public opinion is like the pressure of the atmosphere; you can't see it—but, all the same, it is sixteen pounds to the square inch."

Abraham Lincoln analyzed it best when he observed: "Public opinion is everything. With public sentiment, nothing can fail: without it, nothing can succeed."

The role of publicity in forming public opinion has been known for many, many years. For example, Disraeli said a few years after Lincoln's observation, "Without publicity there can be no public support, and without public support every nation must decay."

About the same time, Joseph Pulitzer was telling his editors: "Publicity, publicity, *publicity*, is the greatest moral factor and force in our public life."

Then, as today, the local, regional and national news media has more power than any other single force in the shaping of public opinion in the United States.

Black Art of Publicity

Naturally, such a powerful force and the techniques of influencing this force have not escaped criticism. Judge Learned Hand always looked at its dark side. He said, "The art of publicity is a black art; but it has come to stay, and every year adds to its potency."

Not only liberal thinkers view the process with alarm. Joseph Goebbels argued (quite successfully for a number of years, I might add) that, "It is the absolute right of the state to supervise the formation of public opinion."

4. SUPPORT

Fortunately for us, the founders of this country attached the following Amendment to our Consititution—they thought so much of it that they gave it the top priority—it is the first amendment: "Congress shall make no law respecting the establishment of religion, or prohibiting the free excerise thereof; or abridging the freedom of speech, or of the press; or the right of the people to peaceably to assemble, and to petition the government for a redress of grievances."

The easy way is to hire an experienced PR man or woman to work with your group, either as a full-time employee or as a consultant. Instead of one individual, you may hire several through a PR agency which will officially serve as your consultant and help develop and execute programs for you. The only hard part about this approach is getting a budget to take on professional staff.

If you haven't any money to pay staff or consultants, the next easy way is to recruit one or more PR professionals on a volunteer basis. Many individuals, either because of their intellectual interest in a field or because of a personal involvement in a field as a parent, etc., gladly will volunteer if prompted to work on an advisory or a task-force basis for a nonprofit organization's PR projects. Additionally, many for-profit companies encourage their PR staff (encourage is too weak a word, they *order* them) to take on PR assignments for nonprofit groups as part of the company's community relations program and, sometimes, as part of the staff member's personal development. In any case, you have the benefit of professional help at no cost. Sometimes you can gather together 10 to 20 people on one PR committee.

I have sat on PR committees where the combined salary of the PR men present was in excess of a half-million dollars. We worked as hard to solve problems, develop programs, and help execute them as we did for our own companies.

This approach works if you are located where a large number of PR people work in the area. If you don't have any contacts with PR people in your area, sometimes the local Public Relations Society of America chapter or the local publicity or advertising club can find volunteers for you.

Occasionally, you also can recruit volunteers from the news media in your community.

What I have just described is the easy way to handle the people problem.

The hard was is to train yourself or one or two members of your staff to handle PR.

PR Workshops or Courses

There are many ways this can be done.

You can attend PR workshops or longer-term courses given by your local Publicity or Advertising Club, the local Chapter of the Public Relations Society of America, Chamber of Commerce or other groups not affiliated with an educational institution. There is usually a fee, often minimal. I have helped conduct PR workshop courses put on by the first four organizations I named and can report that they are well worth the effort to attend.

Sometimes PR or publicity courses are offered by local high schools as part of their adult education evening programs, and by local colleges and universities. Some local newspapers conduct publicity seminars for nonprofit groups.

17. Media

If no formal PR courses are open, then you must go the self-training route. Self-training involves selecting PR books from the public library or a bookstore and actually visiting local newspapers and radio and TV stations. The papers and electronic media will show you the courtesy of having you tour their facilities and telling you how to submit story or program ideas to the appropriate departments.

If you find you have to go this route, larger newspapers have a PR or Public Information Department which will help you make the appropriate contacts. Smaller newspapers without these departments can be approached through the editor. Larger radio and TV stations also have PR or Public Information Departments which will assist you. Smaller stations can be approached through the program director, news editor, or station manager. They are approachable and they will help you, especially if you come from the not-for-profit sector. In fact, if you make a good enough case for your project, they might even assign a "volunteer" from their staff to help you.

Many columnists and radio and TV program hosts "adopt" a specific non-profit organization or project and give invaluable support, especially during the early launch period.

So much for PR personnel.

Now for the second part of consciousness raising—the program—the PR project or projects.

Contrary to what Marshall McLuhan has told you—your message determines the medium you seek. This part of consciousness raising is more subtle and complex than the personnel part.

This is so because you must plan, generate and communicate significant acts which will raise the public consciousness on behalf of education of the gifted. The key here is "significance," Significance for whom? First, for the men and women who run the media you target—but, most importantly, significance for the public you seek to enlist.

Sell Lawn, Not Seed

To put it in crude, commercial terms: The psychology of the salesman must be applied. A grass seed salesman is taught not to sell his **seed**, but rather to sell his **customer's lawn**. Don't sell the seed, sell the lawn. The benefit is sold, not just the bare product. Thus, you can see selling is both a case of education as well as of persuasion. This is the frame of mind you must use when you sit down to plan a program which will use the media to develop support for your programs.

In other words, you must first ask yourself: What's in it for the public you are addressing? As parents? As potentially gifted persons? As neither parent nor gifted persons? As educators? And so on. In whatever form you decide to cast the appeal for your program, it basically must be significant for the public you are addressing. Otherwise no communication transaction will occur.

Let's first take up how you capture the interest of the men and women who run the media—the editors, columnists, commentators, talk show hosts..

You do this by borrowing the tools of the reporter's profession. A reporter writes either a news story or a feature story. A news story is just that. It has some timely element to it, the when—yesterday, today, tomorrow, fleshed out with the who, what, where, why and how. It is in a sense, perishable—like fruits and vegetables in a produce market. The longer it is held, the more likely it will lose its ability to attract a buyer. Its interest

4. SUPPORT

soon perishes as far as the newsman is concerned, and he tosses it into the refuse can—unless you find some way to refresh it, revive it—unless you can turn it into a feature.

A feature by definition is a story not of such an immediate nature that it requires or rates either a press conference or a general release. It is what we call "evergreen", instead of perishable.

Example of a news story would be the announcement of the appointment of a new director of a State Department of Education. Example of a feature would be a later story about him as a personality—his hobbies, special interests, achievements, unusual methods of carrying out his official duties, etc. In both cases, the State Department of Education would figure prominently in the story.

Or, more on point for this Institute, a news story would be the announcement of the inauguration of a special educational program for certain gifted persons in a state or a community. A feature would be a follow-up story reporting on how it was operating. In both cases, the special educational program would be the backbone of the story.

News or Feature Item

In any event, to capture the interest of the news media and thus have a chance to reach the larger public you hope to arouse, your stories must be cast in the form of a news or a feature item.

This would be a good time to point out the basic differences in the structure or the format of the two types of stories. A news story takes the shape of an inverted pyramid, with the point at the bottom. The five *W's*— who, where, what, when, and why—plus how— belong in the first sentence or first paragraph, with details supplied in descending importance.

This rule grew up in the print media, where harried editors and make-up men had to fit stories into the newshole—the space that was available at press time. The rule of thumb was and is for news stories to be cut from the bottom up, dropping sentences and paragraphs as space requirements demand, with the knowledge that the professional reporter allowed for the practice in writing his story. Thus, if you try to write a news story from a conventional essay outline, carefully developing your theme and closing with your dramatic conclusions, you are in danger of having the whole point of your story dropped if it is printed.

The inverted pyramid, then, describes the format of the news story, which is timely and perishable.

The rectangle describes the format of the feature story, which is evergreen, can be used any time, has strong human interest, and is frequently a re-written news story. Unlike the news story, it is assumed that if a feature is used, it will be used in its entireity. Unlike the news story, the feature usually begins with an attention-getting statement to open the story. Then the five *W's* are worked in as the story is developed. Furthermore, the good feature needs a "snapper" for a close. . . .not necessarily as strong as an O'Henry short story closing but something that will snap the reader's interest, focusing it on the main point you wish to make. This increases the likelihood that your feature will be used—and used in its totality.

Your release must be tailored for the medium you have targeted. Written news and feature stories are for newspapers and magazines. Brief, terse script-type releases are for radio, which requires more of a conversational style with your story up-front in the release. News scripts for TV, should have some visual element available, still pictures or film clips.

17. Media

How do you generate these news stories and features which hopefully will build the public awareness and support you seek? Material for stories generally come from three sources:

1. *The development of new programs or services, or the modification or refinement of existing ones.*
2. *The publication or release of local, regional or national research data.*
3. *The use of "names" or visiting personalities connected with the cause you seek to publicize.*

The first two, programs and research, can be timed to fit your schedule. The last is usually connected with the travel schedule of your visiting authority, or your celebrity in residence. The first two generally require that everything be carefully written up in advance. The use of your visiting expert usually requires a few phone calls in advance and then touring with him or her around to the appropriate newspaper office, radio station or TV studio for interviews.

Newspaper and Radio Editorials

In addition to the standard news release technique I have been describing, you can contact editorial page writers to suggest editorials on the subject of your choice, with an offer to help supply relevant background material and/or an expert to supply background advice. You can contact radio and TV stations to suggest subjects for station editorials or offer to write one and record it for them. Also, you can contact stations to demand equal time to respond to an editorial that you wish to challenge. Similarly, you can approach radio and TV program directors and offer to supply public service program material, from 30 seconds worth to a half hour program, as they require.

Another method of reaching selected publics is through the organization and promotion of a speaker's bureau.

And, I would like to point out that many more speeches have changed or shaped the direction events have taken than many people realize. Most of you are aware of Churchhill's "iron curtain" speech at a small college in Missouri which helped refocus the free world's perception of our former allies. He supplied a phrase which permitted great numbers of people to understand on their own levels what was occurring in their world. However, how many of you are aware that a speech given in Chicago in 1963 by Dr. Samuel Kirk at a conference sponsored by the Fund for the Perceptually Handicapped Children first introduced the phrase "learning disability"? It had the staggering impact of causing the convention that very evening to vote to organize itself as The Association for Children with Learning Disabilities (ACLD). Five years later, the Division for Children with Learning Disabilities (DCLD) was organized within the Council for Exceptional Children. (However, as Dr. J. L. Wiederholt has pointed out, the irony is that Dr. Kirk gave that speech to plea for the abandonment of terms which were instructionally useless, not for the creation of another one!)

A century or so earlier, John Milton had set out the rationale defending freedom of speech and freedom to publish unhindered by government censorship. He wrote, "Though all the winds of doctrine were let loose to play upon the earth, so Truth be in the field, we do injuriously, by licensing and prohibiting, to misdoubt her strength. Let her and Falsehood grapple; who ever knew Truth put to the worse, in a free and open encounter?"

I took you on the brief tour for two reasons. . . to make you aware of the power of public opinion and the morally neutral nature of publicity. As

4. SUPPORT

William James once pointed out, "We are all willing to be savage in some cause. The difference between a good man and a bad man is the choice of the cause."

Finally, which is more to the point on our task at hand, I will give one last quote but with a twist, I won't identify its author, because I want you to concentrate on what he is saying—and what it implies for us.

Irrestible Power of Public Opinion

One publisher-editor has said, "Whatever is right can be achieved through the irrestible power of awakened and informed public opinion. Our object, therefore, is not to inquire whether it ought to be done, but to so exert the forces of publicity that public opinion will *compel* it to be done." (William Randolph Hearst)

Now, I'll stop quoting other people and start quoting myself. As everyone knows, there is no pleasure like quoting oneself with approval.

First, I would like to share with you a principle which, on my more modest days, I call the "E" Rule—on my less modest ones, I call it the Ewing Rule: It is simply that public relations follows the substance of an institution's or an individual's act—a significant act will result in significant PR; an insignificant act, insignificant PR.

I lay this rule out early on, because too many people believe that PR is all fluff and no substance. But a moment's reflection will tell you that's not so. Just as a man or a woman does not win a lasting reputation overnight, but over a lifetime, so too does any organization. An organization or an instituion must earn its reputation or right to the public's attention through significant acts professionally communicated.

Thus, PR is a transaction in communications. The communicator gives something—bits of information, entertainment, promises of rewards, plans for action—to the persons in the public he has selected. If a transaction has occurred, the public in return responds immediately or at some future date with some form of support or positive action. The media almost invariably have a role in the more significant transactions that occur.

Personnel and Projects

Next, I would like to take up how you prepare your group or yourself to approach the media with something that would interest them in engaging in a transaction that will eventually bring your desired public consciousness raising.

For simplicity's sake, we will divide this up into two parts: people and plans—PR personnel and PR projects.

Let's take the people first. There is an easy way and a hard way.

Since representatives of the news media best like events unfolding before their very eyes, special events—fairs, expositions, etc., can be staged to dramatize the need or service you wish brought to the public's attention. In fact, you can recruit civic organizations (Jaycees, Kiwanis, women's clubs, etc.) to co-sponsor, support, or even run the events. Don't underestimate the potential impact of a special event—for example the 1913 Armory Show in New York created the background for our first "publicity masterpiece", as art critic Hilton Kramer has pointed out. That was the show which made Marcel Duchamp famous and his "Nude Descending the Staircase" a publicity masterpiece upon which proponents and opponents of modern art focused. It has symbolized a whole cultural shift for almost six decades.

17. Media

My comments to this point relate generally to your local or regional news community. To achieve national or international impact, the wire services, news magazines, and radio and TV networks must be reached.

Generally speaking, working with the two major U.S. news wire the AP and the UPI, is similar to working with newspapers directly, with one major exception. Newspapers have daily editions and as many deadlines during the day as they have editions; wire services on the other hand, have no editions or constant deadlines. They move important news on their general wires all day long.

These wire services maintain their headquarters in New York City, with bureaus in Washington, D.C., state capitals and key cities throughout the country. They also have "stringers" or part-time correspondents in newspaper offices in smaller news centers. Local papers, which are members of one of the wire services generally feed back community news to their services, which in turn may relay these stories to other parts of the country. The two major wire services work in split-second time and do expect equal treatment in receiving news material at the same time. In our workshop session we can discuss how wire service needs and news magazine needs are met by giving them advance copies of important speeches, informing them of interview possibilities, etc.

Celebrity Status of Spokesman

Network TV news and talk shows require more specialized treatment. Headquarters for ABC, CBS and NBC news are located in New York City, also with bureaus in Washington, D.C., and key cities. Generally, if you make contact with your local network bureau manager, indicating your group's area of expertise, you may be contacted from time to time for help on any special programs he is working on. Out of this relationship develops the opportunity to "sell" your news stories when the occasion rises. To place your group's spokesman on a network talk show, you must work with the show's contact in whatever city the show originates. This is hard going and requires almost celebrity status on your spokesman's part. We can discuss this method of media work in detail in our working session, if you wish.

The use of press conferences, films, syndicated columns, mat distribution services, fact sheets, press kits, and so forth all can be discussed in our work sessions, for their use is determined by the program developed.

I would like to briefly outline the basic four-step public relations technique for program development which is used universally by almost all professional PR men.

Step One: Fact-finding. Use research to ascertain the nature of the problem or opportunity, assess attitudes of affected publics, and determine other factors that can be identified.

Step Two: Planning. Establish a public relations program which will coincide with the overall objectives of your group.

Step Three: Communication. Implementation of a planned program through effective communication.

Step Four: Evaluation. Assessment of the results obtained and the techniques used.

This four-step method (research, planning, communication, and evaluation) should be used for each major effort your organization undertakes to reach the specific publics.

4. SUPPORT

Because this is truly the "age of publicity", as various commentators have pointed out, it is important to recognize that you must use publicity techniques to gain for your organization its fair share of public support. Although it is true that the climate of receptivity of our target publics may be minimal, these publics can be reached with significant programs. It is your job to lay bare the significance of your programs so your publics can appreciate them and in turn give you the desired support. They will give it if you remember to tell them what's in it for them.

Fighting "Elitism" is Challenge

Finally, in closing, I would like to suggest that that has been and will continue to be your greatest challenge—correctly identifying "what's in" your programs for the education of the gifted and talented that will somehow benefit the general public you seek to communicate with. Your programs will always, on first impression, smack of "elitism."

If I may be so presumptious to speak from personal experience, I would like to identify the latent hostility your programs may bring forth.

In my lifetime, I have earned letters in three sports—football, basketball and track. I have earned a place on an Army boxing team in Europe, I have earned an A.A. Degree, a B.A. Degree and an M.A. Degree. I have sat for and passed the accreditation exams for the Public Relations Society of America. None of these biographical facts elicit anger from my friends and associates when they learn of them. However, about half of them get angry when they find out I sat for an IQ exam and qualified to become a member of Mensa.

My wanting to see how fast I could run, how skilled I could become at football and basketball and boxing, and how much I could learn held no intrinsic threat to their well being. Somehow, however, my desire to see how high I could jump on the IQ scale represents a threat to their existence and I am usually subjected to a harangue about my ego deficiencies and the fact that IQ tests mean nothing. My usually mild response is I am probably the most insecure under-achiever known to man and that I view IQ tests as any other public measurement—we all come to it with the same basic equipment and we all jump against the same scale—and finally that I really mean them no personal harm when I took the tests and joined Mensa—I just wanted to see if I could do it.

All programs developed to raise the public consciousness about the education of the gifted will have to have the power to overcome the mentality, the mind set, I have just described. I don't think it is an insurmountable challenge, but I do think it is a difficult one. I look forward to trying our hand at doing just that during this two-day Institute.

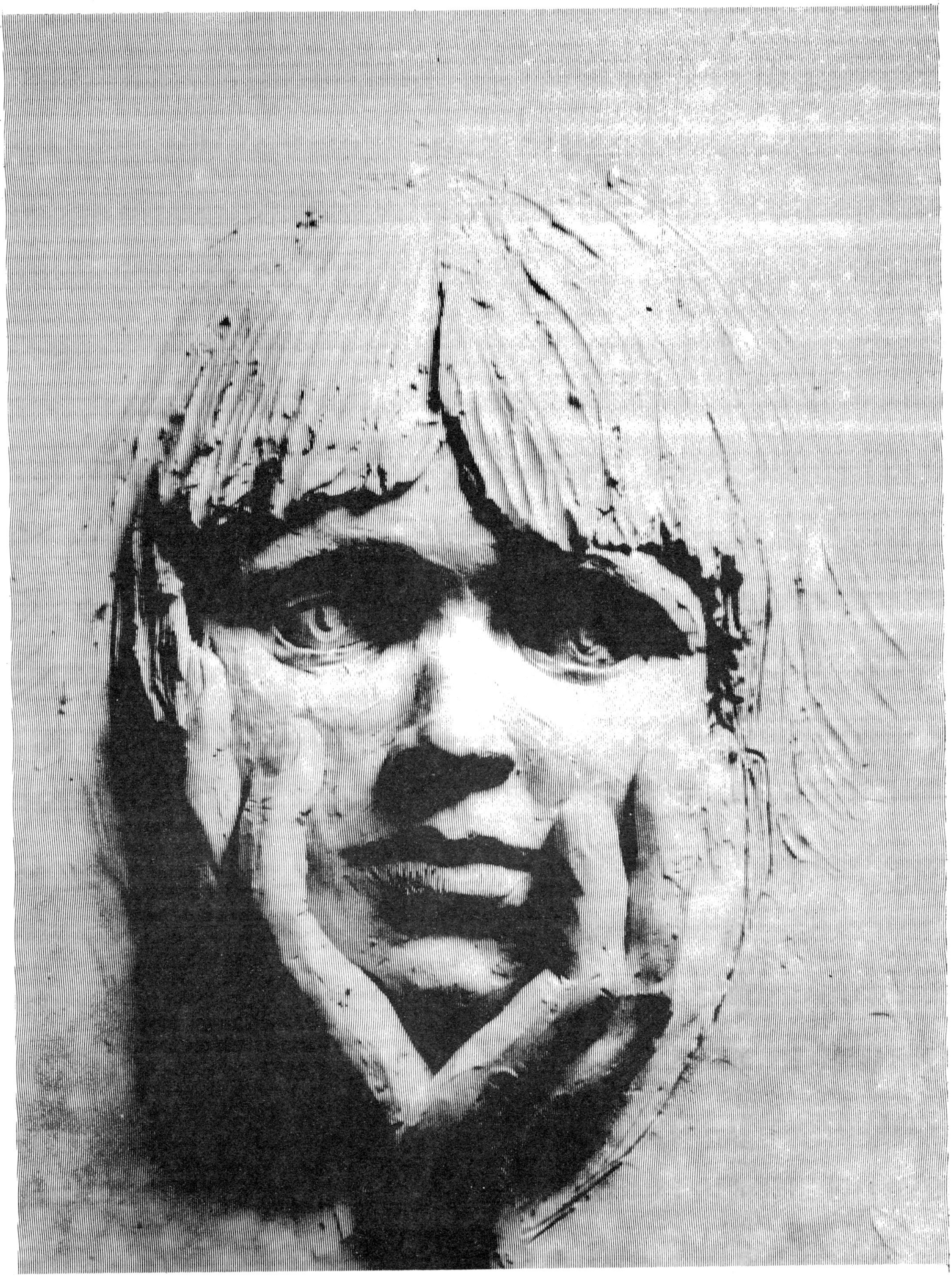

Joseph P. Kennedy, Jr. Foundation
1701 K Street, N.W.
Suite 205
Washington, D.C. 20006

Library of Congress, Division for the Blind and
Physically Handicapped
Washington, D.C. 20542

Mental Health Law Project
1751 N Street, N.W.
Washington, D.C. 20036

Muscular Dystophy Associations of America
810 7th Avenue
New York, New York 10019

National Society for Prevention of
Blindness, Inc.
79 Madison Avenue
New York, New York 10016

The National Association for Gifted Children
8080 Springvalley Drive
Cincinnati, Ohio 45236

National Association for Mental Health
1800 North Kent Street
Arlington, Virginia 22209

National Association for Music Therapy
P.O. Box 610
Lawrence, Kansas 66044

National Association for Retarded Citizens
2709 Avenue E East
Arlington, Texas 76011

National Association of Coordinators of
State Programs for the Mentally Retarded
2001 Jefferson Davis Highway
Arlington, Virginia 22202

National Association of State Directors of
Special Education
1201 16th Street, N.W.
Washington, D.C. 20036

National Association of Private Residential
Facilities for the Mentally Retarded
6269 Leesburg Pike
Falls Church, Virginia 22044

National Association of Private Schools
for Exceptional Children
P.O. Box 928
Lake Wales, Florida 33853

National Association of Social Workers
2 Park Avenue
New York, New York 10016

National Ataxia Foundation
4225 Bolden Valley Road
Minneapolis, Minnesota 55422

National Center for Child Advocacy
U.S. Department of Health, Education and Welfare
Office of Child Development
P.O. Box 1182
Washington, D.C. 20013

National Center for Law and the Handicapped
1236 North Eddy Street
South Bend, Indiana 46617

National Center for Voluntary Action
1735 I Street, N.W.
Washington, D.C. 20006

National Center on Educational Media and
Materials for the Handicapped
Ohio State Unviersity
220 West 12th Avenue
Columbus, Ohio 43210

National Committee
Arts for the Handicapped
1701 K Street, N.W.
Suite 801
Washington, D.C. 20037

National Committee for Citizens in Education
410 Wilde Lake Village Green
Columbia, Maryland 21044

National Council of Community Mental Health
Centers
2233 Wisconsin Avenue, N.W.
Washington, D.C. 20007

National Council for the Gifted
700 Prospect Avenue
West Orange, New Jersey 07052

**National Easter Seal Society for Crippled Children
and Adults
2023 West Ogden Avenue
Chicago, Illinois 60612**

National Epilepsy League
116 South Michigan Avenue
Chicago, Illinois 60603

National Genetics Foundation
250 West 57th Street
New York, New York 10019

National Information and Referral Service for
Autistic and Autistic-like Persons
302 31st Street
Huntington, West Virginia 25702

National Institute on Mental Retardation
Kinsman NIMR Building
York University Campus
4700 Keele Street
Donsview (Toronto)
Ontario, Canada M3J 1P3

National Paraplegia Foundation
333 North Michigan Avenue
Chicago, Illinois 60601

National Rehabilitation Association
1522 K Street, N.W.
Washington, D.C. 20005

National Society for Autistic Children
169 Tampa Avenue
Albany, New York 12208

National State Leadership Training Institute on
the Gifted and Talented
316 West Second Street (Suite PH-C)
Los Angeles, California 90012

National Tay-Sachs and Allied Diseases
Association, Room 1617
200 Park Avenue South
New York, New York 10003

Office of the Gifted
400 Maryland Avenue, S.W.
Washington, D.C. 20202

Orton Society
8415 Bellona Lane
Towson, Maryland 21204

Physical Education and Recreation
for the Handicapped: Information and
Research Utilization Center
1201 16th Street, N.W.
Washington, D.C. 20036

President's Committee on Employment
of the Handicapped
1111 20th Street, N.W.
Washington, D.C. 20010

President's Committee on Mental Retardation
Washington, D.C. 20201

Spina Bifida Association of America
P.O. Box G-1974
Elmhurst, Illinois 60126

Therapeutic Recreation Information Center
University of Oregon
1597 Agate Street
Eugene, Oregon 97403

United Cerebral Palsy Association
66 East 34th Street
New York, New York 10016

"Mainstream on Call"*
1-800-424-8089

***A toll free number for individuals to obtain
answers to questions about Federal legislation
concerning the handicapped.**

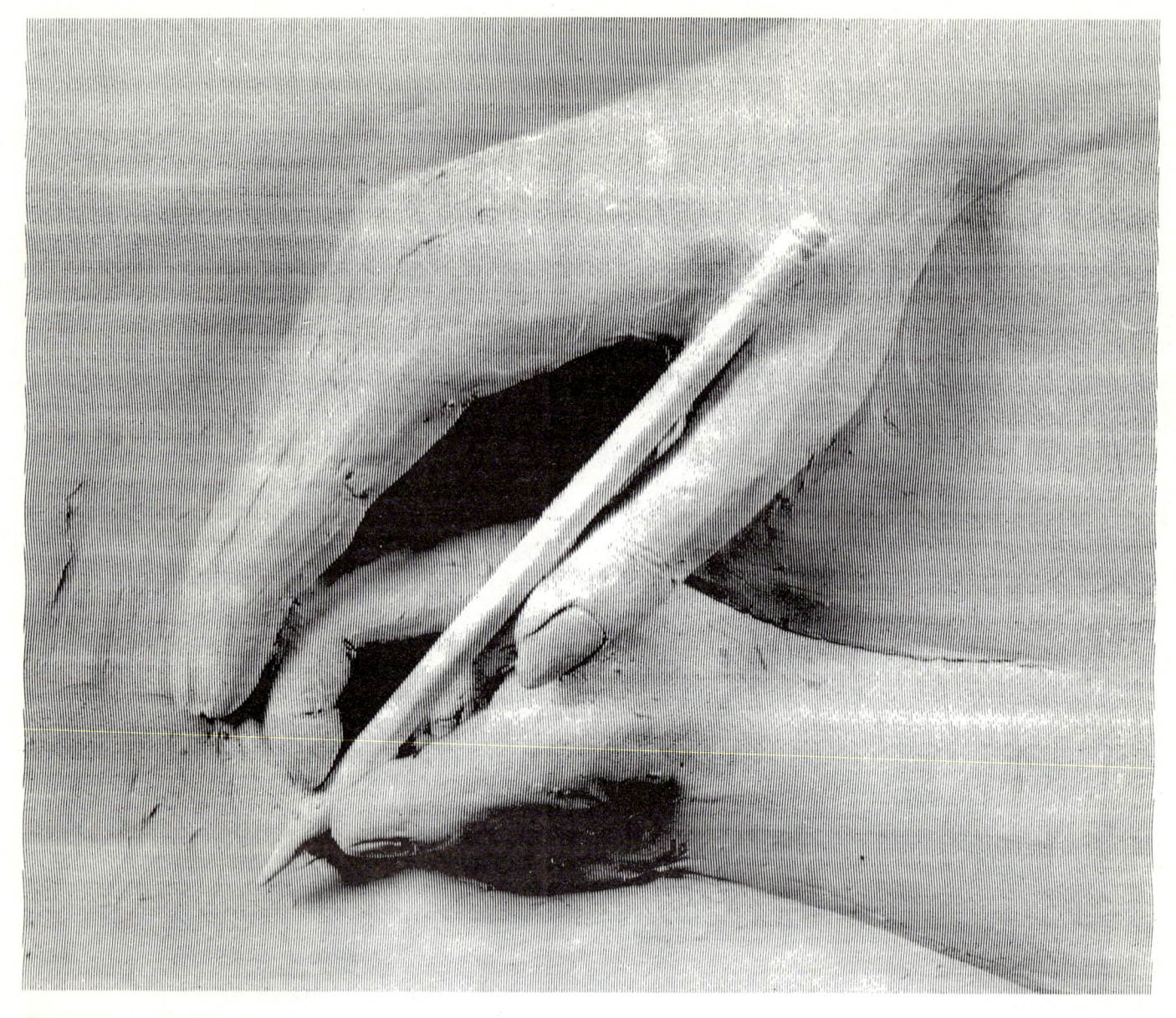

STAFF

Special Learning Corporation

Publisher	John P. Quirk
Director of Design	Donald Burns
Production Ass't.	Mary Kirkiles
Typesetting	Carol Carr
Cover Design	Donald Burns

0-89568-189-7

FOLD THIS DOWN

ORDER FORM

____ Administration of Special Education (8.75)	____ Hyperactivity (8.75)
____ Autism (8.75)	____ Individualized Education Program (8.75)
____ Behavior Modification (8.75)	____ Instructional Media & Special Education (8.75)
____ Career & Vocational Education for the Handicapped (8.75)	____ Law & Special Education: Due Process (8.75)
____ Child Abuse (8.75)	____ Learning Disabilities (8.75)
____ Child Psychology (8.75)	____ Mainstreaming (8.75)
____ Classroom Teacher & Special Education (8.75)	____ Mental Retardation (8.75)
____ Counseling Parents of Exceptional Children (8.75)	____ Physically Handicapped (8.75)
____ Curriculum Development for the Gifted (8.75)	____ Pre-school Education for the Handicapped (8.75)
____ Deaf Education (8.75)	____ Psychology of Exceptional Children (small) (8.75)
____ Diagnosis & Placement (8.75)	____ Psychology of Exceptional Children (large) (19.95)
____ Down's Syndrome (8.75)	____ Severely & Profoundly Handicapped (8.75)
____ Dyslexia (8.75)	____ Special Education (8.75)
____ Early Childhood Education (8.75)	____ Special Olympics (8.75)
____ Educable Mentally Handicapped (8.75)	____ Speech & Hearing (8.75)
____ Emotional & Behavior Disorders (8.75)	____ Trainable Mentally Handicapped (8.75)
____ Foundations of Gifted Educations (8.75)	____ Visually Handicapped Education (8.75)
____ Gifted & Talented Education (8.75)	____ Vocational Training for the Mentally Retarded (8.75)

____ Abnormal Psychology: Problems of Disordered Emotional & Behavioral Development (8.75)

____ Development Psychology: The Problems of Disordered Mental Development (8.75)

____ Human Growth & Development of Exceptional Individual (8.75)

1. Orders will not be processed without *complete* mailing address, including *zip code*.
2. Orders not accompanied by a purchase order number must be prepaid.
3. Orders under $15. must be accompanied by check. Add 10% shipping & handling.
4. Orders less that $100., add 10% shipping & handling.
5. Orders over $100., add 2% handling, shipping will be charged via specific rate.
6. Orders of 5 or more of one title receive 20% discount, less than five will be billed at catalog price.

Checks payable to: SPECIAL LEARNING CORPORATION
Allow 3-6 weeks for 4th Class (book rate) delivery

NO POSTAGE
NECESSARY
IF MAILED
IN THE U.S.

BUSINESS REPLY MAIL

First Class Permit No. 142- Guilford

Postage will be paid by addressee

SPECIAL LEARNING CORP.
P.O. Box 306
Guilford, CT. 06437

STAPLE OR TAPE HERE

SPECIAL LEARNING CORPORATION

COMMENTS PLEASE!!!

1. Where did you use this book?

2. In what course or workshop did you use this reader?

3. What articles did you find most interesting and useful?

4. Have you read any articles that we should consider including in this reader?

5. What other features would you like to see added?

6. Should the format be changed, what would you like to see changed?

7. In what other area would you like us to publish using this format?

8. Did you use this as a
   ( ) basic text? ( ) in-service?
   ( ) supplement? ( ) general information?

———————————— Fold Here ————————————

Are you a ( ) student ( ) instructor ( ) teacher ( ) parent

Your Name _____

School _____

School address _____

_____

Home Address _____

City _____ **St.** _____ **Zip** _____

Telephone Number _____

☐ **ORDER PLACED ON REVERSE SIDE**